THE EVERYTHING® Guide to Buying Foreclosures

Dear Reader,

Acquiring foreclosure properties is not as overwhelming as it might first seem. There are specific things you need to know, and understand, before you get started as a foreclosure investor.

The main reason you want to purchase a foreclosure property is simple. You are acquiring the property for a discounted price. Once you have purchased it, you can then keep it and rent it, or you can immediately sell it for a profit.

The Everything® Guide to Buying Foreclosures will allow you to learn about investing in pre-foreclosure and foreclosure properties. You will know the ins and outs of the process—and how to profit from all kinds of transactions. You will know how to find the properties, how to make purchase offers, and what to do when your offer is accepted.

Investing in foreclosure properties offers the potential for steady profits and financial independence. It's not a get-rich-quick scheme. It takes work, perseverance, and the willingness to learn the strategies that allow you to acquire properties. This book will help you discover the potential that investing in pre-foreclosure and foreclosure properties offers.

Sincerely,

George Sheldon

Lorraine K. Rufe

The EVERYTHING® Series

Editorial

Innovation Director	Paula Munier
Editorial Director	Laura M. Daly
Executive Editor, Series Books	Brielle K. Matson
Associate Copy Chief	Sheila Zwiebel
Acquisitions Editor	Lisa Laing
Development Editor	Brett Palana-Shanahan
Production Editor	Casey Ebert

Production

Director of Manufacturing	Susan Beale
Production Project Manager	Michelle Roy Kelly
Prepress	Erick DaCosta
	Matt LeBlanc
Interior Layout	Heather Barrett
	Brewster Brownville
	Colleen Cunningham
	Jennifer Oliveira
Cover Design	Erin Alexander
	Stephanie Chrusz
	Frank Rivera

Visit the entire Everything® Series at *www.everything.com*

THE
EVERYTHING®
GUIDE TO BUYING FORECLOSURES

Whether you're buying a home or looking for an investment, all you need to know to complete the deal

George Sheldon and Lorraine K. Rufe

Avon, Massachusetts

To Jennifer and George: My two great kids. —G.S.

An Everything® Series Book.
Everything® and everything.com® are registered trademarks of F+W Publications, Inc.

Published by Adams Media, an F+W Publications Company
57 Littlefield Street, Avon, MA 02322 U.S.A.
www.adamsmedia.com

ISBN 10: 1-59869-391-3
ISBN 13: 978-1-59869-391-1

Printed in the United States of America.

J   I   H   G   F   E   D   C   B   A

Library of Congress Cataloging-in-Publication Data

Sheldon, George.
The everything guide to buying foreclosures / George Sheldon.
p. cm. – (Everything series)
ISBN-13: 978-1-59869-391-1 (pbk.)
ISBN-10: 1-59869-391-3 (pbk.)
1. Foreclosure–United States. I. Title.

KF697.F6S54 2007
346.7304'364–dc22
2007019004

This book is available at quantity discounts for bulk purchases.
For information, please call 1-800-289-0963.

Contents

Acknowledgments

Special thanks to everyone that helped assemble this book. I appreciate all the hard work of the editors and staff at Adams Media Corporation. Thanks to Lisa Laing, who always answered my questions promptly and efficiently.

I appreciate the ongoing support and confidence of my agent, Bob DiForio.

I also want to acknowledge everyone that helped in many small ways with the information for this book. Numerous e-mails were sent and phone calls made asking specific questions about different aspects of the book, often just for clarification or verification. Thanks to everyone that provided those snippets of information to me.

Top Ten Things You'll Learn
Through Reading This Book

1. The difference between a pre-foreclosure and foreclosure property.

2. The procedures to purchase a property at a real-estate auction.

3. The nonjudicial foreclosure procedure.

4. The judicial foreclosure procedure.

5. The procedure to deal with defaulting homeowners.

6. How to assess property value before purchasing.

7. How to find both pre-foreclosure and foreclosure properties.

8. How to finance the foreclosure properties you purchase.

9. What to do with the foreclosure properties you acquire.

10. How to maximize your profits when acquiring foreclosure properties.

Introduction

▶ SO YOU WANT to make some money investing in foreclosure properties? You are certainly going to be busy over the coming months.

There's a lot to learn to become a successful foreclosure real-estate investor. You have to learn the local laws, develop contacts, and start searching for properties. There is a certain amount of paperwork involved, too. It takes time to get started, but it is something you can do slowly. You can move as quickly or slowly as you desire.

There is no regulation or licensing to become a real-estate investor. You don't need a college education, a business license, or a lot of money. You simply start and, like the rest of the investors, jump into the sometimes murky waters. Your first foreclosure investment could be just days or weeks away. You will be spending most of your time searching for properties. After you find prospective properties, you need to make a purchase offer. Most of your first offers will be rejected (if not, you may have offered too much!). There will be negotiation, a back-and-forth exchange of offers and counteroffers. You won't buy every property you find, and most of your offers will be rejected.

So why become a foreclosure investor? The answer is simple: profit. The plan is not difficult: You buy properties at a low price and sell them for a higher price. The difference between your buy and sell prices becomes your profit.

When you do put together a deal, you can make thousands of dollars when you sign your name to the documents. Imagine making $10,000 a deal—and completing just one deal a month. And many investors make more than $10,000 on a deal!

You also have a lot of options. You can acquire both pre-foreclosure and foreclosure properties. You can buy and hold properties, or buy and sell them immediately. You can even sell your rights to the property before you actually purchase the property.

In these pages you will learn what it takes to be a successful real-estate investor of foreclosure properties. You will learn the basics of how to acquire foreclosure properties. And with each acquisition you stand to make more money than you ever thought possible.

Chapter 1

The Life of a Mortgagor

As you may already know, a mortgagor is obligated to make a payment every month during the entire term of the mortgage. As long as the mortgagor makes that required monthly payment in full there's no problem. But things don't always go as planned. There can be sudden illness, job loss, divorce, a family crisis, or another life-changing situation that alters everything. Making the monthly payment becomes impossible. However, unless the payments are made as agreed, the life of the mortgagor is about to change drastically.

Mortgagor Versus Mortgagee

A mortgage is a public notice filed in the county courthouse notifying anyone interested that a lien exists on a piece of real property. (A lien is the legal right to keep or sell the property of a debtor as payment for a debt.) The obligation to pay a loan is created by signing a promissory note. The terms and conditions of the loan (the amount of the loan, the amount of the monthly payment, the interest rate, and the number of payments) are described in detail on the note. Some notes are extensive legal contracts, while others are simple to read and written in plain English. The trend has been to make the notes or loan documents consumer friendly and easier to comprehend.

There are many different legal terms used to describe a note. Sometimes called a *promissory note*, a *mortgage note*, a *deed of trust note*, a *real-estate loan note*, or just a *note*, the document creates the legal obligation to repay the amount borrowed and pledges a piece of real estate to guarantee the repayment of the loan. It is a separate and distinct document from the mortgage.

When talking about mortgages there are two entities: the mortgagor and the mortgagee. Most people easily confuse the terms. The mortgagee is the bank or lender. The mortgagor is the person (or the persons) that borrows the money.

ESSENTIAL

The mortgagee (the bank or lender) receives the mortgage from the mortgagor. To remember the terms easily, think of paychecks, employers, and employees. Who gives the money and who receives it? Salary is paid by the employer to the employee. Similarly, with a mortgage, the monthly payment is given from the mortgagor to the mortgagee.

The mortgagor also takes on additional responsibilities when signing a note or installment loan contract. For example, the mortgagor is required to purchase and maintain adequate hazard insurance. Most often the mortgagor purchases a homeowner's policy, which will protect the property against losses from fire, storms, vehicle, or other damage. Other standard obligations include the payment of all property taxes and the adequate maintenances of the property.

The note offered by the mortgagor and presented to the mortgagee is always a written agreement. It is signed by the mortgagor and held or maintained by the mortgagee. The mortgage is always secured by real property (the real estate), and it is pledged as collateral for the loan. Should the mortgagor not make the agreed payments, the mortgagee maintains the right to repossess and take over ownership of the real estate in a foreclosure.

FACT

The promissory note is a legally binding document. It creates an obligation on the part of the borrower to pay back the borrowed funds, plus interest, to the lender. Although different terms are used in different jurisdictions, the purpose always remains the same. Payments on the loan, including interest, must be paid, and failing to do so, the lender has the right to foreclose on the loan.

The mortgage, a public document, alerts anyone searching the title of the property at the county courthouse that a lien exists. The mortgage is the public notice that a promissary note has been signed by the property owner.

A mortgage is often thought of as "the loan." The mortgage does not create the legal obligation to pay back the borrowed money. It simply notifies the public that a note has been signed, pledging the property as collateral on the loan.

The mortgage serves to alert any potential buyer (or another lender) that a loan exists and must be paid in full before a clear title to the property can be obtained. A mortgage notice prevents the property owner from selling the property without the buyer knowing a lien exists. It is up to the buyer to learn of an existing mortgage by searching the property records at the courthouse of the county where the property is located. It also alerts any potentail lender if another loan has been made to the property owner, preventing duplicate loans secured by the same piece of real estate.

Mortgagor's Responsibility

Whenever money is borrowed to purchase real estate, the lender will require the borrower to sign a note and mortgage. The note, no matter what it is called in any given jurisdiction, will specify the obligations and responsibilities of the borrower. The mortgage note legally requires the mortgagor to repay the loan to the mortgagee.

The mortgage note will clearly indicate what the mortgagor must do. Basic terms of the loan are clearly indicated. They include:

- Amount of the loan
- Length of the loan
- Number of payments
- Interest rate
- Amount of each payment
- The date of the final payment
- Any other terms and conditions

As already mentioned, a mortgagor will be required to maintain adequate hazard insurance to protect the property (which is the collateral for the loan) against losses. If there are condominium or homeowner association fees, the note will require the mortgagor to pay those assessments. The note will require compliance with building and municipal property codes, the payment of property taxes, and other similar duties.

There could be other terms or conditions. For example, if the property is located in a floodplain, the note might require the borrower to maintain adequate flood insurance protection.

A mortgage note may also include other important terms and conditions of the loan. For example, it will include any prepayment penalty (assessed if the loan is paid off prematurely).

The mortgagor must make the monthly payments. That sounds simple enough, but too many borrowers overlook this simple requirement. If the borrower makes a payment late, it is customary that a late payment fee must be paid. The amount of that fee is clearly specified in the mortgage note. While most mortgages require payment on the first day of the month, any day of the month can be used.

No one is concerned if the monthly payment arrives a day or two after the specified date (of course, the lender wants the money before the due date). But legally speaking, no action is taken when a loan payment arrives at the lender's office a few days after it was due.

For the vast majority of borrowers, the mortgage process remains simple and unproblematic. The borrower (or mortgagor) makes the agreed monthly payment to the lender (or mortgagee). She sends off the monthly payment on time, the bank accepts it, and over the period of the loan the balance declines until it is paid off. At that point the mortgagor owns the property free and clear. That's the way it is supposed to work, and does, for most but not all borrowers.

Late Payments and Bad Credit

The borrower sometimes makes late payments on his home loan. This can happen for any number of reasons.

When the note is signed by the borrower, it will include the day of each month that the loan payment is due. The note will also include a definition of when a payment is late. After a specific time, a late fee is assessed to the borrower. This is often ten to fifteen days after the due date of the mortgage payment.

The amount of the late fee is also specified. Sometimes it is a set amount. In some notes a percentage of the payment due is assessed (usually, but not always, about 5 percent of the amount of the principal and interest payment). The late fee serves as a penalty to help insure the borrower makes the monthly payment on time.

While most borrowers make the monthly payment on time, some pay late either intentionally or unintentionally. The lender assesses a late fee based on the amount specified in the note, and the borrower pays that fee. The loan account is then brought current.

FACT

Foreclosure problems really begin when a payment is not made within thirty days after it was due. It signals a huge problem for the lender. It indicates the borrower is in financial peril.

Reasons Mortgagors Don't Make Payments

There are many reasons why a borrower does not make the monthly home loan payment. Most borrowers really do want to make their payments as they had agreed to do when they borrowed the money. Most likely something happened that makes it impossible to pay the monthly payment.

For example, there could be a sudden loss of income caused by job loss or some other situation beyond the control of the borrower. There could have been cutbacks at the borrower's employer. There might have been a reassignment of employment duties, a demotion, or some other circumstance that resulted in less income for the borrower.

Or there could have been a sudden and unexpected illness or injury that could have made it impossible for the borrower to work. Without working, there is not enough income to make the payment.

There might have been a death of one of the two borrowers, making it impossible for the surviving borrower to make the monthly payment with the loss of the income. Sometimes the inability of a married couple (co-borrowers) to make the monthly payment results from a separation or dissolution of the relationship.

There could have been some serious overborrowing since the home loan was granted. The borrower may have purchased too much on credit terms. A new car loan or overuse of credit cards and other installment credit may have made it impossible for the borrower to meet all the required monthly payments.

Sudden and unexpected expenses might also affect the borrower's ability to put together the payment. For example, uninsured medical expenses for a sick child could make it impossible for the borrower to have enough funds to make the payment.

Mortgage Products Lead to Delinquency

Over the past several years lenders have aggressively sought borrowers. As the pool of conventional borrowers diminished, the lenders created new mortgage products. This was done to find more borrowers. The problem is that many of these unconventional loan products tend to create a higher rate of delinquency.

Adjustable rate mortgages (commonly called ARMs) often offer an initially lower monthly payment, allowing borrowers to qualify for the loan based on their income level.

To understand these new mortgage products, you must first understand a conventional or "perfect" home loan, at least in the eyes and heart of the lender.

Consider a $200,000 home purchase. To a lender, the perfect loan is one to make to borrowers with:

- Excellent credit
- Sufficient income to make the monthly payment
- Solid employment history
- Few other monthly obligations that must also be paid
- Solid collateral (the property being purchased is easily worth the amount being paid)
- Down payment from the borrower of 20 percent or more
- Reserve funds (three months or more of cash on hand)

When all of these factors come together, the lender has a "perfect" loan. While there is always some risk when money is loaned, by following these simple guidelines the possibility of a loan going into default status is minimized.

In this example the borrowers are making a down payment of 20 percent (or a total of $40,000) from their own funds. They have excellent credit. Their income level is sufficient to handle the monthly payment. They have no other installment loans. Their employment situation is unquestionable: They have been employed for more than ten years and there is no reason to assume their employment will not continue. They have cash in reserve, beyond the amount of the down payment and the closing costs. The property has been appraised for more than the $200,000 purchase. As a lender in the business of making home loans, there is no reason not to lend the money. It is a perfect loan.

It's when any one (or more) of these factors are not perfect that a home loan decision becomes more difficult. For example, the employment history may not be as stable, or there could be some questionable items on the borrower's credit report. It doesn't mean that the borrowers can't get a loan, but it does put more risk when making the loan.

Lenders are not quite as stringent when making home loans for the purchase of the primary residence. They believe that most borrowers will do everything they can to save their primary residence because it is where they live. And everyone needs a home.

FACT

Mortgage insurance is sometimes called PMI, which stands for private mortgage insurance. The federal government, through loan programs administered by the Department of Veterans Affairs (VA), Federal Housing Administration (FHA), and the Department of Agriculture, provides mortgage insurance to allow home purchases with small down payments—from 0 percent to 3 percent.

For years the mortgage industry has made loans to people that do not have a 20 percent down payment. To make the loan, lenders required the purchase of mortgage insurance. This protected the lender, not the borrower, should the loan fall into default. If the borrower has only 5 percent down, the lender would make the loan but only with the purchase of mortgage insurance. Think about the example: a $200,000 home with a $40,000 down payment. Should the loan default, the lender would control a $200,000 property that only needs to net $160,000 if sold. That's a pretty comfortable position for the lender. When a smaller down payment is made by the borrower, the mortgage insurance protects the bank from any loss after a default as if the borrower had made a 20 percent down payment.

ALERT!

Stated income loans, sometimes called no income verification loans or no docs (no documentation), are an easy way to get into debt at a level that the homebuyer cannot afford. Just because someone will lend the money does not mean it makes financial sense to borrow it.

The problem for lenders is that there are not enough "perfect" loans available. So to keep lending money, which is how they make their money, they need to lend to people that don't fit the perfect loan scenario. To do so they create new loan products.

One of the specialized loan products recently marketed is the interest-only loan. This type of loan allows the borrower to pay only the interest for the first few years, which means a lower monthly payment during that time, before the principal is amortized in the loan. Other recent innovations are longer-term mortgages such as thirty-five or forty-year loans.

Stated income loans are available to those that find it difficult to provide verification of their incomes. These loans are particularly popular with the self-employed and allow mortgagors to simply state their income rather than provide documentation that proves their income.

The real problem with these unconventional mortgage loans is that there is a greater chance of default. This can happen easily and unintentionally. For example, a homebuyer agrees to an ARM loan, and an adjustment of the interest rate occurs. The monthly payment could increase hundreds of dollars. The difference between the old loan payment (the adjustment of the adjustable rate mortgage) and the newer one makes it impossible to make the monthly payment.

Mortgage lending ratios are the key as to how much money can be borrowed. Usually expressed as 28/36, these two numbers are the percentage of the homebuyer's gross monthly income. The first number is the maximum amount of the proposed housing payment. It includes principal, interest, taxes, insurance, and any homeowner's association fees. This means the total monthly housing payment cannot exceed 28 percent of the total monthly gross income. The second number is the amount of all the monthly loan obligations. This includes credit card payments, student loans, car loans, and other monthly debts combined with the proposed monthly housing payment. This combination (or total of all the monthly payments) cannot exceed 36 percent.

Decades of lending experience have proven the 28/36 ratios to be worthy measures of what someone can afford when it comes to housing expenses. Lenders have over time loosened these ratios, all in an effort to lend more money. Some lenders have offered lending programs where as much as 50 percent to 55 percent of the borrower's total income can be allocated toward a housing payment.

To qualify for one of the specialized lending programs, the borrower must seek a loan from a subprime lender. A subprime loan usually costs more by charging the borrower higher interest rates.

Other loan products also make it easier to finance a piece of real estate. Notorious are the mortgage products that offer 100 percent financing. Sometimes lenders offer first and second mortgages: an 80 percent first mortgage and a 20 percent second mortgage. This eliminates the necessity of needing any down payment. It is usually sold to a borrower as a method to avoid paying mortgage insurance. Some lenders go further. They offer 103 percent loans, or actually lend more than the property is worth. The extra 3 percent is used to pay closing costs.

All of these special financing plans or specialized mortgage products make it easier for the borrower to get the money needed to buy a property.

The problem is that it is also easier for the borrower to get into a precarious financial position.

When Late Payments Are a Real Problem

A payment thirty days late can signal a growing problem for the borrower. The first issue is how to make up the past-due payment and late fee plus make the next payment.

At the beginning of the next month, when the next payment is due, the lender rightfully becomes concerned over the past month's payment. It's a matter now that two payments are due: the current month's and the past month's payment. Depending on the lender's policies, certified letters, phone calls, or correspondence from a legal department or attorney may be part of the communications forwarded to the borrower. At this point the lender really does want the borrower to catch up on the late payment and make the current payment. Some lenders will be more lenient than others. Some will threaten immediate legal action while others will encourage communication, all for the purpose of bringing the loan current.

ALERT!

Too many borrowers facing foreclosure go into hiding. They refuse to speak or communicate with the lender. It's probably the biggest mistake they can make. The best way out of the tough situation is to find a solution with the lender. Ignoring the warnings and hoping the situation will get better never works, even though many people facing foreclosure do just that.

When the payments are missed, foreclosure may occur at any time. Each state has its own laws and procedures that the lender must follow when commencing foreclosure. Foreclosure is a legal process that a lender uses to repossess or take over the real estate. The property is, after all, the collateral of the loan.

Foreclosure is not an instant process. It takes time to foreclose on a loan because it is a legal process. Depending on the jurisdiction, it can take four to eight months for a routine foreclosure to proceed through the court system. Foreclosures that do not proceed through court—the nonjudicial foreclosures—can be completed in half the time.

Lenders will usually do everything possible to assist borrowers to become current with their payment. It is far better, in the eyes of the lender, to have a loan return to current status than it is to foreclose.

Banks and Nonperforming Assets

Lenders do not want nonperforming assets on their books. They lend money to make money. Lenders are quite willing to take the risk of lending money, especially for the purchase of real estate. Because the value of the real estate serves as the collateral for the loan and because real estate is likely to retain its value (or increase), lenders actively seek borrowers.

But the one thing they do not want is a borrower that will not or cannot make the monthly payment. Without the payments coming in to the lender, the value of the loan is diminished. Lenders want (and need) those monthly interest payments to make their money.

QUESTION?

When can a defaulting homeowner sell the property if it is in foreclosure?
The owner of a property that is in the process of foreclosure can sell the property anytime up to the point the title is transferred from the borrower to the lender. As long as the borrower can sell the property and pay the loan off to the satisfaction of the lender, he can do so until the time of the public foreclosure sale.

Foreclosure is never easy for the borrower or the lender. The goal of the foreclosure is to force the borrower out of the home and turn the title of ownership over from the borrower to the lender. When a nonperforming loan reaches the point where foreclosure proceedings are commenced, the goal is to get the borrower out of the property as quickly and inexpensively as possible.

For the homeowner in financial difficulty, it is more than just a property; it is her home. There are often many emotions involved ranging from anger to embarrassment.

Many borrowers do not realize that if their property is worth less than the total amount owed on their mortgage loan a deficiency judgment could be pursued by the lender. This means that if the property cannot be sold for the amount of the balance of the loan, the lender may require the borrower to pay the uncovered amount. If that happens, not only do they lose their home, they could owe the lender an additional amount.

F A C T

Another option for the homeowner facing foreclosure is to surrender the property to the lender. This is often referred to as "deed in lieu of foreclosure." In order to enter into a deed in lieu of foreclosure, the homeowner should have first tried to sell the property, and the fair market value of the property has to be equal to the indebtedness of the buyer.

Foreclosures are never easy. Something happened to the borrower (remember that she did qualify for the loan, and her credit and financial condition was good when she borrowed the money). For the borrower it's an emotional, mind-numbing time. For the lender it's business: make the payments or face foreclosure. And for the astute real-estate investor, there are opportunities available to make money by investing in foreclosures.

Chapter 2
Types of Legal Commitments

When a homebuyer borrows money to purchase real estate, she has to make a legally binding commitment to repay the loan being made to her. The lender will require her to pay back the money borrowed, along with interest, in monthly payments. There are other requirements also, such as maintaining the property and insuring it against damage. All of these promises are legal commitments the borrower makes to her lender.

Notes and Security

When a homebuyer borrows money to purchase a home, he signs a promissory note. The promissory note is his promise to pay back the money he borrowed, plus interest, over a specific period of time and at regular intervals (usually monthly and most often on the first of each month). The repayment plan requires the interest be paid up front. This is why the initial loan payments are mostly applied to interest with very little being paid on the principal.

To guarantee the loan (and to assure the lender that it will be repaid), the homebuyer offers security for the money he borrows. This security is the actual property he is buying. The promissory note is simply an IOU.

The note is one of the most important documents signed when purchasing property with borrowed money. It's what creates the legal obligation on the borrower's part to pay back the money she has borrowed plus interest.

The original note is retained by the lender. The borrower receives a copy of the note at the time of settlement. The original is returned to the borrower, marked paid, when all the money borrowed plus interest has been paid back.

Legally speaking, over the years other terms have been used to describe the parties involved with a note. Common terms are:

- **Promisor**—The promisor is the person who makes a promise. With a promissory note, the promisor is the person promising to repay the loan (in other words the borrower).
- **Promisee**—The promisee is the person to whom a promise is made. With a promissory note, the promisee is the person who receives the payments for the loan (the lender).
- **Obligor**—The obligor is the person who binds herself to another by a contract or legal agreement. This is another word for promisor or borrower.

- **Obligee**—The obligee is the person to whom another is bound by a contract or legal agreement. This is another word for promisee or lender.

Depending on the locale, any one of these terms might be used to describe the parties of a promissory note.

A promissory note is typically known as an unsecured obligation. This means should the borrower declare bankruptcy, the debt secured by the note is repaid only after all the other debts to secured creditors have been paid. When lending money to purchase real estate, most promissory notes are made secure with a lien or mortgage against the real estate.

Sample Promissory Note

Most notes are easy-to-read documents. They do vary from state to state, and some jurisdictions require special provisions.

The following example is a typical note format recommended by Fannie Mae and Freddie Mac (government-sponsored enterprises whose policies the real-estate industry follows) and commonly used with loans guaranteed by both:

1. BORROWER'S PROMISE TO PAY

   In return for a loan that I have received, I promise to pay U.S. $_____ (this amount is called "Principal"), plus interest, to the order of the Lender. The Lender is _____. I will make all payments under this Note in the form of cash, check or money order.

   I understand that the Lender may transfer this Note. The Lender or anyone who takes this Note by transfer and who is entitled to receive payments under this Note is called the "Note Holder."

2. INTEREST

   Interest will be charged on unpaid principal until the full amount of Principal has been paid. I will pay interest at a yearly rate of _____ percent.

The interest rate required by this Section 2 is the rate I will pay both before and after any default described in Section 6(B) of this Note.

3. PAYMENTS
   (A) *Time and Place of Payments*
   I will pay principal and interest by making a payment every month.

   I will make my monthly payment on the _____ day of each month beginning on _____, _____. I will make these payments every month until I have paid the entire principal and interest and any other charges described below that I may owe under this Note. Each monthly payment will be applied as of its scheduled due date and will be applied to interest before Principal. If, on _____ _____, 20____, I still owe amounts under this Note, I will pay those amounts in full on that date, which is called the "Maturity Date."

   I will make my monthly payments at _____

   or at a different place if required by the Note Holder.
   (B) *Amount of Monthly Payments*
   My monthly payment will be in the amount of U.S. $_____.

4. BORROWER'S RIGHT TO PREPAY
   I have the right to make payments of Principal at any time before they are due. A payment of Principal only is known as a "Prepayment." When I make a Prepayment, I will tell the Note Holder in writing that I am doing so. I may not designate a payment as a Prepayment if I have not made all the monthly payments due under the Note.

   I may make a full Prepayment or partial Prepayments without paying a Prepayment charge. The Note Holder will use my Prepayments to reduce the amount of Principal that I owe under this Note. However, the Note Holder may apply my Prepayment to the accrued and unpaid interest on the Prepayment amount, before applying my Prepayment to reduce the Principal amount of the Note. If I make a partial Prepayment, there will be no changes in the due date or in the amount of my monthly payment unless the Note Holder agrees in writing to those changes.

5. LOAN CHARGES

If a law, which applies to this loan and which sets maximum loan charges, is finally interpreted so that the interest or other loan charges collected or to be collected in connection with this loan exceed the permitted limits, then: (a) any such loan charge shall be reduced by the amount necessary to reduce the charge to the permitted limit; and (b) any sums already collected from me which exceeded permitted limits will be refunded to me. The Note Holder may choose to make this refund by reducing the Principal I owe under this Note or by making a direct payment to me. If a refund reduces Principal, the reduction will be treated as a partial Prepayment.

6. BORROWER'S FAILURE TO PAY AS REQUIRED

(A) *Late Charge for Overdue Payments*

If the Note Holder has not received the full amount of any monthly payment by the end of _____ calendar days after the date it is due, I will pay a late charge to the Note Holder. The amount of the charge will be _____ percent of my overdue payment of principal and interest. I will pay this late charge promptly but only once on each late payment.

(B) *Default*

If I do not pay the full amount of each monthly payment on the date it is due, I will be in default.

(C) *Notice of Default*

If I am in default, the Note Holder may send me a written notice telling me that if I do not pay the overdue amount by a certain date, the Note Holder may require me to pay immediately the full amount of Principal which has not been paid and all the interest that I owe on that amount. That date must be at least 30 days after the date on which the notice is mailed to me or delivered by other means.

(D) *No Waiver by Note Holder*

Even if, at a time when I am in default, the Note Holder does not require me to pay immediately in full as described above, the Note Holder will still have the right to do so if I am in default at a later time.

THE EVERYTHING GUIDE TO BUYING FORECLOSURES

(E) *Payment of Note Holder's Costs and Expenses*

If the Note Holder has required me to pay immediately in full as described above, the Note Holder will have the right to be paid back by me for all of its costs and expenses in enforcing this Note to the extent not prohibited by applicable law. Those expenses include, for example, reasonable attorneys' fees.

7. GIVING OF NOTICES

Unless applicable law requires a different method, any notice that must be given to me under this Note will be given by delivering it or by mailing it by first class mail to me at the Property Address above or at a different address if I give the Note Holder a notice of my different address.

Any notice that must be given to the Note Holder under this Note will be given by delivering it or by mailing it by first class mail to the Note Holder at the address stated in Section 3(A) above or at a different address if I am given a notice of that different address.

8. OBLIGATIONS OF PERSONS UNDER THIS NOTE

If more than one person signs this Note, each person is fully and personally obligated to keep all of the promises made in this Note, including the promise to pay the full amount owed. Any person who is a guarantor, surety, or endorser of this Note is also obligated to do these things. Any person who takes over these obligations, including the obligations of a guarantor, surety, or endorser of this Note, is also obligated to keep all of the promises made in this Note. The Note Holder may enforce its rights under this Note against each person individually or against all of us together. This means that any one of us may be required to pay all of the amounts owed under this Note.

9. WAIVERS

I and any other person who has obligations under this Note waive the rights of Presentment and Notice of Dishonor. "Presentment" means the right to require the Note Holder to demand payment of amounts due. "Notice of Dishonor" means the right to require the Note Holder to give notice to other persons that amounts due have not been paid.

10. UNIFORM SECURED NOTE

    This Note is a uniform instrument with limited variations in some jurisdictions. In addition to the protections given to the Note Holder under this Note, a Mortgage, Deed of Trust, or Security Deed (the "Security Instrument"), dated the same date as this Note, protects the Note Holder from possible losses which might result if I do not keep the promises which I make in this Note. That Security Instrument describes how and under what conditions I may be required to make immediate payment in full of all amounts I owe under this Note. Some of those conditions are described as follows:

    If all or any part of the Property or any Interest in the Property is sold or transferred (or if Borrower is not a natural person and a beneficial interest in Borrower is sold or transferred) without Lender's prior written consent, Lender may require immediate payment in full of all sums secured by this Security Instrument. However, this option shall not be exercised by Lender if such exercise is prohibited by Applicable Law.

    If Lender exercises this option, Lender shall give Borrower notice of acceleration. The notice shall provide a period of not less than 30 days from the date the notice is given in accordance with Section 15 within which Borrower must pay all sums secured by this Security Instrument. If Borrower fails to pay these sums prior to the expiration of this period, Lender may invoke any remedies permitted by this Security Instrument without further notice or demand on Borrower.

    WITNESS THE HAND(S) AND SEAL(S) OF THE UNDERSIGNED.

    _____ (Seal)

    Borrower

    _____ (Seal)

    Borrower

    As you can see, the note is straightforward, clear, and easy to understand. It includes all the terms and conditions of the loan and repayment obligations.

Mortgages

The mortgage is the public notice of the lender's interest or lien on the property. While the note creates the legal obligation on the part of the borrower to pay back the money with interest, the mortgage makes the loan public. This is done so the buyer of a property knows if there are any encumbrances or liens that would prevent a clear title to the real estate. When a borrower receives money to purchase a home, two documents are signed: the promissory note, which you've just seen, and the mortgage.

The mortgage alerts the public—anyone who looks at the property records in the county courthouse—that a loan exists and the lender has an active interest in the property. It prevents the property from being transferred without the mortgage first being satisfied.

Sample Mortgage Contract

Each state where mortgages are used has established its own laws regarding their use and what legal language needs to be included within the mortgage document. The mortgage is usually recorded in the county where the property is located. The actual mortgage form varies for each locale. The mortgage document establishes the security for the loan, in other words it creates the collateral for the loan by pledging the real estate. The lender places a lien on the property, granting rights to repossess it should the borrower not make required loan payments.

Today's mortgage document usually varies from fifteen to twenty pages. A shorter, more generic mortgage document is offered here and gives you a basic understanding of what language is usually included in the document:

This Mortgage is made by _____, an individual with an address of _____, ("Mortgagor"), to _____ _____, an individual with an address of _____ _____, ("Mortgagee").

Mortgagor is indebted to Mortgagee in the principal sum of $_____ _____, with interest at the rate of _____ percent per year, payable as provided in a certain dated _____. The terms and conditions of such promissory note are incorporated herein by reference.

Therefore, to secure the payment of the above indebtedness, Mortgagor hereby mortgages and conveys to Mortgagee all the following real estate:

(legal description of property)

Subject to all valid easements, rights of way, covenants, conditions, reservations, and restrictions of record, if any.

To have and to hold the same, together with all the buildings, improvements, and appurtenances belonging thereto, if any, to the Mortgagee and Mortgagee's heirs, successors, and assigns forever.

Mortgagor covenants with Mortgagee that:

1. Mortgagor will promptly pay the above indebtedness when due;

2. Mortgagor will promptly pay and discharge all real estate taxes, assessments, and charges assessed upon the property when due, and in default thereof, Mortgagee may pay the same and such amounts will also be secured by this Mortgage;

3. Mortgagor will keep the buildings and improvements on the property, if any, insured against loss by fire and other casualty in the name of Mortgagee in such an amount and with such company as shall be acceptable to Mortgagee, and in default thereof, Mortgagee may effect such insurance and such amounts will also be secured by this Mortgage;

4. Mortgagor will neither make nor permit any waste upon the property and will maintain the property and any improvements in good repair;

5. Mortgagor will not remove or demolish any building or improvement on the property without the consent of Mortgagee;

6. If Mortgagor shall sell, convey, or transfer, voluntarily or involuntarily, all or any interest in the above property, Mortgagee may, at its option, declare the entire indebtedness secured hereby to be immediately due and payable;

7. Mortgagor hereby assigns to Mortgagee all rents and profits of the property, if any, as additional security for the above indebtedness;

8. Mortgagee shall be entitled to the appointment of a receiver in any action to foreclose this Mortgage; and

9. Mortgagor will warrant and defend the title to the property against the lawful claims and demands of all persons.

If any payment required under such promissory note is not paid when due, or if default shall be made by Mortgagor in the performance of any agreement, term, or condition of this Mortgage or such promissory note, Mortgagee may, at its option, declare the entire indebtedness secured hereby to be immediately due and payable and may enforce payment of such indebtedness by foreclosure of this Mortgage or otherwise, in the manner provided by law. Mortgagor shall pay all costs and expenses, including reasonable attorney's fees, incurred by Mortgagee by reason of Mortgagor's default.

Provided, however, that if Mortgagor shall pay the above indebtedness and faithfully perform all agreements, terms, and conditions of this Mortgage and such promissory note, then this Mortgage shall be null and void.

The rights and remedies of Mortgagee herein are cumulative, not exclusive, and are in addition to all other rights and remedies available to Mortgagee at law or equity. Failure of Mortgagee to exercise any right or remedy at any time shall not be a waiver of the right to exercise any right or remedy on any future occasion.

If any provision of this Mortgage shall be invalid or unenforceable, the remaining provisions shall remain in full force and effect.

This Mortgage is made upon the STATUTORY CONDITION, for any breach of which Mortgagee will have the STATUTORY POWER OF SALE, if existing under applicable law.

IN WITNESS WHEREOF, this Mortgage is executed under seal on the _____ day of _____, 19____.

Signed, sealed, and delivered

in the presence of:

_____ (Seal)

(Signature of witness)

STATE OF _____

Deed of Trust

While many states only use mortgages to place liens against property, others use deeds of trust (sometimes called trust deeds). The deed of trust is placed "in trust" with a third party, usually a title or a trust company.

QUESTION?

What if the state where the property is located permits both morgages and deeds of trust?
Many states authorize both forms of liens against real estate. Most often the lender will offer a loan based on one form or the other of indebtedness. Usually in those states where both mortgages and deeds of trust are available, the lender will offer a loan based on a deed of trust rather than a mortgage.

Sample Deed of Trust

Each state where deeds of trust are used has established its own laws regarding their use. The trust deed is usually recorded in the county where the property is located. The actual trust deed varies for each locale. A deed of trust is a legal contract used in the same way as a mortgage. It creates a lien so the property cannot be sold until the loan is paid in full, and it grants the property to the lender should payments not be made as agreed. Notice that the deed of trust preauthorizes the foreclosure should the property owner default on the loan.

Today's typical deed of trust is usually a fifteen- to twenty-page document. A more generic trust deed document is presented here:

This DEED OF TRUST, made _____, between _____ herein called TRUSTOR, whose address is

_____

TITLE INSURANCE COMPANY, a California corporation, herein called TRUSTEE, and _____, herein called BENEFICIARY,

WITNESSETH: That Trustor grants to Trustee in trust, with power of sale, that property in the _____, County of _____ _____, State of California, described as:

together with the rents, issues, and profits thereof, subject, however, to the right, power, and authority hereinafter given to and conferred upon Beneficiary to collect and apply such rents, issues, and profits for the purpose of securing (1) payment of the sum of $_____ with interest thereon according to the terms of a promissory note or notes of even date herewith made by Trustor, payable to order of Beneficiary, and extensions or renewals thereof, (2) the performance of each agreement of Trustor incorporated by reference or contained herein and (3) payment of additional sums and interest thereon which may hereafter be loaned to Trustor, or his successors or assigns, when evidenced by a promissory note or notes reciting that they are secured by this Deed of Trust.

To protect the security of this Deed of Trust, and with respect to the property above described, Trustor expressly makes each and all of the agreements, and adopts and agrees to perform and be bound by each and all of the terms and provisions set forth in subdivision A, and it is mutually agreed that each and all of the terms and provisions set forth in subdivision B of the fictitious deed of trust recorded in Orange County August 17, 1964, and in all other counties August 18, 1964, in the book and at the page of Official Records in the office of the county recorder of the county where said property is located, noted below opposite the name of such county, namely:_____ shall inure to and bind the parties hereto, with respect to the property above described. Said agreements, terms, and provisions contained in said subdivisions A and B, (identical in all counties, and printed on pages 3 and 4 hereof) are by the within reference thereto, incorporated herein and made a part of this Deed of Trust for all purposes as fully as if set forth at length herein, and Beneficiary may charge for a statement regarding the obligation secured hereby, provided the charge therefore does not exceed the maximum allowed by law.

The undersigned Trustor, requests that a copy of any notice of default and any notice of sale hereunder be mailed to him at his address hereinbefore set forth.

_____

Signature of Trustor
STATE OF CALIFORNIA
COUNTY OF _____}

On _____ before me, _____
_____, a notary public, personally appeared
_____
_____ personally known to me (or proved to me on the basis of satisfactory evidence) to be the person(s) whose name(s) is/are subscribed to the within instrument and acknowledged to me that he/she/they executed the same in his/her/their authorized capacity(ies), and that by his/her/their signature(s)

on the instrument the person(s) or the entity upon behalf of which the person(s) acted, executed the instrument.

WITNESS my hand and official seal.

Signature _____

The following is a copy of Subdivisions A and B of the fictitious Deed of Trust recorded in each county in California as stated in the foregoing Deed of Trust and incorporated by reference in said Deed of Trust as being a part thereof as if set forth at length therein.

A. To protect the security of this Deed of Trust, Trustor agrees:

1) To keep said property in good condition and repair, not to remove or demolish any building thereon; to complete or restore promptly and in good and workmanlike manner any building which may be constructed, damaged, or destroyed thereon and to pay when due all claims for labor performed and materials furnished therefor, to comply with all laws affecting said property or requiring any alterations or improvements to be made thereon, not to commit or permit waste thereof; not to commit, suffer, or permit any act upon said property in violation of law; to cultivate, irrigate, fertilize, fumigate, prune, and do all other acts which from the character or use of said property may be reasonably necessary, the specific enumerations herein not excluding the general.

2) To provide, maintain, and deliver to Beneficiary fire insurance satisfactory to and with loss payable to Beneficiary. The amount collected under any fire or other insurance policy may be applied by Beneficiary upon any indebtedness secured hereby and in such order as Beneficiary may determine, or at option of Beneficiary the entire amount so collected or any part thereof may be released to Trustor. Such application or release shall not cure or waive any default or notice of default hereunder or invalidate any act done pursuant to such notice.

3) To appear in and defend any action or proceeding purporting to affect the security hereof or the rights or powers of Beneficiary or Trustee; and to pay all costs and expenses, including cost of evidence of title and attorney's fees in a reasonable sum, in any such action or proceeding in which Beneficiary or Trustee may appear, and in any suit brought by Beneficiary to foreclose this Deed.

4) To pay; at least ten days before delinquency all taxes and assessments affecting said property, including assessments on appurtenant water stock; when due, all encumbrances, charges, and liens, with interest, on said property or any part thereof, which appear to be prior or superior hereto; all costs, fees, and expenses of this Trust.

Should Trustor fail to make any payment or to do any act as herein provided, then Beneficiary or Trustee, but without obligation so to do and without notice to or demand upon Trustor and without releasing Trustor from any obligation hereof, may; make or do the same in such manner and to such extent as either may deem necessary to protect the security hereof, Beneficiary or Trustee being authorized to enter upon said property for such purposes; appear in and defend any action or proceeding purporting to affect the security hereof or the rights or powers of Beneficiary or Trustee; pay, purchase, contest, or compromise any encumbrance, charge, or lien which in the judgment of either appears to be prior or superior hereto; and, in exercising any such powers, pay necessary expenses, employ counsel, and pay his reasonable fees.

5) To pay immediately and without demand all sums so expended by Beneficiary or Trustee, with interest from date of expenditure at the amount allowed by law in effect at the date hereof, and to pay for any statement provided for by law in effect at the date hereof regarding the obligation secured hereby any amount demanded by the Beneficiary not to

exceed the maximum allowed by law at the time when said statement is demanded.

B. It is mutually agreed:

1) That any award of damages in connection with any condemnation for public use of or injury to said property or any part thereof is hereby assigned and shall be paid to Beneficiary who may apply or release such monies received by him in the same manner and with the same effect as above provided for disposition of proceeds of fire or other insurance.

2) That by accepting payment of any sum secured hereby after its due date, Beneficiary does not waive his right either to require prompt payment when due of all other sums so secured or to declare default for failure so to pay.

3) That at any time or from time to time, without liability therefor and without notice, upon written request of Beneficiary and presentation of this Deed and said note for endorsement, and without affecting the personal liability of any person for payment of the indebtedness secured hereby, Trustee may: reconvey any part of said property; consent to the making of any map or plat thereof; join in granting any easement thereon, or join in any extension agreement or any agreement subordinating the lien or charge hereof.

4) That upon written request of Beneficiary stating that all sums secured hereby have been paid, and upon surrender of this Deed and said note to Trustee for cancellation and retention or other disposition as Trustee in its sole discretion may choose and upon payment of its fees, Trustee shall reconvey, without warranty, the property then held hereunder. The recitals in such reconveyance of any matters or facts shall be conclusive proof of the truthfulness thereof. The Grantee in such reconveyance may be described as "the person or persons legally entitled thereto."

5) That as additional security, Trustor hereby gives to and confers upon Beneficiary the right, power, and authority, during the continuance of these Trusts, to collect the rents, issues, and profits of said property, reserving unto Trustor the right, prior to any default by Trustor in payment of any indebtedness secured hereby or in performance of any agreement hereunder, to collect and retain such rents, issues, and profits as they become due and payable. Upon any such default, Beneficiary may at any time without notice, either in person, by agent, or by a receiver to be appointed by a court, and without regard to the adequacy of any security for the indebtedness hereby secured, enter upon and take possession of said property or any part thereof, in his own name sue for or otherwise collect such rents, issues, and profits, including those past due and unpaid, and apply the same, less costs and expenses of operation and collection, including reasonable attorney's fees, upon any indebtedness secured hereby, and in such order as Beneficiary may determine. The entering upon and taking possession of said property, the collection of such rents, issues, and profits and the application thereof as aforesaid, shall not cure or waive any default or notice of default hereunder or invalidate any act done pursuant to such notice.

6) That upon default by Trustor in payment of any indebtedness secured hereby or in performance of any agreement hereunder, Beneficiary may declare all sums secured hereby immediately due and payable by delivery to Trustee of written declaration of default and demand for sale and of written notice of default and of election to cause to be sold said property, which notice Trustee shall cause to be filed for record. Beneficiary also shall deposit with Trustee this Deed, said note and all documents evidencing expenditures secured hereby.

After the lapse of such time as may then be required by law following the recordation of said notice of default, and notice of sale having been given as then required by law, Trustee, without demand on Trustor, shall sell said property at the time and place fixed by it in said notice of sale, either as a whole or in separate parcels, and in such order as it may determine, at public auction to the highest bidder for cash in lawful money of the United States, payable at time of sale. Trustee may postpone sale of all or any portion of said property by public announcement at such time and place of sale, and from time to time thereafter may postpone such sale by public announcement at the time fixed by the preceding postponement. Trustee shall deliver to such purchaser its deed conveying the property so sold, but without any covenant or warranty, express or implied. The recitals in such deed of any matters or facts shall be conclusive proof of the truthfulness thereof. Any person, including Trustor, Trustee, or Beneficiary as hereinafter defined, may purchase at such sale.

After deducting all costs, fees, and expenses of Trustee and of this Trust, including costs of evidence of title in connection with sale, Trustee shall apply the proceeds of sale to payment of: all sums expended under the terms hereof, not then repaid, with accrued interest at the amount allowed by law in effect at the date hereof; all other sums then secured hereby; and the remainder, if any, to the person or persons legally entitled thereto.

7) Beneficiary, or any successor in ownership of any indebtedness secured hereby, may from time to time, by instrument in writing, substitute a successor or successors to any Trustee named herein or acting hereunder, which instrument, executed by the Beneficiary and duly acknowledged and recorded in the office of the recorder of the county or counties where said property is situated shall be conclusive proof of proper substitution of such successor Trustee or Trustees, who shall, without conveyance from the Trustee predecessor, succeed to all its title, estate, rights, powers, and duties. Said instrument must contain the name of the original Trustor, Trustee, and Beneficiary hereunder, the book and page

where this Deed is recorded and the name and address of the new Trustee.

8) That this Deed applies to, inures to the benefit of, and binds all parties hereto, their heirs, legatees, devisees, administrators, executors, successors, and assigns. The term Beneficiary shall mean the owner and holder, including pledgees, of the note secured hereby, whether or not named as Beneficiary herein. In this Deed, whenever the context so requires, the masculine gender includes the feminine and/or neuter, and the singular number includes the plural.

9) That Trustee accepts this Trust when this Deed, duly executed and acknowledged, is made a public record as provided by law. Trustee is not obligated to notify any party hereto of pending sale under any other Deed of Trust or of any action or proceeding in which Trustor, Beneficiary or Trustee shall be a party unless brought by Trustee.

TO TITLE INSURANCE COMPANY, TRUSTEE:

The undersigned is the legal owner and holder of the note or notes, and of all other indebtedness secured by the foregoing Deed of Trust. Said note or notes, together with all other indebtedness secured by said Deed of Trust, have been fully paid and satisfied; and you are hereby requested and directed, on payment to you of any sums owing to you under the terms of said Deed of Trust, to cancel said note or notes above mentioned, and all other evidences of indebtedness secured by said Deed of Trust delivered to you herewith, together with the said Deed of Trust, and to reconvey, without warranty, to the parties designated by the terms of said Deed of Trust, all the estate now held by you under the same.

Dated _____

_____

Chapter 3
Foreclosure

When a borrower misses mortgage payments, he can expect the lender to commence a foreclosure action. Foreclosure is the process that takes the house away from the owner and forces him to move out. This is a legal process that varies from state to state. Each state has set up specific rules and procedures of how a foreclosure should be conducted. It is also common for lenders to provide additional time, beyond statutory requirements, in their lending contracts and forms. For example, a state law might require fifteen days' notice, but the lender grants thirty days.

When Remedies Don't Work

No legitimate lender wants to proceed with a foreclosure. It is a costly and lengthy process. Lenders would rather receive their monthly payments. That's why they are willing to find a way to help a borrower make up missed payments.

But it doesn't always work out. When the income stream is interrupted and it does not seem to show any promise of resuming to the level required to make the payments, foreclosure becomes a necessity. It is a business decision to start the foreclosure and is often the last resort for the lender.

Lender Communications

After a loan payment is forty-five days past due, the phone calls from the lender's mortgage collectors become frequent. Each of the fifty states have established rules regarding collection activities. Threats are not permitted. Telephone calls—including their frequency, content, and timing—are also regulated. For example, early morning and late-night calls are usually never permitted. But the calls from the lender's collection department will continue nonstop. Always within the established legal boundaries, they will be unrelenting and the tone will vary from just wanting to help to aggressively demanding the payments.

FACT

It is best for a defaulting borrower to stay in the property and not move or abandon it. If the defaulting property owner moves, she may no longer be eligible for assistance from any number of sources.

Before foreclosure is formally commenced, the lender will have tried to communicate with the borrower via letters (both by regular and certified mail or overnight carriers) and numerous telephone calls. It is always best for the borrower to respond to the communications; ignoring them never helps. The defaulting borrower should be prepared to discuss his financial difficulty and to provide current income information as well as other data to the lender. Without it, the lender cannot help. Borrowers may even qualify for grants of assistance. These are sometimes available from state or local agencies, charitable organizations, and other government programs.

Borrowers in trouble should seek assistance from local housing agencies. They will have the information about all available programs and offer counseling services. Some of the agencies also offer credit counseling. There is usually no charge for the housing agency service. If they do charge, it is often a nominal amount. Most lenders, when contacted by a housing agency, will not proceed with a foreclosure. They will wait to see if the housing agency can find a solution to the nonpayment problem. The borrower should be ready to cooperate fully with the counselor.

Some defaulting borrowers are just not comfortable talking with a lender's representative. A good option for these borrowers is to contact a HUD-approved housing counseling agency and arrange an appointment with an experienced counselor. The list of agencies available is on HUD's Web site at *www.hud.gov.*

Finding Solutions

Remember that lenders are looking for a solution that will work for the borrower and themselves. They are not in the business of buying and selling homes. They want the borrower to be able to stay in her home and have her make her monthly payments. That is the ultimate solution. But it doesn't always work out that way in the pre-foreclosure stage.

If the borrower cannot afford the monthly payment, he always has the option of selling the property. There are many unscrupulous people ready to take advantage of the homeowner because of his current financial condition. These people prey upon those facing foreclosure. They often advertise in real-estate classified ads, offering fast purchases. They are looking for borrowers that just want a fast solution to the foreclosure nightmare.

While the defaulting borrower may not want to go from property owner to renter, it might be the best move financially. Sometimes it makes sense to start over, rebuild credit, improve the financial situation, and then when the time is right buy another property.

Each situation is unique. There may be no solution or anything workable for both the borrower and lender. When the lender realizes this, it will commence with a foreclosure.

ALERT!

Signing a deed to the property to someone else does not relieve the homeowner of the responsibility of his loan payment. Until that loan is paid in full, the borrower is still obligated to pay the money borrowed plus interest and any legal expenses.

Why Borrowers Hide

So why don't borrowers communicate with lenders when they are in financial trouble? A 2005 survey conducted by Freddie Mac and Roper Public Affairs and Media discovered that 75 percent of late-paying borrowers recall being contacted by their lenders but a substantial percentage neglected to follow up to discuss workable solutions. This lack of borrower follow-up with the lender may explain why more than six out of ten (61 percent) borrowers paying their mortgage payments late said they were unaware of the existence of options that are available to help them. Some of the reasons given by the late payers for not contacting their lenders included:

- Can take care of the situation without involving lender
- There is nothing they can do
- Don't have the money to make the payment
- Embarrassed
- Never had trouble paying mortgage before
- Scared
- Don't know whom to call

Nonperforming Asset

Investors do not want nonperforming assets in their portfolio. A mortgage where monthly payments are not received is a nonperforming asset. To fully understand a nonperforming asset, consider a typical mortgage:

- 30-year loan (360 monthly payments)
- 6.5 percent interest rate
- $200,000 loan
- Monthly payment: $1,264.14

On this mortgage, the total amount of interest to be collected over the term of the loan is $255,088.98. The borrower would pay a total of $455,088.98 (the original loan amount of $200,000 plus the interest of $255,088.98).

The loan note—an asset to the holder of the note—produces monthly income to its owner. It is an asset so long as the borrower regularly makes those monthly payments.

When the borrower stops making the payments, the loan becomes a nonperforming asset. Not only is the amount loaned at risk, but the expected monthly income is no longer available.

Disposing of Nonperforming Assets

To lenders, the best thing to do is to get rid of this nonperforming asset (commonly referred to as an NPA). Rather than have their money tied up in a loan that is not producing any income, it makes far more sense to foreclose and get their money back. They can then use their money to invest in a performing asset—one that makes money each month.

When a mortgage payment is overdue by several days it is not automatically classified as a nonperforming asset. Payments that have not been paid on time are usually called past due if not received within fifteen days of the due date. After thirty days the loan payment is overdue. Payments not received for ninety or one hundred twenty days usually cause the loan to be identified as a nonperforming asset.

Nonperforming assets are never good for lenders. When income diminishes, stockholders and investors become impatient. Too many

signs a loan of $175,000 on a property with monthly payments required and the borrower stops making the monthly payments, the lender has the right to demand the borrower immediately make good on the entire balance of the $175,000 loan.

Borrowers can avoid the lender accelerating the loan by keeping in contact with the lender's customer service department. If the payment will be late, the borrower should alert the lender as soon as possible. Being honest and forthright with the lender makes it more likely for the lender to cooperate with the borrower and not accelerate the mortgage. Many borrowers hide rather than contact their lender.

FACT

Few mortgages today do not have this vital acceleration clause. Although it is possible the acceleration clause is not included in a mortgage, it is unlikely. This important clause in a mortgage contract is what allows the lender to speed up the mortgage payments.

Acceleration of a mortgage is not specifically authorized by a state or federal law but rather by the loan agreement signed by the borrower and lender when the loan was granted.

Acceleration sometimes occurs through the natural aging of the overdue payment. Some lenders have a strict policy of accelerating a mortgage. For example, the lender might accelerate all loans that are ninety-one days overdue.

Consider a typical scenario where the borrower is obligated to make a $1,200 monthly payment on a $150,000 loan balance and review this payment requirement:

- After 30 days the borrower owes…$1,200
- After 60 days the borrower owes…$2,400
- After 90 days the borrower owes…$3,600
- After 91 days the borrower owes…$150,000 (the entire balance of the loan) plus late fees and any other expenses.

ALERT!

The mortgage acceleration is often referred to as *calling in the loan*. It is done when the lender decides there is no further sense in chasing the borrower for the monthly payments. It's also used by a lender when the borrower can't show that she is likely to be able to make future monthly payments on the loan.

Proceedings Begin

Foreclosure is a process. That becomes abundantly clear as the legal proceedings begin. It is not an instant process however; it takes time to proceed. The ultimate goal is to get the borrower out of the property and the title to the property changed from the borrower to the lender. After that is accomplished, the property can then be sold and the lender can recover its money.

Each state has its own laws and procedures regarding foreclosures. It is all a matter of the lender repossessing the property. The lender is trying to recover the money that was loaned to the borrower by selling the property.

The formal foreclosure process commences after the borrower defaults on the loan payments and the lender seeks to repossess the collateral. The lender files a public notice, usually either a notice of default or a complaint in foreclosure.

ESSENTIAL

The type of legal notice that is filed depends solely upon the laws of the state where the property is located. If the state allows either a judicial or a nonjudicial foreclosure, the lender will usually opt for the nonjudicial foreclosure.

There are two types of foreclosures:

- Judicial foreclosure
- Nonjudicial foreclosure

The judicial foreclosure is carried out by the court, while the nonjudicial foreclosure is carried out through a process not directly supervised by a court. Some states use the judicial foreclosure, others use the nonjudicial foreclosure, and some offer both options to the lender.

The purpose of both the judicial and nonjudicial foreclosure is the same: to get the borrower out of the property and get the title back to the lender. Lenders want and need possession so the property can be sold and they can recover their invested money. Chapters 5 and 6 describe these two foreclosure methods in more detail.

QUESTION?

What is a strict foreclosure?
Some states hold a legal view that the lender is the rightful owner of the real estate. As the owner, the lender can legally order the borrower to vacate the property after a specific period of nonpayment.

All states have enacted laws about how a mortgaged property is to be sold after a foreclosure has been started. Usually a public foreclosure auction is scheduled and advertised. Depending on the locale, the property is sold by the sheriff "by public outcry" on the steps of the county courthouse or by an auctioneer at the property.

The foreclosure usually commences after ninety days of delinquency, or in other words, after the borrower has missed three payments. At this point in the breach of contract, the lender is ready to do something and is no longer willing to wait for payments. The lender usually refers the matter to its local attorney.

Within a short time the legal progress begins in earnest. The local attorney prepares the official documents, files them in the courthouse, and moves the foreclosure process forward. Depending on the state laws and local court rules, the foreclosure may become public knowledge at this point. Notices of the pending foreclosure may be posted in public places or advertised in local newspapers. Hearings may be scheduled, giving the borrower an opportunity to prove the payments had been made as agreed and that the foreclosure should not proceed.

Chapter 4

Foreclosure Processes and Terms

Most people understand the foreclosure process: If they don't make their monthly payment, they lose their mortgaged home. In some states a foreclosure can be completed in a few months, while in others the process can take almost a year. As mentioned in the previous chapter, there are two types of foreclosures: judicial and nonjudicial. Which process is used will determine how long a foreclosure actually takes. When the foreclosure method is nonjudicial, the foreclosure process generally takes less time. In states that allow both judicial and nonjudicial foreclosures, most lenders opt for the nonjudicial method, as it takes less time to gain control of the property.

4

Judicial Foreclosures

The judicial foreclosure is conducted by the court of the county where the property is located. It follows courts rules and established legal procedures. When the foreclosure commences, the pre-foreclosure stage of the loan default ends.

Judicial foreclosures commence when the lender files a lawsuit against the borrower. The lender's lawsuit alleges the borrower is in default on the loan and asks the court for a judgment in the amount due and the return of the property.

For the most part, judicial foreclosures are routine. There is virtually no defense. If the borrower did not make the required payments, the court is going to side with the lender.

After the court rules in favor of the lender (who is the plaintiff in the legal action), the property is scheduled for sale. Local custom and state law determine how the property is sold and how the buyer receives the title for the property.

The defendant can stop the foreclosure by paying off the mortgage and all legal expenses.

Nonjudicial Foreclosures

Those states that allow nonjudicial foreclosure have granted the lender the power to foreclose on a property without court approval. The procedure is clearly established, and it becomes a step-by-step technical process to foreclose on the property.

A nonjudicial foreclosure is usually supervised and conducted by the lender's attorney. Just as in a judicial foreclosure, there is little defense for the borrower who has not made the required payments.

Deeds of Trust

States that have authorized the nonjudicial foreclosure use a deed of trust. It is a legal document used in lieu of a traditional mortgage. With a deed of trust, the title to the property passes from the property seller to a trustee who holds the mortgaged property until the mortgage has been fully paid by the borrower. The trustee is automatically authorized to sell the property should the borrower default on the loan. The trustee then pays the lender the outstanding amount of the loan.

The authorization to institute a nonjudicial foreclosure is typically included in the deed of trust or loan note. The borrower authorizes this type of foreclosure as part of the terms and conditions of the home loan.

The Notice of Default

The nonjudicial foreclosure often commences with the filing of a notice of default. This occurs once the borrower has defaulted on the loan and the lender intends to proceed with a foreclosure. If the borrower does not bring the loan current, a notice of sale is mailed to the homeowner. A notice is usually also posted in public places, recorded at the county courthouse, and published in the local legal publications.

The people who handle foreclosures—both judicial and nonjudicial proceedings—are experienced and know the procedures. What might seem complicated to the outsider is routine work for them.

Following the required period, a public auction or sale is held. The highest bidder becomes the owner of the property.

Breakdown by State

Each state has enacted laws and procedures for foreclosures within their jurisdictions. Table 4-1 lists all the states and the foreclosure types used within the state.

TABLE 4-1
Foreclosure Procedures by State

State	Judicial	Nonjudicial
Alabama	X	X
Alaska	X	X
Arizona	X	X
Arkansas	X	X
California	X	X
Colorado	X	X
Connecticut	X	
Delaware	X	
District of Columbia		X
Florida	X	
Georgia	X	X
Hawaii	X	X
Idaho	X	
Illinois	X	
Indiana	X	
Iowa	X	X
Kansas	X	
Kentucky	X	
Louisiana	X	
Maine	X	
Maryland	X	
Massachusetts	X	
Michigan		X
Minnesota	X	X
Mississippi	X	X

State	Judicial	Nonjudicial
Missouri	x	x
Montana	x	x
Nebraska	x	
Nevada	x	x
New Hampshire		x
New Jersey	x	
New Mexico	x	
New York	x	
North Carolina	x	x
North Dakota	x	
Ohio	x	
Oklahoma	x	x
Oregon	x	x
Pennsylvania	x	
Rhode Island	x	x
South Carolina	x	
South Dakota	x	x
Tennessee		x
Texas	x	x
Utah		x
Vermont	x	
Virginia	x	x
Washington	x	x
West Virginia		x
Wisconsin	x	x
Wyoming	x	x

A complete foreclosure summary of the states is included in Appendix A. Detailed information about each state's practice is offered, including the approximate number of months it takes for a foreclosure to occur. Keep in mind that foreclosures are routine and the procedure is well established. The process is mostly technical and based on a systematic timetable.

Deficiency Judgment

For the borrower, losing a home through foreclosure and being forced to move has to be both emotionally draining and frightening. But the nightmare might not be over yet. If the property is sold for less than the amount of the balance of the loan plus the legal expenses and costs, the lender has lost money. To collect it, the lender has the option to seek a deficiency judgment against the borrower.

The deficiency judgment is a court order requiring the borrower to pay the remaining amount not recovered when the property was sold. The lender can then proceed, according to local state law, to collect on the judgment.

QUESTION?

What if the property is sold for more than the amount of the loan balance and outstanding costs, fees, and expenses?
The amount of the surplus—what is left after the lender pays all expenses and pays off the balance of the loan—is returned to the borrower.

Not all states allow deficiency judgments. Some of the states permit them but only under special circumstances. The judgment may or may not be allowed depending upon the foreclosure processed used by the lender. Table 4-2 lists all the states and whether a deficiency judgment is permitted.

TABLE 4-2
Deficiency Judgments Allowed by States

State	Deficiency Judgments Allowed?
Alabama	Yes
Alaska	Varies by process
Arizona	Varies by process
Arkansas	Varies by process
California	Varies by process
Colorado	Yes
Connecticut	Yes
Delaware	No
District of Columbia	Yes
Florida	Yes
Georgia	Yes
Hawaii	Yes
Idaho	Yes
Illinois	Yes
Indiana	Yes
Iowa	No
Kansas	Yes
Kentucky	Yes
Louisiana	Yes
Maine	Yes
Maryland	Yes
Massachusetts	No
Michigan	Varies by process
Minnesota	Yes
Mississippi	No
Missouri	No

State	Deficiency Judgments Allowed?
Montana	Varies by process
Nebraska	No
Nevada	Yes
New Hampshire	Yes
New Jersey	Yes
New Mexico	Yes
New York	Yes
North Carolina	Varies by process
North Dakota	Yes
Ohio	Yes
Oklahoma	Yes
Oregon	Yes
Pennsylvania	Yes
Rhode Island	Yes
South Carolina	Yes
South Dakota	Varies by process
Tennessee	Yes
Texas	Yes
Utah	Yes
Vermont	Yes
Virginia	Yes
Washington	Yes
West Virginia	No
Wisconsin	Yes
Wyoming	Yes

Reinstatement

After the foreclosure has commenced, there is still a period where the borrower can avoid losing the property by paying the past-due amount and all other fees and costs. This is called the reinstatement period. It is a final chance to get the overdue mortgage payments paid. The sooner the reinstatement is paid and completed, the sooner the growing costs of the foreclosure stop.

FACT

In some states the court clerk (or some other official) must review and certify that a sale was properly held in accordance with law. This can take up to a month in some areas. It may be technically possible to reinstate during this period, too.

Right of Redemption

Some states have enacted laws giving the borrower the right of redemption. This means that after a foreclosure sale has occurred, it is still possible for the borrower to reclaim his property. If the borrower can pay the entire overdue loan payments and the fees, he can keep his property, provided he can do so in a specific amount of time.

Approximately half of the states have redemption periods. Some redemption periods are up to one year after the foreclosure.

Chapter 5

Judicial Foreclosure Processes

In those states that use the courts to foreclose on defaulted mortgages, the process moves through the judicial system routinely and with remarkable speed. The process has been well developed and defined over the past decades. Designed to give the defaulting borrower a chance to save the property, the procedures the courts follow are swift and certain. Most judges look at the foreclosure case as a simple one: either the borrower made his payment or did not. Without proof of payments, there is little defense. Most judges approve the foreclosure, awarding judgment to the lender.

Notice of Intent

When the lender has decided to proceed with a foreclosure, one important communication will be sent to the defaulting borrower. That will be a formal notice of intent to foreclose on the mortgage.

Each state has its own laws about foreclosure and what is required before instituting a lawsuit in a foreclosure action. Some states do not allow foreclosure to begin until thirty days after the notice of intent was sent to the borrower. Some states require the notice to be sent by certified mail, while others permit regular mail sent to the last known address of the borrower. Many lenders will have sent notices and communications via overnight delivery service or personal messenger. The requirements of the states vary. But the issuance and delivery of the notice of intent is the last legal step required before the lender proceeds with the foreclosure.

Often, but not always, the notice of intent is issued by the local attorney that has been hired to institute the foreclosure suit. The notice of intent letter, issued and mailed in accordance with local law, is part of the process of getting the lawsuit ready for filing before the court.

Once the notice of intent has been prepared and delivered, it is just a matter of time—counted in calendar days—before the foreclosure complaint is filed in court. The borrower can still continue to negotiate with the lender and try to work out some kind of solution or repayment plan. However, unless a solution is found within the legal time frame, a foreclosure suit will be instituted as soon as allowed.

Complaint of Foreclosure

The lender's attorney will begin the court action by preparing a foreclosure complaint. The complaint, filed with the court of the county where the property is located, will follow local court rules and custom.

A foreclosure complaint is not an extensive document. It simply states the parties and alleges that the borrower has not made the required payments.

After the complaint has been filed with the court clerk, it will then be served upon the borrower in accordance with state law. Some states require physical service. Sometimes this service is by any adult, while others require official service by the sheriff or a deputy. Some permit service by certified or regular mail.

QUESTION?

What is a courtesy copy of the complaint?
A courtesy copy of the complaint is a copy provided to the borrower by the lender's attorney before the actual complaint, filed in the courthouse, is officially served by the required authority. It provides the borrower with an advance copy of what is coming.

After proper service of the complaint, another clock begins ticking for the borrower. The complaint must be answered within the period required.

A sample complaint follows. Complaints vary from jurisdictions, but the basics are the same. The borrower has defaulted, and the lender wants to repossess the property.

123 MORTGAGE CORP
SUPERIOR COURT VS. JUDICIAL DISTRICT OF ANYTOWN
FRED HOMEOWNER
COMPLAINT

1. Fred Homeowner, an adult, resides at 456 West Main Street, Anytown, Ohio, and further described in this complaint as the "defendant."
2. 123 Mortgage Corp, a corporation established under the laws of the State of Delaware, has established offices at 1 Pennsylvania Plaza, Akron, Ohio, and further described in this complaint as the "plaintiff."

3. On August 11, 2005, the defendant, Fred Homeowner, owed the plaintiff one hundred fifty thousand ($150,000) dollars as evidenced by his note dated on the aforesaid date and payable to the order of the plaintiff, together with interest at the rate of seven (7) percent per annum and together with all costs of collection, including reasonable attorney's fees, in the event of foreclosure of the mortgage securing the note. A copy of the said promissory note is attached to this complaint and described as Exhibit A.

4. On said date, by deed of that date, the defendant, Fred Homeowner, to secure said note, mortgaged to the plaintiff the real estate described in Exhibit A attached hereto and made a part hereof. Said deed is conditioned upon the payment of said note according to its tenor and was recorded on August 11, 2004, in Volume 12, Page 134 of the Anytown Land Records.

5. Said note and mortgage are still owned by the plaintiff and the debt is due and wholly unpaid.

6. The defendant, Fred Homeowner, has defaulted under the terms of the mortgage note and deed.

7. Although the note is in default and demand was made upon the defendant, said defendant has neglected and refused to make payment.

WHEREFORE, THE PLAINTIFF CLAIMS:

1. Monetary damages and that the amount, legal interest, or property in demand is greater than $150,000.00 exclusive of interest and costs.

2. Strict foreclosure of said mortgage.

3. Possession of mortgaged premises.

4. A deficiency judgment.

5. Such other equitable relief as the Court may deem necessary.

6. Reasonable attorneys' fees as authorized in the note.

Dated at Anytown, Ohio, this 23rd of February, 2008
THE PLAINTIFF
BY: _____

Janice Jones, Attorney for
JONES & SMITH PC

Once the complaint is filed in the courthouse, it becomes public knowledge that a foreclosure action has been started. This public information is available to anyone that seeks it.

Lis Pendens

In some jurisdictions the lis pendens is used. It is a Latin term that simply means "action pending." The lis pendens serves as the official notice that a lawsuit has been filed that concerns the title to the real property. The lis pendens is normally filed with the clerk of the court and is then recorded with the county deed recorder. A copy is provided to the borrower, which gives notice that there is a claim on the property. The recording of the lis pendens also informs the general public (and, most important, anyone interested in buying or financing the property) that there is this potential claim against the title of the property.

The lis pendens always includes the legal description of the real property. The lawsuit must involve the legally described property.

ESSENTIAL

If the borrower (defendant) has multiple properties but is in default on only one, the lis pendens cannot be used against the other unencumbered properties. It can only be filed against the one used to secure the mortgage.

The actual form of a lis pendens varies among the states. A sample lis pendens follows.

To whom it may concern: Pursuant to Ohio 33.260, this property is the subject of pending lawsuits. Interested parties should check with both parties as to the status of these cases. This NOTICE is provided for anyone interested in the following property: 456 West Main Street, Anytown, Ohio 49398 - Parcel 77-04-4-200-007

IN THE ANYTOWN COUNTY COURT, OHIO
123 MORTGAGE CORP
VS.
FRED HOMEOWNER
No. 08FC1007666

Contact Information:

For the Plaintiff:
Janice Jones, Attorney
SMITH & SMITH PC
41 Northwest Drive
Anytown, Ohio 49392
417-866-1222

For the Defendant:
Fred Homeowner
456 West Main Street
Anytown, Ohio 49398
Legal description of property: .9 acres
456 West Main Street, Anytown, Ohio - 77-04-4-200-007

COMMENCING AT THE SOUTHEAST CORNER OF THE SOUTHEAST QUARTER (SE 1/4) OF SECTION THIRTY-SIX (36), TOWNSHIP THIRTY-ONE (31) NORTH, RANGE TWENTY-ONE (21) WEST, ANY COUNTY, OHIO, THENCE NORTH 01ø22'12" EAST TO THE SOUTHWEST CORNER OF THE TRACT DEEDED TO W.M. SMITHE IN BOOK 304 AT PAGE 357, IN THE ANY COUNTY RECORDER'S OFFICE; THENCE SOUTH 68ø12'00" EAST A DISTANCE OF 1258.00 FEET TO A POINT FOR CORNER; THENCE NORTH 11ø59'10" EAST A DISTANCE OF 203.31 FEET TO A POINT ON THE NORTH LINE OF THE SOUTHWEST QUARTER (SW 1/4) OF SECTION THIRTY-ONE

(31), TOWNSHIP THIRTY-ONE (31) NORTH, RANGE TWENTY (20) WEST; THENCE SOUTH 8ø22'OO" EAST ALONG SAID NORTH LINE A DISTANCE OF 248.65 FEET TO THE NORTHEAST CORNER OF SAID SOUTHWEST QUARTER (SW 1/4) OF SECTION THIRTY-ONE (31); THENCE SOUTH 01ø12'21" WEST ALONG THE EAST LINE OF SAID SOUTHWEST QUARTER (SW 1/4) OF SECTION THIRTY-ONE (31) A DISTANCE OF 255.98 FEET TO THE CENTERLINE OF OHIO RIVER; THENCE SOUTH 5ø24'14" WEST ALONG SAID RIVER A DISTANCE OF 240.71 FEET.

The filing of a lis pendens makes the pending foreclosure known to the public. Investors interested in investing in real estate being sold at foreclosure sales seek lis pendens notifications as a way of learning about those properties.

Summary Judgment

Following the filing and service of the complaint, it's time for the judge to decide what occurs next. After consideration of the facts of the case, the judge makes the decision. The vast majority of foreclosure complaints end in summary judgment for the plaintiff (the lender).

Foreclosure complaints are made to order for a summary judgment. It all comes down to those monthly payments and whether the borrower made them or not. Summary judgment is likely—in favor of the lender and against the borrower—in the vast majority of foreclosure cases.

FACT

A summary judgment is a court order ruling that no factual issues remain to be tried and therefore a cause of action or all causes of action in a complaint can be decided upon certain facts without trial.

Appearing in Court

The borrower is entitled to his day in court. To appear before the judge, the borrower must file a timely answer to the foreclosure complaint. Within the complaint, the borrower (now the defendant) must raise questions and challenge the facts as stated by the lender (plaintiff). In other words, the defendant must raise a legitimate defense.

Should the defendant fail to respond to the complaint, judgment is routinely entered against the defendant and in favor of the plaintiff.

A summary judgment is based upon a motion by the plaintiff that contends that all necessary factual issues are settled or so one-sided that they do not need to be tried. In foreclosure cases, the facts are simple: the defendant borrowed money, agreed to pay it back in monthly payments, and has not done so. Unless there is an issue of fact (the defendant, for example, provides copies of canceled checks showing the payments), summary judgment is entered.

The theory of the summary judgment process is to eliminate the need to try settled factual issues and to decide without the expense and time of a trial one or more causes of action in the complaint. In other words, summary judgment speeds up the judicial process.

The Judge's Order

Unless there is some factual dispute and legitimate defense, the assigned judge will enter judgment against the defendant. As part of that judgment, the court will direct the property to be sold. In many jurisdictions the sale is conducted by the county sheriff.

Notice of Sale

Following the court order to sell the property, notice of the sale of the property is published. Each jurisdiction follows its own procedures for the public notification of the pending real-estate sale.

Most jurisdictions include some kind of public posting or notification of the real-estate sale at the courthouse. The public notification often includes advertising in the newspapers and legal publications within the county where the property is located.

Even though the property is now scheduled for sale, the owner (borrower and defendant) can still stop the foreclosure process by paying off the loan. Public sales can be prevented up to a specified deadline established by state laws.

Most foreclosed properties are sold by public auction. The highest bidder wins the property and usually only has a very short time (within forty-eight hours) to pay cash for the property. Title to the property usually is given to the buyer by the sheriff or clerk of the court.

Foreclosure Proceedings

During the judicial foreclosure, everything moves forward based on the local court rules and the law. If a thirty-day period is required between steps, then nothing will happen until those thirty days have passed. But on the thirty-first day, the next phase of the procedure moves forward.

The judge has the power to stop or delay the proceedings but cannot speed it up. Most judges will look at a foreclosure complaint as a routine case, and one that is clear against the borrower. When the judge rules, that's pretty much it. If the judge rules on the side of the lender and against the borrower, there is not much else to be said.

ALERT!

With a judicial foreclosure, the judge will make sure that the law is strictly followed. If there is a real issue between the borrower and the lender, the judge will listen to the borrower. Judicial foreclosures give the borrower an opportunity to have a legitimate grievance resolved.

Each state has enacted its own laws regarding foreclosure proceedings. Table 5-1 lists the foreclosure statute for each state.

TABLE5-1
State Foreclosure Statutes

State	Foreclosure Statute
Alabama	§35-10-1
Alaska	§34.20.090
Arizona	§33.807
Arkansas	§51-1106
California	§2924
Colorado	§38-37-113
Connecticut	§49-24
Delaware	§2101
District of Columbia	§45-701
Florida	§702.01
Georgia	§44-14-162
Hawaii	§667-1
Idaho	§6-101
Illinois	§15-101
Indiana	§32-8-11-3
Iowa	§654.1
Kansas	§60-2410
Kentucky	§381.190
Louisiana	§2631
Maine	§6321
Maryland	§7-101
Massachusetts	§19.21
Michigan	§452.401
Minnesota	§500.01
Mississippi	§89-1-55

State	Foreclosure Statute
Missouri	§443.320
Montana	§71-1-228
Nebraska	§25-2139
Nevada	§107.020
New Hampshire	§479.22
New Jersey	§2A-50-2
New Mexico	§48-7-7
New York	§1301-91
North Carolina	§45
North Dakota	§32-19-01
Ohio	§2323.07
Oklahoma	§686
Oregon	§86.010
Pennsylvania	§1141
Rhode Island	§34-11-22
South Carolina	§15-7-10
South Dakota	§21-47-1
Tennessee	§35-501
Texas	§51.002
Utah	§57-1-14
Vermont	§4528
Virginia	§55-59.1
Washington	§61.12.010
West Virginia	§38-1-3
Wisconsin	§846.01
Wyoming	§1-18-101

In addition to the specific statutes governing foreclosures in the states, each court will follow established rules and guidelines.

Although it is possible for a borrower to defend against the foreclosure complaint in court, it is always best to hire a lawyer. Many times the borrower does not have the money available to engage an attorney. Her financial difficulty has caused the foreclosure. Hiring a lawyer is financially impossible.

The Time It Takes to Foreclose

The amount of time it takes to complete a judicial foreclosure varies from state to state, and from case to case. Some states require a longer time, while others move the process faster.

For a timetable of average foreclosure times, see Appendix A.

Part of the determination of the time it takes is what the borrower is or is not doing. The borrower might be doing everything possible to delay the foreclosure. Or the borrower might just give up, surrender the deed and the keys, move, and hope the whole thing is over soon.

Chapter 6

Nonjudicial Foreclosure Processes

The nonjudicial foreclosure differs from the judicial foreclosure in that everything occurs outside of the courthouse. The foreclosure is commenced and conducted by a third party. The foreclosure process has already been preauthorized by the borrower when the loan was accepted. The primary advantage of the nonjudicial foreclosure is the ease in which the foreclosure can be completed. In the states where both nonjudicial and judicial foreclosures are available, most lenders choose the nonjudicial foreclosure as one of the terms of the condition of the loan.

Notice of Default

In those states where nonjudicial foreclosure is used, the lender starts the process by filing a notice of default. That notice is filed at the county courthouse in the deed recorder's office.

With the nonjudicial foreclosure, a trust deed is used in the same way a mortgage is used. The deed of the property had been placed in trust. Most commonly the third party is a trust company or a title company.

Should the borrower become delinquent with loan payments, the lender can request the trustee to file a notice of default in the county where the property is located. The deed of trust contains a power-of-sale provision that authorizes the lender to sell the property through the trustee rather than a judge.

ESSENTIAL

There is no legal action or foreclosure complaint to be filed when the nonjudicial foreclosure process is used. Since the trustee has already been determined at the time the deed was prepared, foreclosing on a property by a lender is faster and costs much less than a judicial foreclosure.

To start the foreclosure, the lender forwards a declaration of default along with the instruction to the trustee to proceed with the notice of default. The trustee creates the notice of default, records it at the county courthouse, and sends copies to the lender and borrower. If the borrower in default does not pay off the default within a specific time frame, the trustee will schedule a public sale of the property.

The trustee is required to be a neutral third party. The trustee must not favor either the lender or the borrower. In some areas title companies or trust companies act as the trustees. In other areas lawyers act as the trustee.

Notice of Sale

Depending on the state where the property is located and that state's law, the nonjudicial foreclosure cannot proceed until after a certain period. This gives the borrower time to cure the default by making all payments and paying all owed late fees and expenses. In some jurisdictions the sale cannot be scheduled before ninety days. In some states there is only a thirty-day waiting period.

There is a requirement to advertise the sale. For several weeks before the scheduled sale, the sale is advertised in the local newspaper and legal journals, and required public notices are posted. It is also common to post a notice of the sale on the property being foreclosed. At anytime during the process, the lender and the borrower can continue to negotiate and attempt to find a way to avoid the sale by bringing the loan current.

QUESTION?

Is the lender allowed to profit from the sale of foreclosed property?
By law the lender is never allowed to profit from a foreclosure. The lender is only permitted to recoup the loan amount and legitimate fees. Any excess received is required to be turned over to the borrower.

The date, time, and place of the sale is always required to be included in the sale notice. It is common that multiple properties are scheduled for sale on the same day by the trustee.

The lender and borrower who were mailed a copy of the notice of default are now sent a copy of the notice of sale. Any taxing agencies entitled to receive notice will also be provided with a copy of the notice of the sale. The Internal Revenue Service (IRS) is also routinely provided with a notice of sale.

As part of the process, an affidavit of nonmilitary status is prepared. The affidavit is a sworn statement that to the best of the lender's knowledge the subject property owners are not in active military service. This signed affidavit is routinely required before the actual sale because of certain protections granted to military personnel by the Soldiers' and Sailors' Civil Relief Act of

1940. It is rare when a property owner claims protection under the act, but it could happen.

Quicker Process

As mentioned, nonjudicial foreclosures are faster and cost less (no lawyers involved), so it is obviously a preferred method for lenders. In those states where both judicial and nonjudicial foreclosures are permitted, the nonjudicial foreclosure is usually used by the lender. Once the lender has determined the borrower is in deep financial trouble, the sooner the loan can be foreclosed, the sooner the lender can repossess the property and sell it, and the better it is for the lender.

Although the amount of time it takes to complete a nonjudicial foreclosure varies from state to state, some states require more time than others. This is because specific procedures or rules must be followed. Often the time delay is based on notification requirements. The amount of time it takes to foreclose in nonjudicial states often is determined by how much time is required to advertise the property before it is sold at a public sale. For an approximate timetable of average nonjudicial foreclosure times, see Appendix A.

Th following form depicts a typical notice of default and foreclosure sale used by HUD in those cases where a deed of trust secured the property. The form shows the type of notice that is recorded at the county courthouse. A copy of the form is delivered or served on the defaulting borrower. Notice that it also includes the date of the public sale.

NOTICE OF DEFAULT AND FORECLOSURE SALE

WHEREAS, on _____, a certain Deed of Trust was executed by _____ as mortgagor in favor of _____ _____ as mortgagee, and was recorded on _____, in Book _____, Page _____ in the Office of the _____, _____ County, _____; and

WHEREAS, the Deed of Trust was insured by the United States Secretary of Housing and Urban Development (the Secretary) pursuant to the National Housing Act for the purpose of providing single family housing; and

WHEREAS, the beneficial interest in the Deed of Trust is now owned by the Secretary, pursuant to an assignment dated _____, and recorded on _____, in Book _____, Page _____, in the office of the _____, _____ County, _____; and

WHEREAS, a default has been made in the covenants and conditions of the Deed of Trust in that the payment due on _____, was not made and remains wholly unpaid as of the date of this notice, and no payment has been made sufficient to restore the loan to currency; and

WHEREAS, the entire amount delinquent as of _____ is $_____; and

WHEREAS, by virtue of this default, the Secretary has declared the entire amount of the indebtedness secured by the Deed of Trust to be immediately due and payable;

NOW THEREFORE, pursuant to powers vested in me by the Single Family Mortgage Foreclosure Act of 1994, 12 U.S.C. 3751 et seq., by 24 CFR part 27, subpart B, and by the Secretary's designation of me as Foreclosure Commissioner, recorded on _____ in Book _____, Page _____ notice is hereby given that on _____ _____ at _____ local time, all real and personal property at or used in connection with the following described premises ("Property") will be sold at public auction to the highest bidder:

Commonly known as:

The sale will be held at _____.

The Secretary of Housing and Urban Development will bid $_____.

There will be no proration of taxes, rents, or other income or liabilities, except that the purchaser will pay, at or before closing, his prorata share of any real estate taxes that have been paid by the Secretary to the date of the foreclosure sale.

When making their bids, all bidders except the Secretary must submit a deposit totaling $_____ [10 percent of the Secretary's bid] in the form of a certified check or cashier's check made out to the Secretary of HUD. A deposit need not accompany each oral bid. If the successful bid is oral, a deposit of $_____ must be presented before the bidding is closed. The deposit is nonrefundable. The remainder of the purchase price must be delivered within 30 days of the sale or at such other time as the Secretary may determine for good cause shown, time being of the essence. This amount, like the bid deposits, must be delivered in the form of a certified or cashier's check. If the Secretary is the highest bidder, he need not pay the bid amount in cash. The successful bidder will pay all conveying fees, all real estate and other taxes that are due on or after the delivery date of the remainder of the payment, and all other costs associated with the transfer of title. At the conclusion of the sale, the deposits of the unsuccessful bidders will be returned to them.

The Secretary may grant an extension of time within which to deliver the remainder of the payment. All extensions will be for 15-day increments for a fee of $500.00, paid in advance. The extension fee shall be in the form of a certified or cashiers check made payable to the Secretary of HUD. If the high bidder closes the sale prior to the expiration of any extension period, the unused portion of the extension fee shall be applied toward the amount due.

If the high bidder is unable to close the sale within the required period, or within any extensions of time granted by the Secretary, the high bidder may be required to forfeit the cash deposit or, at the election of the foreclosure commissioner after consultation with the HUD representative, will be liable to HUD for any costs incurred as a result of such failure. The Commissioner may, at the direction of the HUD representative, offer the property to the second-highest bidder for an amount equal to the highest price offered by that bidder.

There is no right of redemption, or right of possession based upon a right of redemption, in the mortgagor or others subsequent to a foreclosure completed pursuant to the Act. Therefore, the Foreclosure Commissioner will issue a Deed to the purchaser(s) upon receipt of the entire purchase price in accordance with the terms of the sale as provided herein. HUD does not guarantee that the property will be vacant.

The scheduled foreclosure sale shall be canceled or adjourned if it is established, by documented written application of the mortgagor to the Foreclosure Commissioner not less than 3 days before the date of sale, or otherwise, that the default or defaults upon which the foreclosure is based did not exist at the time of service of this notice of default and foreclosure sale, or all amounts due under the mortgage agreement are tendered to the Foreclosure Commissioner, in the form of a certified or cashier's check payable to the Secretary of HUD, before public auction of the property is completed.

The amount that must be paid if the mortgage is to be reinstated prior to the scheduled sale is $_____ as of _____, plus all other amounts that would be due under the mortgage agreement if payments under the mortgage had not been accelerated, advertising costs and postage expenses incurred in giving notice, mileage by the most reasonable road distance for posting notices and for the Foreclosure Commissioner's attendance at the sale, reasonable and customary costs incurred for title and lien record searches, the necessary out-of-pocket costs incurred by the Foreclosure Commissioner for recording documents, a commission for the Foreclosure Commissioner, and all other costs incurred in connection with the foreclosure prior to reinstatement.

Tender of payment by certified or cashier's check or application for cancellation of the foreclosure sale shall be submitted to the address of the Foreclosure Commissioner provided below.

Date:_____

_____
Foreclosure Commissioner

Setting the Sale

Pushing for the sale of the property becomes the priority of the lender when the borrower defaults and does not appear likely to be able to make the past-due monthly loan payments. The nonjudicial foreclosure allows the lender to force the sale to recover the money that was loaned.

Because the trustee's sale date is set at the time of the notice of default (or shortly thereafter), the scheduled sale can occur much faster than with a judicial foreclosure. It is always scheduled as soon as legally allowed.

When the Sale Occurs

The foreclosure sale is public. There is often a minimum bid required, which is the amount of the overdue loan plus costs. The successful bidder must usually pay by cash or certified check at the time of the sale or within a few hours after the sale. Although personal checks are not accepted, attorney's checks are accepted.

In fact, you will be amazed at how fast a sale of the property can occur. Someone's home can literally be sold and transferred within minutes. It is both a swift and efficient method for the lender. The sale can be accomplished quickly and smoothly with a nonjudicial foreclosure. If there is not an acceptable bid at the public auction, the property is taken back by the lender.

Redemption by the Borrower

In some states, after a nonjudicial foreclosure sale takes place the borrower can still keep her property. This is called the right of redemption. If the borrower can pay all the past-due payments, plus all the additional fees, she may keep her property. The amount of days that redemption can occur is called the redemption period. Should the borrower exercise her right of redemption, whoever bought the property at the public auctions is given his money back. After the borrower's redemption period has expired, a trustee's deed is drafted and presented to the successful highest bidder of the public sale.

New Nonjudicial Foreclosure Laws

Nonjudicial foreclosures caught the attention of the legislature in California. Laws and regulations were established to control and stop unscrupulous people from taking advantage of borrowers facing nonjudicial foreclosure. Because of high-pressure tactics used by some less-than-honorable real-estate investors to get the wearied homeowners to sign sales agreements, California law now requires the right to rescind the sales agreement. The homeowner can easily cancel the sales contract within five days.

Other states are enacting similar legislation, allowing any sales contract offered during the pre-foreclosure process to be canceled for a specified period.

Stopping the Process

The lender is in control of the nonjudicial foreclosure. Accordingly, the lender can stop the process and reinstate the loan, especially if the lender and borrower can agree to a reasonable payment plan. Not only does the borrower need to bring the back payments current, but the borrower must also pay all unpaid fees and expenses. Refinancing, and paying off the current loan, always stops the nonjudicial foreclosure.

Another option available to the borrower is to seek replacement financing. Sometimes this is a good alternative because it allows the borrower to start over, often with a lower monthly payment.

As a real-estate investor investing in foreclosure properties, it is important for you to realize that property owners (defaulting on their home loan) can stop the foreclosure at any time by finding alternative financing or selling their property. Either option pays off the borrower's defaulted loan. Of course, that payoff can stop any deal or transaction you are working on as a real-estate investor to acquire the property.

Chapter 7

Investing in Foreclosures (the Good and the Bad)

Properties that are at risk of being in foreclosure are often desirable investments to real-estate investors. The main reason is simple: You can often acquire the property for less than the actual market value. The only reason to invest in a foreclosure property is to make money from the acquisition. With the issues and problems that can arise from acquiring a foreclosed property, it would not make sense to purchase foreclosure properties without the opportunity to make a profit. Buying a property at a wholesale price should always be your goal when investing in a foreclosure property.

The Fantasy

You've heard the stories: Someone bought a $150,000 house at a public foreclosure auction for only a couple thousand dollars. He became a millionaire within the year. He moved into a mansion with swimming pools and tennis courts. It is a huge fantasy.

Investing in foreclosures can generate profits. There are people that have made money on each transaction. Some people specialize in foreclosing investing and do quite well at it. Many people want to be foreclosure investors but quickly become discouraged.

That's because it is not as easy as it might first appear. There are many pitfalls and problems along the way. How well you handle those problems and find workable solutions to them will likely determine your success as a foreclosure investor. It takes work, knowledge, and a willingness to stick to your goals.

Get Rich Quick

There is a fantasy among many that are interested in investing in foreclosure properties. They think this is a get-rich-quick opportunity. They believe it is an easy way to make big money quickly. They falsely believe that it is a simple, effortless road to riches.

There is a fantasy sold by late-night infomercial real-estate gurus that you don't need a job and that you can be broke and have horrible credit yet can still buy all the real-estate investment properties you want for just a few dollars. Now that is a real-estate fantasy! Why would anyone lend you thousands of dollars if your credit report shows repeated bad marks and you have no apparent way whatsoever to pay the loan?

No Money Down and Bad Credit

Is it impossible to buy an investment property with no money down and bad credit? Of course it is possible. The real question is how likely it is. And unfortunately, the days of buying a property with a total cash outlay of $50 or $100 are long gone. It's always possible, but highly unlikely.

This daydream of growing rich (quickly) is mere flight of the imagination. It makes far more sense to seek steady employment and rebuild your credit by paying your bills on time. As you do, save some money and have some cash to work with so you can acquire investment properties.

Leave Your Job?

A part of the dream about investing in foreclosures is the possibility of leaving your job to be a full-time real-estate investor. Many would-be foreclosure investors assume they can, and will, become full-time, self-employed people earning significant incomes.

The vast majority of real-estate investors are part-timers. Most buy properties when they can, as they can, and don't look at real-estate investing as a full-time endeavor.

This doesn't mean that you can't become a full-time real-estate investor. Many investors have started part-time and moved into full-time investing. Because of their business activities in operating and managing their real-estate investments, it became necessary for them to become full-timers.

ALERT!

Beware of real-estate gurus that tell you that you can quickly leave your job and become a full-time real-estate investor. It is more likely they are selling a dream to you than worthwhile information that is likely to allow you to leave your employment.

You could do the same thing: become a full-time, self-employed real-estate investor. There could be a day when you, as a savvy real-estate investor, will leave your job and earn all of your income by investing in foreclosures.

Helping Others

One of the advantages of being in the foreclosure investment business is your ability to help people. The person that owns a property about to be foreclosed is motivated to sell and is looking for help to make the nightmare go away.

Remember that these homeowners are good people. They were able to qualify for a mortgage and paid for the costs of closing as well as made a down payment for their purchase of the property.

But something went wrong. It was most likely something out of their control. Most foreclosures occur because of:

- Job transfer, relocation, or loss
- Separation or divorce
- Bankruptcy
- Serious illness or disability
- Property tax escalation
- Retirement
- Real-estate investor burnout

Property owners facing foreclosure want out of the deal, and the sooner the better. They are experiencing many different emotions, from being angry about losing the property to being scared and worried about the future. Helping them resolve their current financial problem is something you can feel proud about doing.

Keep in mind that the property owner is experiencing financial difficulty. Trying to help the property owner out of his current situation should be a side benefit of your involvement in the foreclosure investment. The deal must make sense to you as an investor.

Buying Under Market Value

Another part of foreclosure investing is the huge discounts available on distressed properties. Investors buy foreclosure properties for less than their market value.

A distressed property is one that is in poor physical condition or in poor financial condition. However, it is not the property that is in bad financial condition, it is the owner of the property that is suffering from poor financial shape.

That is part of the foreclosure investment game. Most foreclosure experts agree that 20 percent discounts are common. More rare, but always possible to find, are properties that can be acquired at even larger discounts below market value.

Sometimes the discounts can be 30 percent to 50 percent below market value. Even a property obtained at 10 percent off current market value can offer significant value. For example, a $250,000 foreclosure property purchased at 90 percent of market value offers the buyer a $25,000 discount.

There is no compelling reason to invest in a foreclosure property that is not discounted. Without the benefit of a near instant gain of equity, the hassles and problems are probably not worth it. When there is an opportunity to purchase real estate at a wholesale price and sell at a retail price, profit exists. That profit is what attracts real-estate investors to acquire foreclosure properties.

Buying Over Market Value

One of the problems when buying foreclosure properties is the ease in which you can purchase the property over its real market value. You might overpay because of what is owed on the property, or even because of the frenzy involved with a public foreclose sale.

Buying over market value never makes sense. This is especially true for a real-estate investor. The old adage of "buy low, sell high" never made more sense than it does to a foreclosure real-estate investor.

The main reason you want to invest in foreclosure properties is the ability and likelihood that you are going to acquire the property for less than current market value. In other words, you want a bargain. Paying too much for the property erases its bargain status. The amount of what the property owner owes has nothing to do with the true market value.

Overpaying for a property can easily occur in what the media calls a "hot" real-estate market. That's when the sellers are in control of the market, and the buyers get into a sharklike feeding frenzy. They pay more than the listing price of the property. They become enamored with the idea of owning a property in a specific region. Then it happens: The market turns. What had been a seller's market becomes a buyer's market.

ALERT!

Don't get wound up in a bidding war at a public foreclosure auction. Public sales, with an auction driving up the price, are exciting events. It's easy to get involved in the fast pace and overbid or pay too much for the property. Set your limit and pay no more.

There is any number of reasons why the local real-estate market might swing directions. As the market changes, price corrections occur. It is easy, if the real-estate investor is not careful, to overpay for a property.

Paying Too Much

Some foreclosure investors wrongfully believe that any property can be a good investment if they can acquire it with little or no money out of pocket. They believe that if they hold the property long enough, it can become a good investment. They also believe that if they can purchase the property with favorable terms, price doesn't matter.

Buy-and-hold advocates often overlook the current market value of the property. They focus on the potential cash flow that rent payments could generate. Not considering the market value and what could happen if the property needed work is flawed foreclosure investing advice.

Overpaying for a property never makes sense. Any purchase must be based on the actual market value. Properly valuing the potential investment property is fundamental.

Buy Foreclosures at Wholesale Prices

Amateur foreclosure investors often overpay for the properties they acquire. Professional, experienced foreclosure investors never pay retail prices for the properties they purchase. They always and only invest in properties they can purchase at wholesale prices and sell at a retail profit.

Did you ever hear of the old real-estate adage about getting rich? It says, "You make your profit when you buy and you get paid when you sell." This wise saying clearly demonstrates that you make your profit based on what you pay for the property.

Competition

Foreclosure investing attracts many real-estate investors. Everyone wants to make a profit on his or her investments. Buying for less and selling for more always means a fast profit. For this reason alone there can be fierce competition among real-estate investors to buy a particular property.

Increased competition drives the price of the property up and your profit potential down. The more people interested in buying the foreclosure property, the higher the final price will be. This increased competition does not make it any easier for you to acquire the property and earn a respectable profit.

Even though there can be fierce competition on some properties from both investors and noninvestors, other times there is little or no competition. Each foreclosure is unique.

Gauge the Market

Consider the competitive market where the property is located. If the foreclosure property you want to purchase as an investment is in a highly competitive local real-estate market, acquiring the property might become futile. Others may be quite willing to pay more for the property. Your hopes of acquiring the property at a price where you can collect a profit might be dashed in this type of real-estate market.

If you are investing in an area where there is a good supply of foreclosure properties, the competition among investors will be less. If few properties are available, the competition for the current property inventory will be greater.

Evicting Folks

Throwing people out of their home is never easy. Even from a cold-hearted business point of view, forcing a defaulted buyer out of the property is an emotional issue.

The problem is that many of the people you are likely to be evicting have a sympathetic story. It could be a young parent with small dependent children. Or a middle-aged person with a medical condition that prevents him from working. Or you might need to evict a newly retired, gray-haired individual that can't afford the home on his meager retirement benefits.

To be a successful foreclosure real-estate investor, you have to be willing and able to do whatever is necessary to evict the unfortunate people living on the property. This can be emotionally draining and even expensive. When the former buyers become squatters, they have nothing to lose. They could damage the property—deliberately or unintentionally. Some foreclosed property owners may deliberately strip the property. They sell everything they can, from the appliances to the copper pipes. The result of their efforts to find money from their lost property can mean expensive repairs for the foreclosure investor.

They might delay their vacating of the property to the last possible minute, which makes it hard for you to take control, get repairs or updates completed, and to sell or use the property.

ESSENTIAL

Evictions can become involved legal issues. It is possible that a court-ordered eviction will be necessary to get control of the property. While the owner of the property will win the court case—no judge is going to allow anyone to stay in the property that is not paying for it—the only way to get the defaulted owner out of the property is with a court order and the sheriff physically carrying the people off the premises.

Pitfalls You Might Miss

Foreclosure investing is full of other pitfalls that can be costly or cause tremendous time delays. It is easy to make mistakes, and unfortunately some of those errors can be expensive to the foreclosure investor.

Investing in foreclosures can also be downright frustrating at times. For example, you might have found a perfect property, one that makes financial sense to purchase. You successfully bought it at the public sale and are ready to take control. Then the defaulted buyer takes advantage of the redemption period and the property reverts to the buyer. Although it is good for the defaulted property owner, it is not good for you. You get your money back and have nothing to show for your time and effort.

Property Liens

Foreclosure properties often have liens in place. The property owner's financial condition often has caused other problems beyond not being able to make the monthly loan payment. Other bills are likely to have been unpaid.

A lien is a legally binding claim filed against a property. The lien must be paid off when the property is sold and transferred to the new owner.

ALERT!

Postponed Sales

Another frustrating pitfall occurs when the actual sale of the property is postponed. This can happen for any number of reasons. The property owner may have worked out some sort of payment plan with the lender. Perhaps he came up with enough money to save his home, or a buyer has come forward with an acceptable offer to purchase the property. For the real-estate investor ready to purchase a foreclosure property, these kinds of sale postponements can be exasperating.

Avoiding Legal Problems

One other important consideration for the foreclosure investor is to make certain he is not making himself legally vulnerable. It is often too easy to sign papers without understanding the complete legal ramifications. With the stroke of the pen, you could find yourself on the hook for payments you never expected.

Don't forget, too, that this is a lawsuit-prevalent society. Today, everyone is ready to sue anyone for whatever reason. Frivolous lawsuits are filed every day. Even if you win, the expense and lost time can create a pricey ordeal. Foreclosure investors must take every possible precaution to protect themselves and their assets.

Negotiating with distressed homeowners often becomes difficult. Many defaulting borrowers are not ready to admit defeat. They hang on to a false hope, thinking there is some easy way out of their bleak situation. As a foreclosure investor, you must negotiate with borrowers that are unable to afford to pay their current monthly home payment. They are going to have to move sooner or later. The reality of their current financial condition may not be as clear to them as it is to you. They are likely not to negotiate, at least initially, because their desire to hold on to their home clouds their judgment of their current financial condition.

Chapter 8

Risks in Dealing with the Prior Owner

You need to be careful when you are planning to buy a foreclosure property from a defaulting borrower. The property owner is under tremendous emotional pressure; it's not easy to lose your home. Remember, the cause of the financial problem—loss of employment, divorce, death—is still negatively affecting the owner's life. Someone facing foreclosure often does not think straight. The property owner might be in denial and refuse to accept his plight. He is likely confused and agitated, and you are probably not the first person he has spoken to about his worsening financial situation.

Run a Title Report

Never take the word of the defaulting property owner about the condition of the title of the property. Always check for yourself. This is critical, and it's the first thing you should do before considering the property as an investment. Order an updated title report.

Determine What Liens Are Placed Against the Property

The only way to discover what issues you might be facing is to check the title of the property at the county courthouse. A title search can reveal lots of information quickly and easily. With this information you can decide if the foreclosure property could be a viable real-estate investment. The title search should uncover:

- Tax liens—federal, state, or local unpaid taxes
- Unpaid judgments
- Secondary or subordinate liens, such as second mortgages or home equity loans
- Government liens—from unpaid student loans to overdue water bills
- Mechanics' liens
- State or federal welfare, child support, or medical liens

Liens can be either voluntary (such as a mortgage) or involuntary (such as a mechanics lien) when placed against a property. Some liens the property owner accepts, while others are placed because of unpaid bills. All the liens must be paid before the property can be successfully transferred.

ESSENTIAL

The liens, those beyond the mortgage, can make a foreclosure unappealing to the real-estate investor. What might first look like a good deal could turn out to be one without any profit potential after the title is searched and you review the title report.

If the local municipality has placed tax liens against the property, it could be scheduled for auction at a tax sale. The local municipality could be the city, borough, or township; the county; or the school district. All of these entities need to be checked and a determination made if the taxes are current. If they are delinquent, it must be ascertained what amount is needed to pay all the owed taxes.

Due Diligence Is Important

The term *due diligence* is used often when buying foreclosure properties. You will hear people saying that you need "to perform your own due diligence on foreclosure properties." Due diligence is the process of investigation, research, and analysis of your investments. You are looking for any skeletons in the closet, and the fastest way to find those skeletons is to complete a title search. It is a basic part of your due diligence with the acquisition of any foreclosure property.

FACT

The deed recorder offices in the courthouse can be very busy places. However, most of the clerks working in the offices can help you and answer any questions. Once you learn how to search the records, extracting the information you need becomes fast and simple. With this information you can quickly decide to pursue or drop any potential foreclosure property as an investment.

The title search is done by checking the records at the county courthouse where the property is located. The deed recorder's office is where the records are maintained. They are public documents and open for examination during regular business hours. Some jurisdictions now have their records online. You can either examine the deed records yourself or hire a title company, attorney, or abstract company to do the title search for you.

You cannot have too much information about a foreclosure property. In addition to the courthouse records, look for any public information that might be available. This is easier with the powerful and free search engines available on the Internet.

Family Squabbles

Other issues beyond unpaid bills, taxes, and liens could place a cloud on the title. Family squabbles can create serious problems for the foreclosure investor. Always be on the lookout for any signs that could indicate there is an underlying issue with family members that could affect the sale of the property.

QUESTION?

What is a clouded title?
A *cloud* is any condition discovered during a title search that could negatively influence the property's salability or value. Any outstanding encumbrance or claim could affect the title.

The death of the homeowner can often create a clouded title to a prospective property. Heirs may try to claim the property. It is quite possible that another legal battle is being waged that could affect the title of the property.

The family battle may not be public information. There could be a lot of wrangling going on behind the scenes as different family members try to resolve their issues. Often this takes time, and it only takes one stubborn relative to stop the inevitable sale of a property. Any potential heir that did not (or is not) willing to sign off the property and release any potential claim to it could create a serious cloud on the title.

Squabbles can also occur between children and grandchildren, especially when the property owner is older and needs assisted living care. Until the bickering is over, it might be impossible to proceed with any plan to acquire and invest in the property.

Separation and Divorce

Another real problematic situation you can encounter when investing in foreclosure properties is when the owners are separating and divorcing.

These situations can create untold complications and extended negotiations for you.

When you are dealing with only one spouse but the title report indicts there are two owners, you must get the second spouse to agree to any deal. Sometimes this is easy, and other times it is difficult. This is especially true if there is a nasty or deteriorating separation and divorce situation occurring behind the scenes. Dealing with both spouses separately can become frustrating. You can spend a lot of time, energy, and money in hopes of acquiring the property and watch the deal fall apart because of the issues involving the divorce situation.

When you realize there is a separation and divorce situation, it is always best to get both parties to agree with the terms of the sale. If you don't get a fast acceptance from both parties, consider how difficult assembling the deal might become.

When there are attorneys involved and a nasty divorce is ongoing, getting both parties to agree to the terms of a foreclosure purchase is involved. The attorneys are usually difficult to deal with, especially when they are charging hundreds of dollars of fees to their clients. They are not likely to resolve the sale of the real estate quickly.

Become skeptical of any deal where a separation and divorce is the underlying cause of the foreclosure. Most experienced foreclosure investors will not get involved in these kinds of real-estate deals.

Recorded Papers

The best source for accurate information is the papers recorded in the courthouse. Consider these official documents as the final status of any situation, no matter what the property owner says or claims.

People facing foreclosure seem to have all kinds of excuses, explanations, and stories as to why something should not be on their credit report or why a lien should not be on their property. Some of the stories are unbelievable. Others sound plausible.

But as a working real-estate investor seeking foreclosure properties, believe none of the property owner's stories. Assume the recorded papers at the courthouse are always accurate.

Without strong written proof, there is no way to overcome those recorded documents. For example, the title search might reveal an $800 unpaid water bill. The local water authority placed a lien against the property. When you ask the property owner about the lien, the response is, "I paid that." Your response should be, "Prove that it is paid." Short of a canceled check that proves the payment, the lien stands. If the property owner cannot find the canceled check, you have to assume the water bill was never paid. Even if it was paid, without irrefutable proof that the payment was made, the bill will need to be paid, since a municipal lien has been placed against the property. And without the proof, it's likely the property owner is not telling the truth about the lien.

FACT

Clerical errors and mistakes occur. However, you will rarely find them when dealing with foreclosure properties. The error is almost exclusively on the part of property owners. Don't believe their story over the recorded documents.

Review the documents recorded in the courthouse carefully. They can tell you a lot about the liens and the amount owed.

Fix-the-Problem Solutions

Property owners facing foreclosure often are willing to fix the problem. The problem is that they can't afford to do so. If they could, they would have. So beware when you hear them say they will fix it.

Perhaps it is part denial or just the hope that things will work out, but borrowers who have defaulted on their home payments are always thinking they can fix it. They falsely believe that a lien will go away or a large sum of money will appear suddenly in their bank account that will allow them to pay off a second mortgage so a deal can be made.

The smart foreclosure investor learns quickly not to trust the false promises of the borrowers fixing their problems. It just doesn't happen in the real world.

It makes far more sense for the foreclosure investor to take the steps necessary to solve the problems necessary to make a deal work. For example, if there are various mechanics' liens on the property, it is better for the foreclosure investor to call those holding the liens and negotiate for a partial payment. Depending on the harried homeowner to do so could result in nothing happening. The likelihood of you closing the deal will dwindle as the days of inaction continues.

ESSENTIAL

Don't rely on borrowers in foreclosures to do anything necessary to move an investment purchase to a conclusion. While they may want to end the foreclosure proceeding, they are often mentally drained and simply worn out.

The less you rely on the borrower to get things completed, the better off you will be in acquiring the property. Consider that most defaulting borrowers will just vacillate and that nothing will be done, especially not on time or when required.

Property Condition

Foreclosure properties come in all sizes, shapes, and conditions. Because of the failing financial condition of the property owner, routine maintenance and necessary repairs are often postponed. As an investor of foreclosure properties, you need to inspect carefully any property you are considering purchasing.

If the property is still occupied by the defaulting owner, you can assume it is livable. But there could be extensive dirt, grime, damage, and neglect that could cost thousands of dollars to make the property acceptable to any other potential buyer. Sometimes referred to as an "ugly" property by investors, you will be surprised at how a previously qualified buyer may have suddenly trashed a property when his financial condition changed for the worse.

You also need to be wary of the deceitful homeowner that is now quite willing to hide a substantial property defect. Perhaps only discovered after occupying the property, the unscrupulous property owner is now willing to allow you to buy the property and find the problem for yourself.

ALERT!

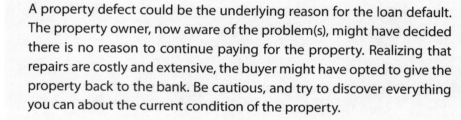

A property defect could be the underlying reason for the loan default. The property owner, now aware of the problem(s), might have decided there is no reason to continue paying for the property. Realizing that repairs are costly and extensive, the buyer might have opted to give the property back to the bank. Be cautious, and try to discover everything you can about the current condition of the property.

The physical condition of the property is crucial for the real-estate investor. As an investor of foreclosure properties, you need to ascertain the extensive repairs versus cosmetic problems. The difference, of course, determines the cost of the repairs and your eventual profit. Unfortunately, when investing in foreclosure properties, the range of needed repairs can be quite large.

You will certainly fail as a foreclosure real-estate investor if you do not properly inspect each potential investment property. Too often foreclosure investors forget or overlook the basics. This can lead to costly mistakes and lost profits. For example, a simple termite inspection, something routinely completed in a nonforeclosure real-estate transaction, could be overlooked by the inexperienced foreclosure investor. It could cost thousands of dollars to repair the property, something that could have been avoided had you taken the time to order a property termite inspection.

Use a Professional Property Inspector

As part of your resources and your effort to perform your own due diligence on any property you are considering buying, you need to use the services of a competent and professional property inspector. These are the people that you hire to inspect and snoop around the property. Their goal is to find the property's flaws and defects and report them to you.

There are many professional property inspectors, and there are those that are not. It may take you a little while to find and build a relationship with a property inspector that you can trust and rely upon. Many states do not have any special requirements, beyond paying for a license, to become a home inspector. Some inspectors are more concerned about where their next dollars are coming from than attempting to do a good inspection on the property. Many inspectors offer video or DVD reports, using flashy technology to prove their services.

Rather than bells and whistles, you want an inspector that is not afraid to get on the roof and walk on it or get into a crawl space with spiders and rodents to see what is going on with the proposed property.

One place to locate qualified property inspectors is the American Society of Home Inspectors (1-800-743-ASHI (2744)). Their Web site is *www.ashi .org*. Using their Web site, you can quickly locate member inspectors in your area. Interview several, and work to build a good relationship with a professional inspector.

The home inspector will not pass or fail a property. Rather she will endeavor to find all the potential problems with the property. Once she has located a problem, she will note it on her report. You will then have to decide what to do about the property after you have reviewed your inspector's report.

Always make sure that your purchase agreements include a property inspection clause. You always want the right to inspect a property when purchasing it, and you want the right to cancel the purchase based on defects or problems discovered during the inspection.

The cost of the home inspection will vary depending on geographic location and will depend on the services you order. With a home inspection service, it is not always best to pick an inspector based solely on price. You want to pick an inspector that is going to work with you, be objective and fair, and let you know exactly what the problems are with the property.

You may question if the cost of the inspection is necessary. The answer is obvious. It only takes one sour deal, caused by the lack of inspection, to validate the costs of many inspections. Don't overlook the importance of the inspection process on any potential foreclosure property investment.

Property Defects

Assume there are defects with the foreclosure property and that the current defaulted owner will do everything possible to keep you and your home inspector from finding those problems. Your inspection should look for these kinds of problems:

- Electrical problems and hazards
- Fire hazards
- Termite infestation
- Rotting wood
- Cracked or sinking foundations
- Structural damage
- Roof damage and leaks
- Mold problems
- Stripped, nonworking, or damaged mechanical systems
- Damaged, leaking, or collapsed water line
- Damaged, leaking, or collapsed sewerage line
- Damaged or missing roof gutters and downspouts
- Water damage
- Moisture problems
- Safety issues
- Building code violations

It is usually a good idea for the property owner to be present when you and your home inspector are looking at the property. As your experience with inspecting properties matures, you may want to do your own preliminary inspections. As you learn what to look for, you can determine if a particular property is one that you want to have professionally inspected.

You need basic tools to complete inspections. From the obvious—clipboard, flashlight, checklists—to the tools of the inspector—ice pick, digital camera, voice recorder—you need these items to determine the condition of the property. One of the advantages of having the property owner present is to question the problems and concerns you have. When you find a defect, ask a question like, "How long has this been damaged?" Most likely your reply will be, "I didn't know there was a problem." Nevertheless, you are starting the process of setting up the expectation that you will not be paying top dollar for a defective property.

Environmental Issues

Mold issues can stop a prospective homebuyer from proceeding with a sale. The Environmental Protection Agency (EPA) offers free information about mold. It is readily available from the agency's Web site: *www.epa.gov/mold/moldresources.html*. Look for their publication, *A Brief Guide to Mold, Moisture and Your Home*. It provides information on how to prevent and clean up any indoor mold growth. You can also request a copy of the publication by contacting the EPA at 1-800-490-9198.

You can also use the EPA to determine if the foreclosed property is located near any known hazardous waste site. The agency's Web site offers information about problem sites at *www.epa.gov/superfund/sites*.

The EPA Web site also includes good information about lead paint. Properties built before 1978 may pose a lead paint hazard. You can learn more about the Residential Lead-Based Paint Hazard Reduction Act, as well as learn how to abate the problem, on the EPA Web site.

According to the EPA, lead from paint chips, which you can see, and lead dust, which you can't always see, can be serious hazards. Peeling, chipping, chalking, or cracking lead-based paint is a hazard and needs immediate attention.

Lead-based paint may also be a hazard when found on surfaces that children can chew or that get a lot of wear and tear. These areas include:

- Windows and windowsills
- Doors and doorframes
- Stairs, railings, and banisters
- Porches and fences

For more information on lead paint, visit: *www.epa.gov/lead/pubs/lead info.htm.*

Check Out the Neighborhood

Consider the location of the foreclosure property. What could look like a good deal during the day could be a terrible choice at night or vice versa.

You need to understand what the neighborhood is like during the different hours of the day. Some neighborhoods fill with intoxicated persons, noisy cars, and loud music in the evening hours. Others are quiet at night but are loud during the day because of business activities. Visit the property, and the neighborhood, at different times to gauge any other problems.

It is always good to visit after major weather storms. Check out flooding, standing water, and drainage. See for yourself how the water flows near the foreclosure property. Look for any environmental issues during your neighborhood visits.

Chapter 9

Investor Pitfalls

As an investor of foreclosure properties, you must proceed carefully with all your transactions. This is business, clear and simple. Just because this transaction involves a foreclosure, it is not reason for you to let your guard down. Excitement over the acquisition of a property often fogs common sense. There are many pitfalls and traps for the hapless real-estate investor seeking foreclosure properties. Failing to complete your due diligence can be a costly mistake, and can cause you to lose any potential profit.

Expecting It to Be Easy

New foreclosure real-estate investors expect foreclosures to be an easy business. They approach it as a chance to make money quickly and rapidly and expect the process to be repeated as often as they want. They expect fast, easy, and large paydays.

Expecting the foreclosure investment business to be easy is probably the norm. In reality, it is a business, with pitfalls and traps, that offers rewards and successes. Just like any business, it needs to be worked and developed.

The general misconception remains that the foreclosure business is a fast path to big fortunes with little work. Entry into real-estate investing is easy and quick. However, producing constant and consistently profitable results requires ever-expanding knowledge and constant work.

Finding properties in various stages of foreclosure is just part of the work. Evaluation of the foreclosure properties, the due diligence part of the transaction, is something too many real-estate investors overlook as a necessary piece of each acquisition.

Operating as a Business

To be successful as a foreclosure investor you must start and operate as a small business. The purpose of your enterprise is simple: to make reasonable profits from investing in both pre-foreclosure and foreclosure properties.

Creating and maintaining accurate records is the only way to claim legitimate business deductions.

Operating your real-estate investment venture requires proper bookkeeping and record retention. With the use of a personal computer, most of the work becomes manageable and much easier.

Maintaining receipts and invoices, as well as files for those properties you are buying and selling, is necessary work. A home office helps to make it easier to separate your home life from your business. Keeping your work in one room maintains organization. You will need some office supplies, such as paper, envelopes, pens, pads, and so on. You will certainly gather books and other materials, so some storage is needed. You will need a desk to work on and a phone. Other essentials include things such as a fax, printer, and a shredder.

ALERT!

If you are not a small-business expert, seek competent professional advice. You should discuss your obligations with your tax advisor, and you should consult with an attorney about your business operation. Remember that it always costs less to stay out of trouble than it does to get out of a legal mess.

Your business operation, as far as record-keeping is concerned, is relatively easy. You simply need a system that allows you to record all your business-related expenses and your income. You are likely to have few income transactions, especially compared to expenses. In other words, you have far fewer paydays and far more days where you are paying expenses.

Claim every legitimate expense that you are entitled. Be sure to have the receipt carefully stored away in your record system so you can prove what you paid. Some expenses are obvious, such as office supplies and postage. Others are less obvious, such as a receipt for $200 to AB Enterprises. However, attaching a note that AB Enterprises was paid the money for a property inspection at 12 West North Street makes the expense legitimate and deductible. Your files should always speak for themselves. When they do, you can sleep at night knowing you can pass any tax audit. Your goal is to make it easy to show what you paid to support your real-estate investing business.

It's perhaps all too easy to slide into a lackadaisical attitude when working as a foreclosure real-estate investor. Developing and maintaining a positive, productive work ethic is going to pay you great dividends. Sometimes the work is lonely and boring, especially when deals don't come together as expected. Keeping to your work and maintaining a never-give-up attitude will go far to turn dry periods into fruitful profits.

Be Prepared to Walk Away

A tough part of being a foreclosure real-estate investor is walking away from a potential deal. This is especially true for the newer or inexperienced foreclosure investor.

Once you have spent a lot of time on what looked like a profitable deal, it just hurts to walk away. It's human nature to stay with the deal and try to salvage something for all the time you've got in the deal.

It's too easy to get knee-deep in the thrill of the chase. It's fun, exciting, and the lure of profit often clouds your best judgment. A business-minded investor folds and walks away to search for another, better deal. This isn't easy, but it is what makes the most sense.

You should always be ready to walk away from any deal, even if it means losing the money you paid for property inspection or title searches. When it becomes apparent there is little or no profit potential, allow your competitors to compete over the deal. You should go searching for another property to acquire.

Not Knowing Market Value

In theory, a property is worth what someone is willing to pay for it. As you progress with your foreclosure investments, the main question for you when considering any property is its true market value. One of the biggest mistakes foreclosure investors make is not knowing the market value of a property they are considering purchasing.

There are hundreds of books available about how to set the market value of real estate. You can be sure there are many different ways of evaluating the market value of a foreclosure investment property. You can be just as certain that the defaulted property owner will have a far different opinion from yours as to the value of his property.

One of the best ways to develop a sense of the market value of the property is to concentrate your investment area. Rather than trying to invest in properties in a 200-mile radius from your home, you are likely to be more successful by narrowing the distance. If you can shorten the radius to a few miles, you will soon become an expert on what specific home values in that area are. Sometimes it makes sense to invest only within a specific school district, county, or some other political division.

There is no reason why you cannot expand into other areas after you gain more experience as a foreclosure investor. Initially it often makes the most sense to concentrate in one small, easily defined area.

The reason is simple: The more you know, the more likely you will be to successfully acquire properties at the right price. For example, suppose that your selected investment area includes a recent townhouse development. They are mostly three-bedroom, one-and-a-half-bath units, and most sell for $150,000. With this knowledge, you know right away that a townhouse in this development with an acquisition cost of $165,000 makes no sense. One that you can acquire for $125,000 is an attractive investment.

No Contract

Verbal contracts may be legally binding, but trying to enforce them is an exercise in how to spend money on legal fees. It makes no sense to operate your foreclosure investment business without written contracts.

ESSENTIAL

Find a local lawyer that specializes in real-estate transactions. Ask for referrals to locate a well-regarded attorney. Having access to a knowledgeable and astute lawyer is an invaluable asset for you to have as a real-estate investor specializing in acquiring foreclosures.

Deals are not really deals until you and the property owner put everything in writing. This is also true of someone that is buying a property from you. Until a purchase offer is placed in writing, there is no deal.

Intentions are good, and people are often able to talk big, making grand statements. But it all comes down to what is, and isn't, on the paper.

The agreements you use should be first reviewed and approved by your attorney. Each state and court jurisdiction has its own rules and customs. You want your contracts to be enforceable and withstand any court challenge. The mere fact that your contract is legally binding can stop someone from contesting it.

Your attorney can (and will) advise you not to rely on verbal contracts but rather to reduce any contract and agreement to writing. If someone is not willing to put an agreement in writing, something is wrong. This is a huge signal not to do business with that person.

Contracts and agreements are often fill-in forms. By writing the names, addresses, terms, and dates, an agreement is formed between yourself and the other party. There is also a trend to use boilerplate documents created in word processing software on a personal computer. The details of each deal are filled in at the appropriate location within the document. Following printing, the document is signed by both parties. Your attorney should approve of the basic form and language of whatever type or style of document you use.

Giving Too Much Too Fast

When negotiating with a property owner, inexperienced real-estate investors often give up too much. The idea of negotiation is a give and take, and the going back and forth between the parties is part of the buying process.

FACT

Those real-estate investors that specialize in foreclosure that are the most successful seem to have the common trait of being willing and able to negotiate their deals. They hone their skills, and send signals to the other party. They master how to set expectations, and then work their deals to maximize their position.

Experienced foreclosure investors take their time, working the negotiation as long as necessary to structure the best possible deal. Inexperienced beginners often give up too much all in an effort to make a deal quickly.

Taking your time to make a decision is always a good move when you are negotiating. Don't be afraid to ask, "May I think about this and get back to you?" While it is common for the other side to come up with some reason why you should make an immediate decision, don't allow yourself to be rushed.

Offering full price and paying for everything is a quick way to acquire properties, but that certainly isn't an intelligent method to maximize profits. Every concession and every dollar of price reduction you can achieve improves your position as an investor.

Becoming a skillful negotiator takes time. But it is something most people can master. It just takes some practice and effort on your part.

Underestimating What the Home Needs

Beginning real-estate investors too often underestimate what a property needs to turn it into a desired home. While some things are easy to estimate, others are more complicated.

Computer software programs are available that can help you create more accurate estimates of the materials and time needed to complete necessary repairs to properties. Some Web sites, especially those of the home improvement stores, often offer helpful tools to determine accurate estimates and realistic time schedules.

For example, homes today should be equipped with working smoke detectors. It is relatively easy for any investor to determine if a property is properly equipped with a detector. If not, the cost of a detector can be quickly ascertained. Installation is simple and fast.

A sparsely equipped kitchen is a very different issue. A property without a working stove, refrigerator, garbage disposal, and dishwasher might be impossible to sell or rent. Inadequate storage cabinets could also be problematic. It is easy for you underestimate what it would actually cost to add all of these items to the property. In addition, you may be off on the amount of time it would take to do the work of remodeling a kitchen. It usually always takes longer and costs more than you first think.

Underestimating what a home needs and how much money it would take to get it marketable or livable can be a disastrous mistake for a foreclosure investor. Never overlook the importance of an accurate assessment of what a property needs.

Working with Family

Most new foreclosure investors rely on family members to launch their new venture. Relying on family for expertise or capital can be a huge undertaking, and a major problem.

As long as everything is working and no problems develop, working with family can be rewarding. It's also a way to get started quickly and easily in real-estate foreclosure investing. But when problems occur and things do not go as planned, having family members as partners can become a nightmare. The problem is the family dynamic. Families can be destroyed when money and business are involved. Family members can blindly enter into haphazardly constructed business deals that turn sour. When that happens, the families are never the same.

ALERT!

Resist the temptation to forget the formalities of a regular business relationship with a relative. In fact, because you are working with a relative, and you want to preserve that familial relationship for the rest of your life, you need a solid, well-thought-out business plan and partnership agreement. Handshakes are great, but not for partnership agreements.

The only way to avoid family issues clashing with a business venture is to have a well-thought-out plan before starting. The plan should include not only how to form the partnership but also how to dissolve it. Putting together a business is always more fun than dissolving the enterprise. When it becomes necessary to take a business apart, the enthusiasm is often gone, and there could be bitterness and resentment. The family dynamic makes this even more difficult. It is for this reason that starting a partnership with a family member should be done only with caution and a well-designed plan to dissolve amicably should it become necessary.

QUESTION?

How important is a partnership agreement?
It may help to think of your partnership agreement as a sort of prenuptial agreement between you and your partners. At the beginning you will certainly want to believe that your partnership will last as long as you live. But things can and often do change, and the written agreement determines what will happen if things don't go exactly as everyone has planned.

Any agreement with a relative should be put in writing. The agreement should also be reviewed by attorneys. All parties need to understand their duties and obligations. Just because you are working with a relative, do not overlook the basics of good business practices. Of course you know the family member, but it only makes sense to reduce any business activity to writing.

Your partnership agreement, whether with a relative or a nonfamily member, is not complete without a buyout provision. This part of the agreement clearly states what will happen when a partner leaves the enterprise. Many new partners, inexperienced with partnership agreements, neglect to make a buyout or buy-sell agreement. This is a critical part of the relationship and is important to protect your investment in a partnership. When you create buyout provisions within your partnership agreement, you and your partner(s) are prepared if one partner wants or needs to leave the business. Things can happen to partners, from disabling illnesses or injuries to death, bankruptcy from other business dealings, divorce, and other life-changing events.

Your attorney will certainly be able to produce a well-crafted and binding written agreement. It is important that everyone understand and agree to it. To get the best agreement from the attorney, be sure to explain your goals and issues that you want solved. Formal partnership agreements can be as short as several pages to hundreds of pages in length. Some are very complex documents.

Partnership arrangements can vary in profit splits. Most people think partners always get equal splits. This is not always the case. An agreement could be a 35-65 split between the partners. Another variation is one partner gets 100 percent of the profit until a specific level is reached. For example, partner A takes 100 percent of the first $50,000 profit, then partner B takes the next $50,000, and any profit beyond $100,000 is split 50-50. Anything that is agreeable to the partners can be created and protected in a partnership agreement.

This should not be an adversarial situation but rather one where you and your relative(s) are working hard to make sure everything is up front, proper, and clearly defined. And when working with relatives, it is also good to take extra effort to keep both the business and family relationships healthy.

Working with Untrustworthy Partners

Greed is a powerful emotion, and it's important to realize that not everyone will deal openly and honestly with you. It's unfortunate, but this is the reality of the foreclosure investing business.

ALERT! Consider that you could be held 100 percent liable for your partner's misconduct. For example, if you paid your half of the taxes of the partnership and you partner did not pay, you could be held responsible for your partner's payment. Your partner could legally bind you to agreements and contracts that you did not want. Your credit and ability to operate your business activities could be adversely affected.

Obviously you do not want to work with partners that you cannot trust. You only want to enter into business partnerships that will work for you and your partner. The ultimate goal, of course, is to make the maximum amount of profit that you and your partner can from honest and fair dealing and investing. You need partners that have the same values, desires, and goals that you do.

Conflicts over money usually cause most business partnerships to fail. Control of the money, work, and business decisions also cause conflict. Mix in the inability to trust a partner and the partnership is doomed for failure.

The best solution is to screen your partners carefully. Only enter into a partnership with a written agreement, and make sure there is a way out of the agreement.

If you suspect something is wrong after the partnership is formed, don't ignore the trouble signs. Get into the issue right away. Time never makes problems smaller, it only allows them to grow out of control.

Rental Properties

Owning and operating a property for producing income from rent can be a profitable endeavor. It can also be a costly undertaking.

Most first-time landlords are only concerned about finding a responsible tenant that is willing and able to make monthly rent payments. Of course, having that tenant is important, but there are other considerations.

There are considerable costs that can be incurred when owning a property for rental income. Maintenance and repairs are often needed because of:

- Heating problems
- Indoor decoration (paint, wallpaper, cleaning)
- Replacement of carpets
- Electrical appliances that need repairs or replacement (washing machine, refrigerator, dishwasher, stove)
- Landscaping issues
- Plumbing, including drains and gutters
- Door and lock repairs and replacement
- Exterior maintenance, including painting

What you cannot do yourself you need to hire someone to do. Appliances such as stoves, hot water heaters, and dishwashers need to be repaired or replaced when they stop working. And there is just no way around that expense when they stop working.

Property taxes need to be paid when due, as do any special assessments. If there are homeowner or condominium association fees, they too need to be paid each month. All of these kinds of expenses can suddenly make what would have been a profitable rental property investment a problem property. At best, the property can become a marginal income property. And if the tenant is problematic, such as not paying rent or causing damage, any hope of profit is lost.

Proper management of any rental property can make the difference between loss and profit. If you cannot properly manage the property, the next best solution is to hire a property manager.

Keep in mind that rental properties can be a source of income and significant profit, or they can become costly problems.

Chapter 10

Present Market Conditions

There is one thing you need in order to invest in foreclosure properties: a supply of properties that you can purchase. The current real-estate market and the local economy determine the number of properties that are available at any given time. As the local real-estate market changes from a buyer's to seller's market, and vice versa, there are always opportunities for investing in foreclosure properties. Sometimes there are more, sometimes less, but there are always foreclosures no matter the current market conditions.

Inventory

Real-estate market conditions always change. That is one constant with real estate. There are good times and there are bad times. The market speeds up or slows down depending on various factors. Depending on what the local market is doing, the inventory of available properties moves up and down.

You have certainly heard of the terms "a buyer's market" and "a seller's market." A buyer's market occurs when properties are not selling. The available properties are staying on the market longer, and offers from buyers are not forthcoming. Property owners are forced to reduce their asking prices. Some offer buyer incentives, such as a contribution to closing costs, to try to sell their property. Some sellers get creative to attract buyers by offering big screen televisions, golf carts, cars, vacations, or whatever they can think of to sell their property in a buyer's market.

In a seller's market there is a shortage of available properties. In other words, there are more buyers than there are sellers. Buyers pay more for a property, and sometimes offer more than the asking price, just to get the property. Properties on the market do not last long and are often sold within a few days, if not in a few hours. Sellers do not need to offer any incentives in a seller's market.

ESSENTIAL

The availability of employment determines the trends of a local real-estate market. When unemployment is low and employers are hiring, expect the housing market to trend toward a seller's market.

Keep in mind that the markets move back and forth. It is not an instant movement, and it may take six to twelve months to realize a change of direction in any local real-estate market. Trends are used to evaluate a market condition. If a trend continues, such as sellers offering many buyer incentives to sell a property, the local market is slowing and becoming more of a buyer's market.

Local Economy Determines Inventory

Nothing has a bigger impact on the inventory of properties on the market than the local economy. If the economy is booming, properties are likely to be in short supply. When the local economy slows, there is more likely to be a larger supply of properties offered for sale.

Say there is a major employer called ABC Corp. that employs 1,000 people in an area. ABC Corp. suddenly announces it is shutting down, forever closing its local operation. One thousand employees are out of work. The impact of ABC Corp.'s shutdown is devastating on the local real-estate market. Many people will sell their properties because they can't afford them. Some will need to move to other areas to seek employment. Some will likely find employment nearby and hold on to their property.

Don't overlook the impact of ABC Corp.'s shutdown on others that are not their employees. There are hundreds of people that relied on ABC Corp. for their incomes, or part of it. From the waitress at the nearby restaurant where the ABC Corp. employees dined to the computer technician that worked on the company's computers as an employee of the local computer store, these are people that are also going see their income decrease or even disappear. This also places pressure on the local market, depressing the housing prices. The offered-for-sale inventory increases. There are too many house for sale and not enough buyers.

Consider also that none of this happens overnight. Even with the ABC Corp.'s sudden closure, it would take several months before the housing market would slow. The affected employees would collect unemployment benefits. Some would try to hold on longer than others. But a trend would develop moving the local market to a buyer's market. Many of the homes are moving into a pre-foreclosure status.

Assume that eighteen months after ABC Corp. shut down, major news breaks. The XYZ Company is going to purchase the ABC Corp.'s property and open operations there. Within twelve months, the XYZ Company will be employing 1,500 people.

The impact of XYZ Company's opening will be the exact opposite of ABC Corp.'s shutdown. As employees are hired they need a place to live. The local housing market will move from a buyer's market to a seller's market. The housing will become in demand, not just from XYZ Company's new employees but also from others that are providing services to the company and their employees. It will not happen overnight, but the trend will move to a robust local real-estate market.

Foreclosure Bargains in Any Market

By now you might be thinking that there are only foreclosure bargains in a buyer's market. There is good news: Foreclosures occur in any market. No matter how the local market is trending, you can be sure there are foreclosures.

And when there are foreclosures, the owners of those properties want to sell them, the sooner the better, and this creates foreclosure bargains for you as a real-estate investor specializing in foreclosure properties.

Because foreclosures occur for many reasons, not just employment loss, there are always foreclosure properties available, no matter what the local real-estate market is doing. You need to be aware of the local real-estate market, as you might change your plans as to what to do with a property that you acquire. If the local market is depressed and properties are not selling quickly, you must consider that when buying a property to resell. If you are purchasing the property to hold and rent, consider that a seller's market could make it a bit more difficult to find a renter.

Other Influences on the Local Market

Other things can influence the local market. One major category is interest rates. When the interest rates rise, potential homebuyers are nudged out of the market. The monthly payment increases enough that they cannot qualify for a loan. This creates fewer buyers and slows down the local market.

As markets transition it is harder to realize if you are in an up or down trend, but national events can affect the economy abruptly. The impact can occur suddenly when a major event breaks. For example, the 9/11 attacks and Hurricane Katrina influenced local housing markets.

Energy costs impact the market, too. When gas prices suddenly rise, consumers spend less because they have less money. When the prices fall, they are ready to spend again and take on contracted debts such as a mortgage.

FACT

If you think there are not many foreclosure investment properties in your area, you are wrong. The National Delinquency Survey conducted by the Mortgage Bankers Association (MBA) found that between 1 percent and 2 percent of all mortgages are in danger of foreclosure. That means that millions of pre-foreclosure and foreclosure properties are available at any given time.

Some properties and specific areas are not affected by economic factors. For example, properties located in resort areas are generally desirable and often do not fluctuate in value. Multifamily properties such as apartment buildings are generally not influenced by local economic factors.

Of course, these types of properties could suffer price fluctuation. Recently there has been an overbuilding of condominium units in southern Florida. Investors drove the prices higher. Inflated selling prices were the norm. In some communities, investors bought yet-to-be-built units from a developer and could then sell the purchase contracts to other investors, flipping the paper for thousands of dollars. Investors drove the prices up in a buying frenzy. Then the market corrected itself, and some investors were badly burned by purchasing condominium units at inflated prices.

Present Economy

The American economy, by its very nature, changes regularly. Good and bad economic news, as well as projections and predictions, are broadcast and reported daily by the nation's media.

In October 2006, the National Association of Realtors (NAR) issued a press release stating that home sales appeared to be bottoming out, with lower home prices attracting buyers in many areas of the country. According to David Lereah, NAR's chief economist, the housing market was showing signs of new life and that sales may be leveling out. "Many potential home buyers who have been taking a wait-and-see attitude or taking their time and being methodical in the search process are being enticed by lower home prices," Lereah said. "Given a positive economic backdrop of lower interest rates and job creation, we expect sales activity to pick up early next year."

The thirty-year fixed-rate mortgage was averaging about 6.5 percent in the fourth quarter of 2006. Coupled with an unemployment rate of about 4.8 percent and an inflation rate measured at 3.4 percent based on the Consumer Price Index, and the economic outlook was good. Personal income was likely to grow 3.4 percent for 2006.

Of course, this was 2006. The economy can change directions, and when it does, local real-estate markets move in different directions. Factors such as unemployment, interest rates, stock market indexes, inflation, and world news can influence the current economy.

OFHEO Indices

There is a little-known yet important government agency that provides useful information to the foreclosure investor. The Office of Federal Housing Enterprise Oversight (OFHEO) was established as an independent entity within the Department of Housing and Urban Development by the Federal Housing Enterprises Financial Safety and Soundness Act of 1992.

FACT

Combined assets and off-balance-sheet obligations of Fannie Mae and Freddie Mac were $4.2 trillion at year-end 2005.

OFHEO's mission is to promote housing and a strong national housing finance system by ensuring the safety and soundness of Fannie Mae (Federal National Mortgage Association) and Freddie Mac (Federal Home Loan Mortgage Corporation). OFHEO works to ensure the capital adequacy and financial safety and soundness of the two housing government-sponsored enterprises (GSEs).

Fannie Mae and Freddie Mac are the nation's largest housing finance institutions. They buy mortgages from commercial banks, thrift institutions, mortgage banks, and other primary lenders and either hold these mortgages in their own portfolios or package them into mortgage-backed securities for resale to investors. These secondary mortgage market operations play a major role in creating a ready supply of mortgage funds for American homebuyers.

Fannie Mae and Freddie Mac are congressionally chartered, publicly owned corporations whose shares are listed on the New York Stock Exchange. Under terms of their GSE charters, they are exempt from state and local taxation and from registration requirements of the Securities and Exchange Commission. Each firm has a backup credit line with the U.S. Treasury. OFHEO's responsibilities include oversight of both Fannie Mae and Freddie Mac.

As part of their work, OFHEO issues comprehensive reports and statistical information. One particularly useful report is the OFHEO House Price Index (HPI). It is designed to measure changes in the value of single-family homes in the United States. The HPI also includes information about the various regions of the country, in the individual states, and the District of Columbia. The HPI is published quarterly by OFHEO using data provided by Fannie Mae and Freddie Mac. It generally is about eighty-plus pages of information.

QUESTION?

Why is it important to know what Fannie Mare and Freddie Mac are saying?

As an active real-estate investor, you must keep current on the trends and news of the real-estate industry. Because of their size and power in the financial markets, both Fannie Mae and Freddie Mac have tremendous power and influence. What the two entities mandate, the real-estate financial markets follow.

A free copy of the report is available online at *www.ofheo.gov/HPI.asp*.

Table 10-1, produced from information from the OFHEO quarterly report, shows how housing prices are moving in the states.

TABLE 10-1
Percent Change in House Prices through Q3 2006

State	Rank	1-Yr.	1-Qtr.	5-Yr.
Idaho (ID)	1	17.52	3.00	59.99
Utah (UT)	2	17.41	4.70	40.63
Oregon (OR)	3	16.89	2.85	67.61
Arizona (AZ)	4	16.37	1.02	95.91
Washington (WA)	5	16.35	3.14	63.91
Florida (FL)	6	15.10	1.15	110.62
Wyoming (WY)	7	14.39	4.61	60.13
New Mexico (NM)	8	14.10	2.66	53.01
Hawaii (HI)	9	13.33	1.27	110.11
Maryland (MD)	10	13.19	1.84	101.54
Louisiana (LA)	11	13.14	2.17	39.88
Montana (MT)	12	12.91	2.86	59.67
District of Columbia (DC)	13	11.30	0.99	113.13
Mississippi (MS)	14	10.70	2.51	29.82
Alaska (AK)	15	10.41	1.67	52.98
California (CA)	16	10.16	0.62	109.60
Virginia (VA)	17	9.91	0.66	80.95
Vermont (VT)	18	9.35	1.39	64.89
New Jersey (NJ)	19	9.19	0.78	81.36
North Dakota (ND)	20	8.98	2.65	41.39
Delaware (DE)	21	8.92	1.84	71.35
Alabama (AL)	22	8.85	1.75	31.82
Nevada (NV)	23	8.63	0.85	102.70
Pennsylvania (PA)	24	8.44	1.01	55.17
North Carolina (NC)	25	8.44	1.59	29.33

State	Rank	1-Yr.	1-Qtr.	5-Yr.
South Carolina (SC)	26	7.79	1.34	32.34
Tennessee (TN)	27	7.58	1.48	29.48
Illinois (IL)	28	6.95	1.18	41.98
Texas (TX)	29	6.79	1.83	24.02
New York (NY)	30	6.53	-0.33	68.03
West Virginia (WV)	31	6.34	1.98	36.84
Connecticut (CT)	32	6.34	0.72	60.31
Arkansas (AR)	33	6.23	0.58	31.74
South Dakota (SD)	34	5.88	1.35	31.95
Georgia (GA)	35	5.49	1.19	27.90
Missouri (MO)	36	5.02	1.03	32.73
Oklahoma (OK)	37	4.96	0.30	26.13
Maine (ME)	38	4.89	0.94	58.96
Kansas (KS)	39	4.79	1.48	24.73
Rhode Island (RI)	40	4.55	-0.37	86.35
Wisconsin (WI)	41	4.20	0.60	35.24
Kentucky (KY)	42	4.14	0.69	24.71
Colorado (CO)	43	3.72	0.62	22.65
New Hampshire (NH)	44	3.72	-0.14	55.90
Iowa (IA)	45	3.71	1.16	24.15
Minnesota (MN)	46	3.38	0.34	42.80
Nebraska (NE)	47	3.22	1.07	21.71
Indiana (IN)	48	2.33	1.13	17.47
Massachusetts (MA)	49	1.11	-0.48	50.89
Ohio (OH)	50	1.02	0.12	17.30
Michigan (MI)	51	-0.55	-0.52	16.64

Laws in Different States

Each state has established its own foreclosure laws. The approach of the laws is to protect both the borrower and the lender. The concept of the laws is to allow the borrower sufficient time to catch up with past-due payments yet still allow a lender to foreclose when a borrower is no longer making timely payments.

As a foreclosure investor, you must understand the foreclosure laws in the states where you plan to invest. Not only should you read the statute, you should have your attorney explain any portion of the law that you do not understand.

By typing the name of the state along with the words "foreclosure statute" into any search engine, you can quickly locate the state's foreclosure law on the Internet.

Chapter 11

Finding Foreclosures Through Companies

Before you can invest in foreclosure properties you have to find them. That's not as difficult as you might first think. The lenders that own the foreclosed properties want to sell them, and as far as they are concerned the sooner the better. Lenders use all kinds of methods and techniques to market and sell the properties they own from foreclosure. Whether the property was received through a drawn-out foreclosure process or easily turned over in a deed in lieu of foreclosure transaction, the lender wants the property sold quickly.

banks come in all sizes and shapes. Local banks are slowly dis-
ng, giving way to larger community or regional banks. Then there
arger multistate and national banks. All of them have made loans
by real estate, and all have loans that have gone sour.

You can be sure that all banks, regardless of their size, own real estate
that they want sold. And they will be only too happy to make sure you know
about their properties.

FACT

All lenders have a Real Estate Owned department. It is commonly called
an REO. This is the department responsible for protecting the lender's
collateral and for selling any foreclosed properties to recoup the money
loaned to any defaulted borrowers.

Banks notify potential buyers in a number of methods. Once you are
placed on their foreclosure investor lists, the banks will notify you of new
REO properties by:

- Phone calls
- Fax
- E-mail
- Regular mail

Some lenders also post their REO properties on their Web site. Some
offer e-mail notification when a new property has been posted. On occasion, some will tell you they do not have any such list available.

To get on the REO department's investor distribution list, simply ask. It
may take a phone call or two to locate the correct person within the REO
department. The bank wants buyers, and they are only too happy to add
your name and contact information as a potential purchaser of an REO
property.

Keep in mind that you will not be the only real-estate investor on the REO department's list. Other investors will be notified when you are. For that reason you must be willing and able to move swiftly. Your competition, other foreclosure real-estate investors, will also be aggressively seeking promising properties. You need to move quickly before another investor presents, offers, and purchases the property.

Be sure to visit the local branch offices of the banks located within your investment area. Get to know the branch managers. Ask the managers who to contact at their bank's REO department to get on the notification lists.

Some banks now refer to their REO departments as the Loss Mitigation office. Some might also refer to their REO department as the foreclosure department.

Some of the larger banks have established separate entities or companies to originate mortgages. The names of the mortgage divisions will sound similar to the bank's name, yet they are separate divisions. It can all get quite confusing, but what you need to find out is whom to contact to get the REO listings.

Mortgage Companies

In addition to banks, private mortgage companies originate hundreds of thousands of mortgages each year. Some of the mortgage companies are fully owned bank subsidiaries, while others are companies formed solely for the purpose of originating mortgages. Just like banks, they have REO departments.

It might be a little tougher to find the mortgage companies, but with a little detective work it won't take long to locate the ones you want to contact. Keep in mind there are many local sales offices or origination offices that produce mortgages for a company. Many times there are licensed mortgage brokers arranging home loans. These local offices are not the ones with REO departments. Rather, the larger regional or home office is where the

REO department is located. A simple inquiry can usually locate the mortgage company's REO office.

You can often locate a mortgage company's REO department by looking at the mortgage foreclosure complaints in your local courthouse. The legal document includes the name and address (and often the telephone number and fax number) of the REO office.

Mortgage companies work the same as banks: Their goal is to sell the foreclosed property as quickly as possible. They will gladly add your name to their investor's list. All you need to do is ask to be included.

Lenders are not required to provide a list of their REO properties. There is no statutory requirement that a list be prepared and made available to the public. Lenders routinely prepare lists and make them available for their real-estate agents and others involved in managing and selling the properties.

Some lenders use the Internet to market their owned properties. For example, Countrywide, one of the largest mortgage companies, lists their properties on their Web site. On the site the lender says, "A Countrywide owned property (lender-owned), also sometimes referred to as a REO (real estate owned) home or property is often a way to get a good deal on a home or an investment property." The Web site address is *www.countrywide.com/ purchase/f_reo.asp.*

The following is a list of national and regional lenders that post their real-estate owned listings on their Web site. The list is not exhaustive but rather a starting place to locate properties:

National Lenders
- Bank of America: *http://bankofamerica.reo.com/search*
- Beal Bank—Commercial Listings: *www.bealbank.com/Content. aspx?ID=13*
- Beal Bank—Branch Banking & Trust (BB&T): *www.bbt.com/bbt/ applications/specialassets/search.asp*
- CitiMortgage: *www.citimortgage.com/Mortgage/Home.do*

- Compass Bank: *www.citimortgage.com/Mortgage/Home.do*
- Countrywide: *www.countrywide.com/purchase/f_reo.asp*
- Downey Savings & Loan: *www.downeysavings.com/ffs/properties*
- Fremont Investment & Loan: *www.1800fremont.com/REO/ReoProperties_Available.asp*
- GRP Financial Services Corporation: *www.grpcapital.com/properties/index.php*
- Home Loan and Investment Bank: *www.hlbsales.com/index.htm*
- HSBC: *www.us.hsbc.com/½/3/personal/home-loans/properties*
- IndyMac Bank: *http://apps.indymacbank.com/individuals/realestate/search.asp*
- IAS—Integrated Asset Services: *www.iasreo.com/homesforsale.aspx*
- M&T Bank: *http://services.mandtbank.com/personal/mortgage/reomort.cfm*
- Ocwen Financial Corporation: *www.ocwen.com/reo*
- People's Bank: *www.peoples.com/about/community/0,8397,1355,00.html*
- U.S. Home Mortgage: *https://customercare.fnfismd.com/usbank homemortgage/reo/reoReport.asp*
- Wilshire Credit Corporation: *www.wfsg.com/realestate/realestate.aspx*

Regional Lenders

- 1st National Bank of First Scotia: *www.firstscotia.com/repossessions/repossessions.html*
- Coast and Country: *www.coastandcountryreo.com/*
- Lexington State Bank: *www.lsbnc.com/property_for_sale.asp*
- Mortgage Lenders Network USA: *www.mlnusa.com/realestate/listings.asp?*
- National Bank of Arizona: *www.nbarizona.com/BusinessBanking/CommercialRealEstate/BankOwnedProp.htm*
- New South Federal Savings Bank: *www.newsouthfederal.com/reo/*
- nNYRealty.com: *www.nnyrealty.com/nyreo.htm*
- Texas State Bank: *www.texasstatebank.com/property_listing.html*
- Unity Bank: *www.unitybank.com/foreclosures/index.cfm*

- Virginia Housing Development Authority (VHDA): *www.unitybank.com/foreclosures/index.cfm*
- Western Bank: *www.wbpr.com/En/RepossessedProperties.asp*
- Zions Bank: *www.zionsbank.com/foreclosed_properties.jsp*

Each lender works differently, but they all have similar goals. They intend and desire to get the best price possible. They have no interest in dumping the properties they own cheaply. Once you make an offer to purchase a property, most lenders will present a counteroffer. Often the counteroffer a real-estate investor receives is higher than you would expect. This is the lender (and its employees) demonstrating to investors, shareholders, and auditors that it attempted to get the highest price possible for the property owned.

ALERT!

You should be more surprised to get an acceptance than a counteroffer from the lender's loss mitigation department when offering to buy the REO. Lenders generally take the position that they will negotiate hard for any property they own. They will tell you (and anyone else) that they want fair market value.

You should always plan to counter the lender's counteroffer. It is also typical for most lenders to add a condition to your offer, such as "subject to corporate approval within five days." This is because your purchase offer and counteroffers must often be reviewed and approved by several individuals, other companies, or investors before final approval is accepted.

Insurance Companies

Many people do not realize that insurance companies are active real-estate investors. They often make loans for nonresidential properties. While they can (and do) offer loans for typical American homes, they are more likely to invest in other property types.

For example, insurers often invest in rural properties, farms, larger multifamily units, and commercial properties. Some insurers specialize in particular property types, such as small strip shopping centers or standalone commercial buildings, like the type where fast food franchises operate their restaurants.

Insurers also make loans for larger residential properties. One of the reasons they specialize in nonstandard properties is the higher interest rates they can demand for the loan.

It is often more difficult for you to locate REO departments of licensed insurers. These are the companies, not the agents. However, a local agent might be able to help you find the information you need. Just as with larger banks or mortgage companies, you will need to locate the larger regional or home office of the insurer. Small regional insurers, sometimes called mutual companies, often invest in their community and close to their main (and usually only) office. That is where the REO department will be located.

Credit Unions

In many parts of the country, credit unions act like banks and directly compete with other financial institutions. This means they offer all kinds of services and loans, including mortgages.

Credit unions also are found in all sizes and shapes. Some are private, while others operate as public institutions. Some credit unions do not offer mortgages but do offer loans that are secured by real estate. These home loans might be called second mortgages (they are second to the primary mortgage) or HELOC (home equity line of credit).

Just like banks, mortgage companies, and insurers, credit unions are likely to have some loans go bad from time to time. When that happens, they may have properties for sale.

Develop a list of the credit unions with offices in your investment area. Contact those credit unions and find out who operates the REO office. With smaller credit unions, the REO office might be just one person. Making personal contact at a credit union office will usually provide you with the contact information that you need.

Real-Estate Companies

There are real-estate companies that specialize in the handling of REO properties. These companies market the properties and get them sold for the REO departments.

Many times these real-estate companies are real-estate brokerages that specialize in the disposition of the foreclosed properties.

ALERT!

Some real-estate agents specialize in the listing and sale of foreclosure properties. These agents work in regular real-estate brokerage offices but work almost exclusively in these foreclosures. It might take a little time to develop these contacts. As you make inquiries about advertised properties, you will often find these firms.

You may be thinking that it is wise to circumvent the real-estate agent. Beginning foreclosure investors often make this mistake. They think that by not acquiring properties listed by real-estate agents they are able to buy properties cheaper. They believe that by circumventing agents they are not paying money that is the agent's commission. Agents can be a steady source of foreclosure properties. The amount of properties they can find and the profitable deals they can produce far surpasses any savings you might realize on a deal without paying an agent's commission. You should work to develop a relationship with an agent that specializes in foreclosure properties.

Finding the right agent will take time and some perseverance. Ask your friends and relatives for recommendations. Look for an agent that understands your desire to invest in foreclosure properties. Pay particular attention to the agent's enthusiasm to work with a real-estate investor. Some agents seek investor relationships while others do not.

Lenders often use a BPO, broker's price opinion, to determine the value of their collateral. The lender orders the BPO from companies that compile real-estate information. Depending on local regulations, the BPO might be obtained from real-estate agents, REO companies, or brokers. Lenders order the BPO because it is less expensive and faster than ordering a full appraisal. A BPO is like a mini appraisal and a lot easier to complete. Many are only one or two pages in length, compared to the fifteen-page appraisal. BPOs can be created by driving by the property or by inspecting the interior.

Brokers and agents that prepare BPOs are often sources of REO properties. Don't overlook the contacts they have that can provide you with leads of properties in foreclosure.

Don't worry about the BPO or the current asking price of any REO property. The fair market value (FMV) is often the most questionable part of the foreclosure property transaction. The owner of the REO property wants fair market value, or at least wants to try to show that the highest possible sale price was attempted.

Fair market value is determined by the current as-is condition of the property. Lenders usually want to sell the property as is; they do not want to put any more money in the property. Most lenders will also allow any investor (and potential buyer of the REO) as much access as wanted to inspect the property. They will usually agree to formal inspections as long as you pay for the inspection service.

Lenders will seldom, if ever, agree to pay for repairs recommended by an inspector. The inspection report can, however, be used to justify a differing of opinion of the fair market value of a property.

The amount that is owed to the lender is usually more than what the property is worth. Most likely the lender will try to ask for more than the amount they are owed. That is just a starting point.

Keep in mind that the lender received the property because of an unsuccessful foreclosure auction. The lender made a bid for the property in the amount owed by the defaulting borrower. No one else bid more for the property at the public sale. The property reverted to the lender. It became an REO property.

Consider also that the minimum bid included all the extras in addition to the loan balance. That included the interest, late fees, attorney fees, legal costs, and other charges that have nothing to do with the fair market value of the property. Nobody wanted the property for the lender's initial bid, which was the loan balance.

FACT

Most likely the property was not worth the amount of the loan. If it were, the defaulting property owner would have sold the property, paid off the mortgage, and walked away with the equity. Since this didn't happen, the fair market value is probably less than the lender's loan balance and asking price of the property.

One of the reasons REO properties are not bargains is because of how the property was financed by the lender. Consider this scenario:

- $200,000 property (fair market value)
- 20 percent down: $40,000
- Total amount of loan: $160,000

If the homeowner defaulted and the property became an REO property, the property would be offered for sale for approximately $170,000 (the loan plus $10,000 in fees). To any real-estate investor this was a good purchase and an opportunity to earn a profit of $30,000.

Now consider the same scenario but with 100 percent financing:

- $200,000 property (fair market value)
- 0 percent down
- Total amount of loan: $200,000

If the homeowner defaulted and the property became an REO property, the property would be offered for sale for approximately $210,000 (the loan, plus $10,000 in fees). Just because the lender opted to finance the property with little or no down payment and is now the owner of the property that is no reason for you to pay more for the property.

It may take negotiation, and offers and counteroffers, to get the lender to see your side of the fair market value.

Inflated prices for REO properties are not uncommon. For example, an REO property was offered for sale that two years earlier had sold for $295,000. Other similar owner-occupied homes in the area were selling for $315,000. The REO property was offered for sale by the lender in as-is condition; there was no home warranty, no disclosures, no heat, or appliances, and there were burst pipes and water damage, and the house was vandalized and filthy dirty. The lender listed this REO property with a notation that the price was firm. The listing also said that if a real-estate agent was buying the property on their own behalf the lender would not pay a commission.

Don't look at the lender's asking price or what the lender has to recover as a guide to the fair market value of the property. A lender can provide a loan of $500,000 for a $50,000 property. Just because the lender did and now needs to recoup its loaned amount does not make the property worth more.

The lender's list price was $365,000! Real-estate brokers believed the property was now worth $240,000 in its current condition. No real-estate investor should make such a purchase. The property in this example was overpriced even if it were in pristine condition.

REO Companies

Some lenders—banks, credit unions, insurers, and mortgage companies—outsource the REO duties to another company. Those companies specialize in doing all the work of a regular REO department.

They protect the asset and hire an inspector to report on the property's condition. They winterize the property, if necessary, by draining pipes, turning off water, and making sure the heating system is working. They rekey the property, changing the locks to prevent the defaulted owner or others from entering the property. They often provide digital photos for the lender. They create reports, such as pre-foreclosure evaluations, market analysis, and occupancy verification. REO companies also take care of the utilities, including the transfer and connection to the lender's name.

ESSENTIAL

Most REO companies, as part of their ongoing service, provide monthly status reporting on the property. They attempt to preserve the property (and the lender's collateral) by making sure the property is maintained properly until sold.

Some REO companies manage the evictions for the lender. It is not uncommon for them to pay cash for the keys to property—a way to get the defaulted property owner out of the property. Often cheaper than the legal process, and always faster, the property owner is offered a small amount of cash to vacate the property over a weekend and turn all the keys into the REO company.

The REO company, which is familiar with the local market, develops a marketing plan to sell the property. The company often places the property in a multiple listing service, orders print advertising, and determines where to list the property on the Internet. They often negotiate any purchase offers on behalf of the lender. REO companies may list the property for sale with a local real-estate broker or attempt to market the property directly to the public.

Locating an REO company that serves your area may take some work, but once you do, it could become a source of ongoing leads for foreclosure properties that are new to the market. REO companies often carry out the negotiations between you and the lender. Typically the REO company has no authority to sell the property on behalf of the lender. Rather, the REO company can only submit written purchase offers to the lender and await the decision. Some lenders will not provide financing on REO properties, while others will do so. The REO company usually knows what its client lender will accept. Don't be afraid to ask.

Chapter 12

Finding Foreclosures in Other Ways

You can't invest in foreclosure properties until you find them. As an active real-estate investor specializing in foreclosure investments, you will spend a significant amount of your time searching for properties. Finding foreclosed properties takes time. You will need to use traditional and nontraditional methods to search and find possible foreclosure investment properties. This chapter will explore some of the lesser-known options for finding those properties.

Newspapers

The most obvious and first place to commence your search for foreclosure properties is the local newspapers. Most classified sections categorize real-estate advertisements as real estate for sale, for rent, and investment properties.

Pick up the real-estate magazines at the local grocery store or convenience store. Most communities have several of these types of publications. Some also have For Sale By Owner (FSBO) publications. Don't limit your search of properties to the advertisements of just one newspaper. Look for advertised properties everywhere.

Pre-foreclosure Versus Foreclosure Properties

As a real-estate investor, there are two types of foreclosure properties you are searching for and attempting to locate: foreclosure properties and pre-foreclosure properties.

So far you have been learning about foreclosure properties. These are properties that have been or are in the process of becoming foreclosed. They are easy to find, primarily through the public notice required by each state's law. You can find these properties easily by watching the legal notices.

ESSENTIAL

Finding both types of foreclosure properties is crucial to the success of your real-estate investing business. Without both pre-foreclosure and foreclosure properties to purchase, you have no method of making income.

Pre-foreclosure properties are not as easy to locate. No one advertises a pre-foreclosure property as such. The owner of a property about to enter foreclosure doesn't announce to the world that the property is for sale because it's about to be foreclosed. However, you can locate pre-foreclosure properties often by inquiring about properties advertised for sale. Some key words in ads might indicate the seller is in financial difficulty. Some examples are:

- Motivated seller
- Price reduced
- Bring offers
- Owner says sell now
- FSBO—must sell
- Take over payments

In pre-foreclosure properties, you will be most successful if you can get to the property owner first *before* any other foreclosure investor. The sooner you make contact, the more likely you will be successful.

Remember, keep reading the real-estate advertisements. Don't stop after just a few days or weeks. As an active real-estate investor you must constantly be looking for properties advertised for sale.

Develop Your Own Farm

Most new real-estate investors are excited about the prospect of making money and forget the basics. One of the most basic strategies is to develop your own investment area, or farm. Ideally your real-estate investment area should be close to your home (or within an easy drive or commute from it). Usually one or two counties are a large enough area for a real-estate investment farm. As you develop more real-estate expertise, you can expand your investment area and develop a larger area or several areas. In the beginning of your real-estate investment career though, define a specific area and work it.

Many new real-estate investors that remain unsuccessful do not spend enough time searching for foreclosure properties. You must spend most of your time looking for properties that you can acquire. As you get started as a foreclosure investor, plan to spend nearly 90 percent of your time hunting for suitable foreclosure properties.

The idea of a farm is a place where you can constantly look for properties and produce real-estate deals. You farm the area by growing and developing business within that area. It makes sense to get to know one or two areas well rather than trying to put together deals hundreds of miles away from where you live.

When determining where you are going to farm for pre-foreclosure and foreclosure properties, don't overdo it with the size. While there is no hard and set rule about what size your investment farm must be, don't make the mistake most beginners do by choosing too large an area when determining where you are going to farm for pre-foreclosure and foreclosure properties. You will be better served by keeping your farm smaller. This is where you will concentrate your search effort for foreclosure properties.

Usually your farm should be no larger than two counties. A metro area is also fine, as is several school districts. If you live in a rural location, your farm investment area might be in the nearest town, or it might include a larger area just so there are enough property owners. Common sense will tell you that if there are only 100 properties in your community, your development area must be larger. If you live in a large city, your development area can be concentrated. For example, if you live in Manhattan, you might work only the midtown area.

If you locate a property near your farm area—across the county line for example—of course you should grab it. Your goal is to become an expert on your investment area. You should soon know what the neighborhoods are like, parking issues, public safety concerns, the location and quality of the schools, and local issues that affect the quality of life. You will soon learn the style of houses and, most importantly, their current market value.

FACT

New real-estate agents also use the farm concept. Each brokerage assigns new agents a farm area. It is that area where the agent works to develop new business and tries to get listings. Use this simple and proven model to work your real-estate investing business.

You want to concentrate your efforts on properties located in areas where property values are rising, crime is low, schools are good, and local businesses thrive. That doesn't mean you can't make money in other economic conditions, but it is easiest as a real-estate investor when the neighborhoods are stable and property values are increasing.

You do not need to know every block or street in your investment area before you start investing in pre-foreclosure and foreclosure properties. Rather you want to gain general knowledge of the area and have a working knowledge of the average prices in your target area. This allows you to make fast decisions about properties so that you will soon know a bargain when you spot one.

Legal Notices

Public notice of legal procedures is a fundamental and vital principle of fairness in the in the American legal system. Legal notice is the information of all the legal proceedings of a particular case, including the documents filed, decisions, requests, motions, petitions, and upcoming dates. Legal documents notify both parties affected by a lawsuit or legal proceeding, the opposing attorney, and the court.

ALERT!

Legal notices are often posted on public bulletin boards in the courthouse. They are also usually in regularly published newspapers and in the local legal newspaper. (Your area's legal newspaper is often available at your public library.)

The purpose of legal notice is not to help a real-estate investor specializing in purchasing foreclosure properties. Rather it is that neither a party of a suit nor the court itself can operate in secret, make private overtures, or conceal their actions. Notice of a lawsuit begins with personal service on the defendants of the complaint together with instructions to file an answer in court.

As the foreclosure process proceeds through the court, legal notice is made to make sure all interested parties are notified. In the case of a foreclosure, anyone with an interest in the real estate is made aware of pending action. For example, a contractor (called a *mechanic* in legal terms) with a potential lien is notified by the legal notice and must act to protect the lien. If the contractor does nothing, the lien will not be available once the foreclosure is complete.

All of these places can provide excellent leads and sources of information to help locate properties in foreclosure. As an active foreclosure investor you should be reading these legal notices daily.

Public Records

The courthouse is filled with records that are public and available for anyone to view during regular business hours. There is a wealth of information there for the foreclosure investor.

FACT

Public records are considered constructive notice. Anyone interested in the property receives constructive notice via the courthouse records, without delivering specific notice to individuals.

Depending on the jurisdiction and laws of the state, the courthouse is where deeds and other documents are recorded. Mortgages, deeds of trust, easements, leases, and other documents affecting real property title give notice to the public.

Foreclosure Listing Services

There are some companies that provide foreclosure listings. For a subscription fee, their service provides you with an updated list of foreclosures. Their sources for the information are the same as what is available to you: public legal notices and documents filed in the courthouse. Of course, the service saves you the time and inconvenience of daily visits to the courthouse.

There are many of these types of services offered via the Internet. Before you sign up for an extended period, purchase only a trial period of a foreclosure list service. See if it generates good leads in your area. Make sure you can easily cancel the service, too.

The following are the Web site addresses of some of the foreclosure reporting services available on the Internet:

- Daily Business Review   *www.dailybusinessreview.com*
- Florida Foreclosure Report   *www.floridaforeclosurereport.com*
- Foreclosure Access   *www.foreclosureaccess.com*
- Foreclosure Data NW   *www.foreclosuredatanw.com*
- Foreclosure Disclosure Weekly *www.foreclosuredisclosure.com*
- Foreclosure Report   *www.foreclosurereport.com*
- Foreclosure Reporting Service *www.foreclosure-report.com*
- ForeclosureTrac   *www.foreclosuretrac.com*
- Information Resource Service *www.irsfl.com*
- Las Vegas Default Service   *www.lvdefault.com*
- Midwest Foreclosures   *www.midwestforeclosures.com*
- New York Foreclosures   *www.newyorkforeclosures.com*
- PropertyTrac   *www.propertytrac.com*
- Real Data Corp   *www.real-data.com*
- Records Research   *www.countyrecordsresearch.com*
- REDLOC   *www.redloc.com*
- The Daily Record   *www.mddailyrecord.com*

Some title companies offer foreclosure lists for clients. The advantage of using a daily generated list is that you get the information before others. For example, the information you get from the listing service might be published within a week, but you have had the information and been able to make earlier contact than others relying on public published lists in the daily newspaper or the legal newspaper.

Neighbors

As you work your farm, take notice of properties that appear recently abandoned. Don't overlook the information you can get from a neighbor about an adjoining property.

Start working your investment area by driving around it regularly. Always carry a notepad with you and make necessary notes. When you see ugly properties—those that are rundown and need paint or are cluttered with rubbish, trash, and junked cars—write down the addresses. Search for properties that are listed for sale, both by real-estate agents and for sale by owners. Be constantly on the lookout for vacant and empty properties.

Also be sure to look for For Sale By Owner (FSBO, pronounced fizzbow) signs. Property owners facing foreclosure will often first attempt to sell the property themselves, hoping to avoid the embarrassment of a real-estate agent learning of their financial plight.

As you search for properties in your farm area, write down the phone numbers, addresses, and quick descriptions of the properties. When you get back to your office, call the For Sale By Owner properties. (You will learn more about what to ask later.) If there are neighbors near a FSBO property, don't hesitate to ask about the property. The more you ask, the more you will find out. Carry on a conversation with the neighbor. Find out as much as you can about the property and the property owner. Don't be afraid to ask why the property is for sale or why the property owner might be moving.

Advertise

There are many different ways to advertise and alert the public that you are in the business of buying pre-foreclosure and foreclosure properties. None of the methods of advertising requires extensive advertising budgets.

Some investors advertise on a grand scale. Some have paid huge fees to purchase advertising on billboards beside busy highways or streets. Others have paid hefty advertising rates to television stations for fifteen- or thirty-second spots. You do not need to do this. There are ways you can get the word out inexpensively.

Classified Advertisements

Buy small classified advertisements in the local newspapers as well as in any advertising-only, throwaway weeklies that might be published and distributed in your farm area. These advertisements are inexpensive and can generate thousands of dollars of profit for you each year.

Place your ad in the "real estate wanted" section. Your advertisement should be simple. It should say something like "I Buy Houses" and include your telephone number.

Don't advertise that you only want to purchase foreclosure properties. You want people with all kinds of properties for sale to call. Even though you may not want the nonforeclosure properties, you might want to pass along any leads to others in your network of associates.

Be sure you have your phone answered twenty-four hours a day. Voice mail or an answering machine should be attached to the line. However, you should not hide behind an automatic answer system. Potential foreclosure sellers will *not* leave a message, or if they do, you can be sure they are going to call another real-estate investor. It is always best to answer your phone as much as possible. Take your calls, especially if you are advertising your phone number.

Bandit Signs

Another way to locate pre-foreclosure properties is to erect bandit signs at busy intersections. These are yard-type signs that you erect at busy intersections, usually after 5 P.M. Friday, and you remove before 8 A.M. Monday morning.

The idea is to have them up when city hall is closed. Before they get a complaint about them, you have taken them down and they are gone. You are an advertising bandit. The typical bandit signs say something like "I Buy Houses For Cash" and includes your phone number. One source for these signs is *www.banditsigns.com.*

Nontraditional Advertising Methods

There are many other places and methods you can advertise that will cost you little yet can help get the word out about you and your willingness to purchase properties.

Advertise in other unconventional places that are inexpensive. For example, consider testing an advertisement on your community cable TV channel. Church bulletins are often inexpensive. Another inexpensive and effective place to advertise is on menus in the local community's diners. You can also place small ads, often free, on the Internet. One good place to put your advertisement is on *www.craigslist.org*.

Place brochures or small posters on the community bulletin boards. While you are there, be sure to look for FSBO properties.

Word of Mouth

Perhaps one of the best ways to get leads about properties in the pre-foreclosure stage is by word of mouth. You'd be surprised at what information you can get if you let people know you are interested in purchasing foreclosure properties.

Tell everyone that you are an active real-estate investor and looking for properties to purchase now. Ask for referrals from your real-estate attorney, title company, and your accountant. Be sure to tell your relatives and friends that you are actively looking for investment properties.

Business Cards

Purchase printed cards from the local printer. Forget the idea of printing up your own business cards on your inkjet printer from some stock you bought at an office supply store. Don't be cheap in your search for properties. Pay the $30 or so for 500 cards.

You have to look like you have the money to buy real estate. Handing someone a flimsy card printed on your home computer sends the message that you are not a serious real-estate investor, or worse, that you are a flake!

You don't have to dress in silk suits or drive a Rolls Royce, but you have to present an image that you can purchase real estate. Don't do anything that gives the impression you are broke, don't have the money, or that you are an amateur real-estate investor.

Making Contacts

Visit open houses. Every week there will be open houses in properties located in your investment area. You should visit all open houses whether the property owners (FSBOs) or real-estate agents host them.

Gather property information sheets. Inspect the properties. Tell the hosts that you are a real-estate investor and are looking for investment properties.

Real-estate agents sitting in open houses are there to sell the property. (They have to show the property owner that they are working to sell their property; that is how they can justify collecting their commission.) However, the agents are also looking for potential buyers so they can sell any property to them as well as list the properties these potential buyers currently own.

As a real-estate investor, you want to develop relationships with working real-estate agents. Agents in open houses are generally looking for new clients.

The agent will ask if you are working with another agent. Your reply should always be that you are an active investor and will work with any agent that can find the properties you want to buy. You will, of course, over time develop a network of just a few working agents that are actively referring properties to you. You should never do anything that would cut the agent out of her commissions. And whenever possible, refer clients and potential listings to the agent to maintain a good working, professional relationship.

FACT

Don't be surprised if you have to talk to many real-estate agents before you find one that really will work with you. Most agents will move on when they realize you are looking to purchase properties at a substantial discount. But if you are persistent, you will find agents that realize they have a chance of selling your properties for you.

Make contacts with repair people and other trades contractors. Ask them to pass along leads of potential properties, and be sure to refer work back to them. Nothing builds loyalty more than helping someone else find paying jobs or a way to make money.

Network with other real-estate investors. You will certainly find them by calling about properties for sale. Make sure you maintain meticulous contact information so you can get a hold of them again. Ask them to keep you in mind with properties they have for sale.

Another way to network with real-estate investors is to attend real-estate investing clubs and meetings. Larger areas have these associations. You may have to ask around until you locate one near you.

Finding Properties on the Internet

In today's world, it is hard to imagine being an active real-estate investor without using the Internet as a prime search tool. The Web site *www.realtor.com* is a great source for properties in the Multiple Listing Service (MLS). Another source that offers a large real-estate listing service is *www.yahoo.com*.

You can also check out the For Sale By Owner sites, such as *www.fsbo .com*, *www.homesbyowner.com*, or *www.forsalebyowner.com* or the government foreclosures at *www.hud.gov/homes/homesforsale.cfm*.

Countless other Web sites offer listings and information about properties for you. Many real-estate agents maintain their own sites, which connect to local properties. Some well-spent time on the Internet searching for Web sites could pay substantial benefit to you. You will develop your own list of places to find both pre-foreclosure and foreclosure deals.

Chapter 13

Evaluating Your Foreclosure Find

After locating a potential foreclosure property to purchase as an investment property, it's time to consider purchasing it. Your evaluation of the property should be based on a lot more than just the asking price. The current asking price of a property is not the determining factor of the property's value. Some foreclosure properties are priced far out of line for any number of reasons. As an active real-estate investor, you must determine the property value based on your own calculations and not someone else's determination.

Title Search

When you are seriously considering purchasing any foreclosure property, the first step is to check the title of the real estate. There could be many problems with the title, and you do not want to buy any property with a multitude of problems. You only want properties that have clear titles. You do not want any clouds on the title (remember, a cloud is anything that affects the title of the property).

You should accept the fact that defaulted property owners have not been paying their bills. If they had, the property would not have been foreclosed. No matter what the reason for the foreclosure, from the legitimate mistake to the heartstring-tugging situation, the simple fact remains that the title to the property must be checked.

What could look to you like a good deal could suddenly become one to pass on because of liens now on the property. For example, you might have found a property with a potential of $20,000 profit. However, the liens exceed that amount, eliminating any potential payday for you. In this scenario it is obvious that you should simply pass on the property and look for another one.

Buying a foreclosure property does not mean the property will be given to you with a clear title. It only means the lender will deliver the property (and title) to you and have no more interest in the property. There could be subordinate liens that remain against the property.

One of the things you need to understand clearly is your state's laws regarding property liens. The lender that holds the first mortgage always has the controlling interest in the property. When it comes to being paid, the holder of the first mortgage always is paid first. Whatever is left is paid to the other lien holders before any equity is paid to the property owners.

However, you need to consult with your real-estate attorney to understand the laws of your state. Don't assume that secondary lien holders would not have an interest in the title of the property just because the mortgage holder foreclosed on it.

There are often first and a second mortgages placed on a property. The second mortgage is paid only after the first is paid in full. This is the reason that interest rates of second mortgages are higher: There is a bigger risk of default and not being paid.

QUESTION?

Is it possible to foreclose on a second mortgage?
As the holder of a second mortgage, the only way you can foreclose and take control of the property is to pay off the first mortgage. For smaller amounts owed and unpaid, this is often an impractical solution.

Title searches are not inexpensive. A complete title search may cost between $175 to $200 or more. You may want to start your title search with a less expensive and simpler ownership and encumbrances report (sometimes called the O&E report). The O&E report should quickly reveal any potential problems with the ownership or title at a less expensive cost. O&E reports usually cost less that $100.

Never use an O&E report in place of a full title search. The O&E report should only be used as part of your due diligence and to alert you of any potential problems with the property title.

Keep in mind that a title search could be completed today, and tomorrow a new lien might be filed against the property. This is one of the pitfalls of dealing with foreclosure properties.

IRS Liens

The Internal Revenue Service (IRS) has been granted special powers to collect taxes owed to the federal government. If the title report indicates any liens from the IRS, proceed cautiously! You must determine if the IRS was properly notified of the property foreclosure.

Current law, which is always subject to change, grants the IRS the authority to seize the property for up to 120 days following the sale. If the IRS has been properly notified twenty-five days or more before the sale and they decide to seize the property, you would be entitled to a refund of all your money plus interest. Should the IRS decide not to proceed with a seizure of the foreclosed property, the agency's right to do so will expire on the 121st day following the foreclosure sale.

As you learned earlier in this book, scheduled property auctions are often canceled and postponed. You must be certain that the IRS received proper notification of the actual sale whenever it occurred.

Current law has granted a major power to the IRS. If the Internal Revenue Service was not properly notified of the public sale, its lien remains in position as long as the lien is on file in the county's recording office. Under current law, if you purchased the real estate and there was not proper notice given to the IRS when the foreclosure sale occurred, you are sitting on a time bomb.

Why? Because at any point the IRS could opt to enforce its recorded lien against the property. There is only one way you could get clear title to the property: pay the former property owner's lien to the IRS. In other words, you get to pay someone else's taxes! You are not compensated for your loss.

Other Government Liens

Foreclosed properties often have municipal liens placed against the title for unpaid taxes, services, or other reasons. Some municipalities provide water, trash collection, or sewerage service. If the property owner did not pay the bill, the municipality likely filed a lien against the property.

Depending on your local laws, it is likely the property had been assessed. The municipality probably issued property tax bills. There could be county, local municipality (city, borough, or township) taxes, as well as taxes assessed by the local school board. If these taxes were not paid, the municipality likely placed a lien against the property.

Most municipality liens are not wiped out by a foreclosure action. To get clear title, the lien needs to be paid.

Mechanic's Liens

When a tradesperson works on the property, he has a right to be paid for his service and materials. If the property owner does not pay for the work, the contractor places what is known as a mechanic's lien against the property.

Mechanic's liens may or may not be enforceable against a foreclosed property. Your attorney can advise you as to what the current law is in the counties where you are going to invest in foreclosure properties.

Other Liens

There could be other liens placed against the foreclosed properties. For example, homeowner association fees might have been assessed and remain unpaid. It is not uncommon for homeowner associations to levy substantial fees or fines against homeowners for unpaid dues. In an attempt to collect the unpaid amount, the homeowner association can file a lien against the property.

In some jurisdictions you may not be able to acquire the property until the unpaid balance is paid in full. And unlike other liens, the homeowner association is likely to demand payment for each month since the last fee was paid.

Engineer's Reports

One of the common reasons a foreclosure property has become the property of the lender is its condition. The foreclosed homeowner, having lived in the property, learned the property has major defects. The property might require expensive repairs.

Some defects are easily spotted, even for the untrained real-estate investor. Sagging rooflines, cracked walls, uneven doors, rotting wood, and obvious damage tells you to beware of what it will cost to repair the property.

Other defects are not nearly as detectable. Recent repairs may have hidden the underlying problem. Shoddy workmanship may not be as apparent as it should be. It is not uncommon for unscrupulous homeowners, especially those facing financial disaster, to attempt to conceal major defects in their property. They may have hoped to dump their money pit property onto someone else. Property inspections are crucial to protect yourself. For more information see Chapter 9.

Market Research

You must know your local real-estate market to determine the value of any foreclosed property. Don't trust the opinions of anyone else about the value of the property. Conduct your own market research of any foreclosure you are considering purchasing. By comparing your potential foreclosure deal to recent real-estate deals, you can begin to determine values. This is basic market research. It is not that difficult to learn or do.

As an active real-estate investor, you must watch the properties that have already sold in the neighborhoods where you plan to invest. In many areas the real-estate sections of Sunday newspapers report the recently completed real-estate transactions. Real-estate agents also have this information readily available through their local Multiple Listing Service. The agent can search closed transactions quickly and produce an updated report.

Visit open houses and keep yourself informed of what properties are being purchased for in your farm area.

Neighborhood

As you have probably heard, the number one rule in real estate is location, location, location. The neighborhood where the foreclosure property is located is going to determine its ultimate value.

As an active real-estate investor of foreclosure properties, you are either going to buy the property to hold and rent for income or sell it as quickly as possible (often referred to as flipping). Your strategy for making money from the foreclosure property will often be affected by the neighborhood where the property is located.

It is often best to ask yourself who would rent or buy this property. The answer often determines your next steps with the foreclosure process.

If the property, for example, is located in a seedy neighborhood known for prostitution, gangs, crime, and violence, its value is questionable. The same property located in a stable neighborhood with good schools, recreation, and shopping will enjoy a much higher value.

It is also obvious which property is more likely to sell faster or which property is likely to attract a reliable renter. Although the properties can be similar, the neighborhood will always determine the value.

Always determine if the property is located in an acceptable location. If it is in close proximity to a detrimental site, such as a landfill or smelly factory, it is most likely to decrease rather than increase in value.

Understanding Gentrification

Gentrification is the process of reclaiming old deteriorated neighborhoods by changing them into once again vibrant locations. Signs of positive growth often include the magnificently remodeled house in among the derelict properties that are ready to fall down.

Ask yourself how this property in this neighborhood could dramatically increase in value. As you can readily see, if it could increase in value, it could produce higher rent and a better cash flow for you. It could also produce a better bottom line at settlement if you choose to sell it.

It's not always apparent which neighborhoods are undergoing gentrification. It takes some time for the transistion to occur. You do not need to invest only in neighborhoods undergoing regentrification to be successful as a foreclosure real-estate investor.

Know Your Neighborhoods

One of the reasons it makes sense for you to invest only in your farm area is so you get to know the neighborhoods. You should know where the major shopping areas are, the reputation of the local school district, and the major characteristics of the neighborhood. This is one of the reasons why it does not make sense to try to invest in properties hundreds of miles from your home.

You want to be able to visit the neighborhoods during the day and evenings, on the weekends, and on holidays. You want to see firsthand if the neighborhood is scattered with abandoned cars, burned-out houses, and trash. It is just as important to know the neighborhoods that are well maintained with owners that care about their properties and look after them accordingly. The more of an expert you are of the neighborhoods where you invest, the more money you can make from purchasing foreclosure properties.

Owner Still in Home

Foreclosure properties often come with an interesting yet unusual feature: the foreclosed owner. It is not uncommon for an owner to refuse to leave, even after the property has been legally foreclosed. For whatever reason, the lender has not yet forced its borrower to vacate the property.

FACT

Legally speaking, after the property has been foreclosed, the former owner has no legal right to remain in possession of the property. In other words, the borrower has become a squatter.

Depending upon state law, the borrower needs to be evicted. No judge will rule in favor of the foreclosed borrower. The lender will get the eviction order. Following due process rules, there must be service on the former owner. The judge's order to vacate usually gives the borrower some time to get out of the property. Failing to do so could result in arrest for contempt of court. The sheriff and deputies usually must forcibly remove the former owner. It's a messy, heartbreaking situation, especially if the borrower is sick or incapacitated in some form. The lender doesn't like the publicity. Seldom are these orders enforced just weeks before Christmas.

Lenders are at a disadvantage when the property is still occupied. They often can't show the property, and it is often not going to show well because of the current condition. Also squatters aren't known for keeping a property spotless and ready for a quick sale.

You might be able to make a deal faster and easier with a lender when the property is still occupied by the mortgagor. The lender might just want to get rid of the problem, which means the squatter is going to need to be forcibly removed from the property by the county's sheriff.

It is just human nature perhaps, but sometimes the former owner will move quickly and peacefully if the former lender is not the one doing the evicting. You as a real-estate investor are someone different, and they might just move if you ask.

Another way to get the former property owner to move quickly is to offer a payment. Former owners can often be convinced to move if it means some quick cash is paid for them to leave and turn over their keys to you.

ALERT!

Never purchase an occupied foreclosed property unless you plan to start eviction immediately. No matter what the former owner's story is or how sad and compassionate you feel, you must get the former owner out of the property as quickly as possible. If he didn't pay his lender, he isn't going to pay you.

Don't even think about buying the property for former owners and letting them pay you back for the property with some type of repayment plan or a rent-to-own lease. They need to move and start over as renters. Don't give them a chance to fail, with you to follow their path, by keeping them in the property. They could not afford it. No matter what their reasons for failing to pay, if you take possession of the property, get them out.

Make sure you understand the process of eviction in your investment area. Ask your attorney to describe the steps necessary to remove someone from your property. And make sure you are willing to do what is necessary to get a former owner out of the property should you decide to purchase it as an investment.

Valuing Foreclosure Properties

To determine the value of a foreclosed property you'll need to learn how real-estate professionals evaluate a property's current value. You must learn to read and understand operating statements and comparable sales. The operating statement summarizes the income producing capacity of the real estate. Comparable sales are the recently completed transactions on similar properties sold in your farm area. While there are advanced courses available that teach how to place a precise value on a property, you can learn how to determine your own values without a lot of effort using a simplified appraisal theory.

Simplified Appraisal Theory

The appraisal theory is the process by which three value measures are applied to measuring the fair market value of any particular piece of real estate. The three measures are, income approach, market approach, and cost approach

Income Approach

The income approach involves analyzing the property's operating statement. The operating statement is a summary that contains important information for the real-estate investor. Operating statements are a synopsis of the income and expenses the property produces and are sometimes called the P&L (as in profit and loss) sheet.

Here is a typical operating statement.

Rent Income			
	Monthly	Annual	Percent of Gross
Unit 1	$600	$7,200	54.50%
Unit 2	$500	$6,000	45.50%
Gross income	$1,100	$13,200	100.00%
Vacancies		-$660	-5.00%
Adjusted gross income		$12,540	95.00%

Operating Expenses		
Taxes	$1,580	13.00%
Insurance	$382	3.00%
Electric	$450	3.00%
Natural gas	$1,360	10.00%
Water & sewer	$515	4.00%
Repairs/maintenance	$1,200	10.00%
Lawn service	$600	5.00%
Snow removal	$550	5.00%
Trash removal	$950	9.00%
Miscellaneous	$1,000	10.00%
Total expenses	$8,587	68.00%
Net operating income	$3,953	32.00%

Your ever-expanding knowledge of the local market (through your market research) will allow you to detect numbers that do not make sense on the operating statement. For example, annual maintenance should be approximately 5 percent of the property's gross income.

When you are finished you will have a pretty good idea of the value of the property based on the income approach.

Market Approach

The market approach is the process of accumulating and then evaluating recent comparable sales of similar real estate. You know if the property is a good deal from verifiable sales data.

Often called comps (for comparables), you simply compare other recently sold properties to the foreclosure property. Always remember to compare similar properties. For example, a three-bedroom, two-bath, one-story property should not be compared to a three-bedroom, two-bath, three-story property.

Cost Approach

The cost approach is the third measure of value. The cost approach estimates how much it would cost to find a piece of land just like the foreclosure property and build the same building. A depreciation adjustment is made to reflect that the building being evaluated is not new. The cost approach is most effective for those properties that do not have information readily available for the market approach or the income approach. For example, a church building does not produce income, and there are not enough recent sales of churches to make an accurate determination based on comps. Insurance agents can often help with replacement costs. Older buildings often have features or characteristics that cannot be duplicated.

You can verify some of the data on an operating statement from public information. Property taxes and many utilities (electricity, natural gas, and sewer and water) are public information that you can readily confirm. Your insurance agent can quickly provide an estimate of insurance.

Evaluating the Property after Calculations

Now that you know how the pros place values on properties, it is time to apply these techniques to real-world examples. Assume the foreclosure property you want to purchase is available at $100,000. You believe the property's fair market value is $125,000 to $130,000. Look at all three valuation approaches:

1. Using the income approach, you determine this property's annual net income to be $8,000 per year. On a $100,000 investment, this is an 8 percent return not including any appreciation.
2. Using the market approach, other recent comps affirm the property to be in the range of $125,000 to $130,000.
3. Using the cost approach, the replacement cost is $100,000 and the land is worth another $60,000.

From all indications, the purchase of this property for $100,000 seems reasonable.

You will also use other determinations to value property quickly. For example, one fast rule of thumb is to learn what the property costs based on square footage. If properties in a particular neighborhood are being sold for $90 per square foot, you can assume a property offered for sale at $150 per square foot makes little sense. You will also be able to quickly spot a potential bargain if the square foot price is, for example, $75 or less. This type of fast valuation is something you will learn over time as a real-estate investor buying foreclosure properties. There are always exceptions to this simple valuation method, yet it will tell you quickly if the property deserves your further attention or if it is one to pass on.

Financing

One of the other considerations about purchasing any foreclosure property is the financing. How much money will it take to buy the property? Whatever the answer is, it could determine if it makes sense for you to purchase the property.

There are many different ways to finance a foreclosed property. There are traditional methods as well as creative or nontraditional financing options available. Keep in mind that a property might look good from many aspects, but financing it and what it costs you to get the financing could change a prospective foreclosed property into one that you should pass.

Chapter 14
Pre-foreclosures

Most of the information in this book so far has focused on the foreclosed properties. These properties have been returned to the lender either voluntarily by the borrower or involuntarily through a specific legal process. This chapter will cover pre-foreclosure properties. Pre-foreclosure properties offer special investment opportunities. At the pre-foreclosure stage you are primarily working with the troubled borrower and not the lender.

Finding Pre-foreclosure Properties

There are many ways to locate pre-foreclosure properties. Some are obvious, and others require a bit of digging or detective work.

Pre-foreclosure properties are those that are just in the process of falling into foreclosure. Technically speaking, until the property is officially foreclosed it is in a pre-foreclosure status. The earlier you can get to the property owner, the better off you will be. As the property moves through the foreclosure processes, more public notices are issued. Your competition, other active real-estate investors, are also looking for foreclosure deals, too. It's always to your advantage to get to defaulting borrowers as early as possible and be the first rather than the last to contact them.

One of the problems with pre-foreclosure properties, especially in the early stages of a loan going sour, is that no one is willing to admit to financial trouble and that bankruptcy or financial ruin is on the horizon. Accordingly, it is not as easy to identify the pre-foreclosures. It's still possible to find them in the early stage of default, but it's not as easy as reading the legal notices in the local newspaper.

REO Company

REO companies that operate in your farm area are great sources for finding pre-foreclosure properties. As you learned in Chapter 11, these companies specialize in helping lenders protect their investment by properly controlling their collateral. They are in the business of knowing where properties are and disposing of them as quickly as possible for their lender clients.

An REO company wants to keep the cycle going, and so they know the best thing they can do is to dispose of a property quickly for their client. This is why they work with legitimate real-estate investors that are willing and able to close quickly on properties. Make sure you are in contact with your local REO companies and are inquiring about what they might have available in their current inventory.

Bank Hardship Area

Many lenders offer debt counseling and other specialized services for those facing financial hardships. This is an example of how lenders try to do everything they can to stop a loan from falling into foreclosure.

The hardship area is for those with significant hardships. Lenders are not fools. They can quickly determine which borrowers really can't make payments versus those that have decided they don't want to make their monthly loan payment. Generally, the kinds of cases they consider real hardships are:

- The borrower was activated from reserve status into the armed forces, and the difference between the previous employment and the current pay of the armed forces makes it impossible to pay the monthly mortgage payment.
- The borrower has been incarcerated.
- The borrower has been severely injured or stricken by disease and is unable to return to work within a year.
- The borrower's spouse died, and the borrower relied on the spouse's income to make the monthly payment.

There are other situations that may allow a borrower to be classified by the lender as a hardship case. For example, one lender might consider the loss of employment in poor economic conditions (where it is unlikely the borrower will find another job) a hardship case.

Lenders that have a hardship program in place work with their borrowers to get out of the loan without detrimental credit reports. Some of these lenders work actively with real-estate investors to sell the borrower's property quickly, if the borrower agrees. These hardship departments can be a great source of leads for you.

Searching County Records

Probably the best sources of pre-foreclosure and foreclosure properties are the records located in the county courthouse. Although the courthouse is only open during regular business hours, the vast information available there makes it an important place to visit.

Watch for actions filed with the clerk of courts. That is where foreclosure actions are commended. In addition, the sheriff's department will advertise pending property sales. Also look for lists from the tax collector's office. Unpaid property taxes are signs of property owners in financial trouble. Some people never pay their taxes until the last minute, preferring to pay penalties and interest. Others just can't afford to pay their taxes and are in financial straits.

Many county courthouse records are now available online. If your county does not have the records you want online, ask if there are any plans to make them available electronically. Not only can you get the information as early as possible, you can save many trips to the courthouse while working comfortably from your home.

Flyers

Another way to locate properties is to prepare and distribute flyers. These mini posters quickly announce that you are actively purchasing real estate and encourage people to call you. The flyers should be distributed everywhere. The more people that see it, the more phone calls will be generated. The flyers should be sent to:

- Bankruptcy attorneys
- Title companies
- Real-estate agents
- CPA firms

You should also post flyers on community bulletin boards at grocery stores, markets, Laundromats, diners, and other similar places. Use colored paper to make the fliers look unique and professional.

Contact with the Property Owner

Communicating with a property owner in pre-foreclosure is not as easy as it might first seem. After finding an owner in default, contacting him via mail is relatively easy. The reception your correspondence receives is likely to be disappointing to you.

Most property owners facing foreclosure are not likely to want to discuss their failing financial situation with total strangers. The vast majority of defaulting borrowers are more likely to be in denial of their worsening finances than they are of admitting their trouble.

FACT

The best method to contact the defaulting property owner is via the mail. A professionally prepared letter is likely to get the best results.

You might be tempted to make a cold telephone call or an unannounced visit to the property. Few defaulting property owners are going to be receptive to such methods. By the time you learn of their failing financial status, they have been beleaguered by telephone calls. Suddenly appearing on their doorsteps is more likely to result in a slammed door in your face than a meaningful conversation.

Direct mail to the defaulting property owner is more cost efficient than any other method. Persistence will pay off.

Sending Multiple Letters

It often takes several letters before the property owner will contact you. Mailing to property owners on regular intervals often makes sense. Following up and maintaining contact every seven days for a month produces the best results. This requires five letters, based on the following schedule:

- **First letter:** mail immediately
- **Second letter:** mail seven days after first letter
- **Third letter:** mail fourteen days after first letter

- **Fourth letter:** mail twenty-one days after first letter
- **Fifth letter:** mail twenty-eight days after first letter

With use of a personal computer and some simple word processing software, producing the correspondence is painless. Simple mail-merge techniques make it easier to produce personalized and professional looking correspondence. Maintaining your mailing list is also much easier with a personal computer.

Other real-estate investors will also send letters to the defaulting property owner. One of the best things you can do is to make your letter professional and businesslike. It should look like it came from an attorney's office, but it should not be full of legalese. Your message should be simple, friendly, and encouraging.

Sending letters to defaulting property owners requires some work and discipline. Using a personal computer takes a lot of work out of the process, but there is still work for you to do every week.

Professional Appearance of Your Letters

Don't send out any letters that are not professional looking. Avoid cartoons or fanciful fonts; your letter should project a business look. Just because your computer can produce different-looking typefaces or brochures doesn't mean you should use them. Stick to the conservative approach of a plain business letter.

Here are some tips to make your correspondence look better and stand out:

- Use a better grade paper and envelope. Don't send out a letter printed on copy paper.
- Make sure the paper and envelope match.
- Use only white, ivory (or cream), gray, or light blue paper colors.
- Always personally sign the letters.

- Mail on the same day of each week.
- Never send a brochure; send only a well-crafted letter.

Don't be discouraged if you have a low response to your mailing. You might mail out 250 letters and only get five calls. By following up the next week to the remaining 245 on your list you may get another five calls. After the cycle of five letters, if you get five calls per mailing 250 letters, you will have received a 10 percent response of the total 250 names on your list. Of course, you will keep developing new prospect lists by adding, deleting, and replacing names. Take the time necessary to learn how to use the software that will maintain your mailing lists and produce professional correspondence.

What to Say in Your Letters

Here are five sample letters for you to use as a template. Modify them to suit your needs and style.

First Letter to Defaulting Homeowner

George Sheldon
Post Office Box 6238 · Lancaster, PA 17607
Phone (717) 555-6222
E-mail: georgesheldon@msn.com
January 7, 2009
Mr. Frank Debtor
321 Mortgaged Street
Elizabethtown, PA 17022

Dear Mr. Debtor,

Your mortgage lender has filed a lawsuit in Lancaster County Court of Common Pleas to foreclose on your property. As you know, if you cannot bring your loan payments current immediately, your property will be sold at a public foreclosure auction sale at the Lancaster County Courthouse. You will be evicted from the property.

You do have options. You could do nothing and allow your lender to sell the property at the public auction. You'll receive nothing. Your lender does not care if you get anything. They just want their money back.

Another option is for you to try to sell your property yourself, or list it with a real-estate agency. In four or five months, the property might be sold.

Or you can call me. I specialize in assisting people in Lancaster County who are in foreclosure. I can help you, too! When you call me, we can discuss how this nightmare can end within the next seven days. I can stop the foreclosure process quickly. After making an offer to buy your property, I can also help you locate another place to live. I handle everything, from working with your lender to pay off your loan to handling all the paperwork at the title company.

To get started, all you have to do is call me at (717) 555-2666. Let's talk and set up an appointment to meet at your property.

I look forward to hearing from you. I am most eager to work with you to stop the foreclosure on your home.

Sincerely,
George Sheldon

Second Letter to Defaulting Homeowner

George Sheldon
Post Office Box 6238 · Lancaster, PA 17607
Phone (717) 555-6222
E-mail: georgesheldon@msn.com
January 14, 2009
Mr. Frank Debtor
321 Mortgaged Street
Elizabethtown, PA 17022

Dear Mr. Debtor,
The clock is ticking. Each day limits your options. As I mentioned in my last letter, I assist people in Lancaster County who are in foreclosure.

Your lender is going to sell your property and evict you. Let's stop your foreclosure now.

Call me so we can discuss how to stop the foreclosure within the next seven days.

When you call me at (717) 555-2666, we can talk about your situation. There is no obligation on your part. Let's discuss your options before it's too late.

Sincerely,
George Sheldon

Third Letter to Defaulting Homeowner

George Sheldon
Post Office Box 6238 · Lancaster, PA 17607
Phone (717) 555-6222
E-mail: georgesheldon@msn.com
January 21, 2009
Mr. Frank Debtor
321 Mortgaged Street
Elizabethtown, PA 17022

Dear Mr. Debtor,
Your mortgage lender has scheduled a public foreclosure auction sale at the Lancaster County Courthouse. You will be evicted from your property. You will receive nothing, and in fact, your lender may try to collect more money from you even after the sale of your property.

In my previous letters, I informed you that I help people in Lancaster County who are facing foreclosure. I can help you, but only if you call me. I can stop the foreclosure process quickly by buying your home.

There is not much time before the auction, so call me now at (717) 555-2666. Let's talk and set up an appointment to meet at your property.

I am eager to work with you to stop the foreclosure on your home.

Sincerely,
George Sheldon

Fourth Letter to Defaulting Homeowner

George Sheldon
Post Office Box 6238 · Lancaster, PA 17607
Phone (717) 555-6222
E-mail: georgesheldon@msn.com
January 28, 2009
Mr. Frank Debtor
321 Mortgaged Street
Elizabethtown, PA 17022

Dear Mr. Debtor,
As I mentioned in my last letter, your mortgage lender has scheduled a public foreclosure auction sale at the Lancaster County Courthouse. You are going to be evicted from your property. When this happens, you will receive nothing. In fact, your lender may try to collect more money from you even after the sale of your property. The nightmare will not be over even after the public sale and eviction.

In my previous letters, I told you that I can often help people in Lancaster County who are facing foreclosure. I can most likely help you, too, but only if you call me now. I can stop the foreclosure process quickly by purchasing your home from you before the scheduled sale.

Since there is not much time before the scheduled auction, call me now at (717) 555-2666. Let's chat, and make up an appointment to meet at your property.

I am still quite eager and willing to work with you to stop the pending foreclosure on your home.

Sincerely,
George Sheldon

Fifth Letter to Defaulting Homeowner

George Sheldon
Post Office Box 6238 · Lancaster, PA 17607

Phone (717) 555-6222
E-Mail: georgesheldon@msn.com
February 5, 2009
Mr. Frank Debtor
321 Mortgaged Street
Elizabethtown, PA 17022

Dear Mr. Debtor,

Doing nothing about the foreclosure on your property is the worst thing you can do. By now you realize your lender cares nothing about you and your situation.

Although this is my last letter to you, I want you to know that I am still willing and able to assist you. But it is up to you to take the next step.

My invitation to call me still stands. We can discuss your options with no obligation on your part.

Each day that passes means less time to stop the foreclosure. Don't ignore the problem. We can still resolve your foreclosure and get you back on the road to home ownership again, but you need to call me at (717) 555-6222.

Sincerely,
George Sheldon

Your Marketing Approach: Pushing and Pulling

Your marketing accomplishes one of two things: pushing your message to pre-foreclosure property owners, or pulling owners to you by having them contact you. This two-pronged approach can produce a constant flow of investment properties when effectively used by a real-estate investor.

By using direct mail, you are pushing your message that as an active real-estate investor you purchase foreclosure properties. By using advertising, you are sending the same message but are encouraging direct contact to you.

Marketing campaigns can be expensive. Fortunately for real-estate investors seeking foreclosure properties, the cost of marketing is not prohibitive. Mailing letters, placing small advertisements, posting brochures, and taking other steps necessary to get your message out takes more work than deep financial resources.

The most important part of your marketing campaign is to start it and then maintain it. Don't give up. If you are not finding enough potential properties and subsequent deals, it is probably because your marketing efforts needs some fine tuning.

Approaching the Property Owner

How you initially contact property owners and their first impression of you can directly relate to how successful you are as an investor. It's often easy to offend or turn off a property owner facing financial devastation.

Consider the story of one owner that was approached by a real-estate investor. When the investor arrived at the property, he pulled up in his car with plastic signs stuck on the doors that read "I Buy Houses." The property owner, overly embarrassed by the sight of the car parked in front of his house, immediately dismissed the investor.

You are likely to proclaim that you only want to help the property owner. Of course, this is not true. What you really want to do is earn a profit from purchasing the property. Your attitude should be that you hope your purchase of the real estate helps the current property owner solve his current crushing financial situation.

ALERT!

Don't hide the fact that you are a real-estate investor and that your purpose is to make a reasonable profit on any transaction. An honest approach will usually always work best with a distressed property owner.

Consider your appearance when you meet with the owner. Don't project the stereotypical used-car salesperson look so prevalent in cheap Hollywood movies. Fast talking and gaudy dress is not going to impress the beleaguered homeowner. Choose a business casual look. Don't try to appear as if you are flaunting wealth or accomplishment. Present a clean, successful look. Don't overdo it with flashy jewelry or expensive clothing. Don't drive to meet the homeowner in a glitzy sports car or luxury vehicle.

By the same token, don't present an appearance that you cannot afford to buy the property. Driving up to the property in a $500 clunker wearing threadbare clothing is not going to project your ability to purchase real estate as an investor.

Empathy for the Property Owner

Although business is what connects you with the property owner, you can't help but feel some sympathy for the property owner. Your compassion level is likely to increase when you hear some of the stories of these bewildered borrowers.

As you work on deals and meet the property owners, you will hear all kinds of stories. From the newly single parent with kids to support whose spouse disappeared to the borrower with a devastating illness, expect to hear all kinds of excuses and reasons why the house payments are not being made. It won't be easy to hear all the reasons and the stories. Many are more involved than the plot line of a TV soap opera.

Don't get involved emotionally with the borrower's financial difficulties or personal problems that have contributed to his loan default. Remain businesslike in all your dealings with the borrower.

Rememberm this is simply business. The borrower used someone else's money to purchase the home and agreed to make monthly payments. Without the monthly payment, the borrower cannot continue to live in the property and now has to give up the property. It is that simple.

Eviction

Defaulting borrowers must leave the property. Either voluntarily or by eviction, they have to go. Depending on their mindset, the borrowers may think they can still stay in the property. Perhaps because of denial or because of something they read on the Internet, they think there is some secret plan that will allow them to continue living in the property. It doesn't work that way. They will have to leave.

If they could not afford the property before the foreclosure proceedings began, they can't afford it now. Remember that most lenders would have willingly agreed to restructure the debt by allowing a payment or two to be skipped and paid later.

Property owners seem to cling to the hope that they can keep living in the property. At some point in the process, they suffer from the delusion that an investor will buy their property for them, cut their monthly payment by renting it to them, and then allow them to buy it back at a reduced price. This doesn't even happen when the property is located in fantasyland.

Vacating the Property

Keep in mind that the property owner is going to have to move, no matter what. If he has not accepted that fact, consider that it might take the legal eviction process to get him out of the property.

Make sure you understand the eviction process for the jurisdiction where you are investing in foreclosure properties. Have your attorney describe the steps necessary to evict, as well as the time and expense involved.

Keep in mind as you speak and deal with the defaulting property owner that he must move. What could start out as an amicable relationship between you and the defaulting borrower might turn into a nasty and belligerent situation, all because you need the borrower to move and he doesn't want to leave.

No matter how good his story or how heartbreaking it is, he must move. There is no other way for your purchase of the property to work.

Put It in Writing

As you negotiate with the defaulted property owner, remember to put any agreement in writing. Handshakes and verbal agreements are fine, but don't rely on them to hold up in court. Put every agreement and understanding in writing. Your transaction should speak for itself through the letters, agreements, and contracts.

The test is that any stranger could pick up your file, read it, and fully understand every aspect of the sale and purchase. Strive to make your files readable and clear.

Special Acknowledgments

Ask your attorney if you should use any special acknowledgments in your agreements with defaulting property owners. Two important acknowledgments are:

- Not signed under pressure or duress
- Not a loan

These special acknowledgments, usually prepared on a separate sheet of paper, require the signature of the borrower to acknowledge your agreement. The acknowledgment of your agreement not being signed under pressure or duress is designed to avoid any later claims that you forced or pressured the weary property owner to sign your agreement.

Probate

Some foreclosure properties become available because of probate. When a person dies, the legal process of settling the estate of the deceased person is known as probate. During the process, probate resolves all claims and distributes the decedent's property.

When the person that died owned real estate, the property must be sold. Sometimes because of the death, or the reason that caused the death, the property has been foreclosed. This always complicates the foreclosure and the legal process.

ALERT!

Each state has its own laws about probate. These laws are extensive and involved. Many attorneys specialize in probate law. You need to understand the probate laws of your state and how they affect a foreclosed property.

When a foreclosure property becomes available because of the death of the borrower, the acquisition can be entangled because of surviving family member squabbles. Heirs might suddenly think the property is worth far more than anyone would ever agree to pay for it. Often it takes only one family member with a differing opinion to stop a sale from proceeding.

In other cases, the family members might be just as willing to get rid of the property as quickly as possible. The decedent's estate may be anxious to dispose of the property because it is costing money each month, and they want to stop these expenses. For this reason it pays to pursue foreclosure properties in probate. Don't hesitate to contact the estate of any foreclosed property. Understand that you might have different problems to close on the property.

Value

In the last chapter you learned how to determine the value of a property. Your opinion of the value may vary greatly from the property owner. Defaulting borrowers often think their property is worth a lot more than it actually is. Perhaps this is because they are in denial of their deteriorating financial condition. Obviously you need to work from your opinion of value and not theirs.

As you consider making offers on foreclosed property, there must always be a margin of profit to you. The margin of profit you want to make on each deal is your personal choice.

Don't focus on a specific percentage before you will make an offer. If, for example, you determine the value of a property to be $150,000, don't disregard the property because you can't make 25 percent on the deal. While a profit of $37,500 would be a great payday for you, suppose you could walk away with $20,000. Would you really pass on that deal?

If you set the goal of making $20,000 per deal and could do two deals per month, consider what your annual income would be from investing in foreclosure properties.

Remember also that without the potential for profit there is no reason for your pre-foreclosure or foreclosure investment. The defaulting property owner needs to understand this too.

Chapter 15

Foreclosure Auctions

At the auction you won't be negotiating with the defaulted property owner or the lender's representative. The law of the state where the property is located determines the procedure followed at the auction. The sheriff, a deputy, auctioneer, attorney, or trustee conducts the foreclosure auction in strict compliance with the law. No matter how you purchase a foreclosure property—directly from the borrower, the lender, or at auction—your strategy as a real-estate investor remains the same: buy low, sell high.

Risks of Foreclosure Auctions

Real-estate investors make money by acquiring properties at real-estate auctions. It is a source of potential investment properties. But you should not attempt to purchase properties at public auctions without fully understanding your duties, obligations, and the local laws that cover purchasing real estate at an auction.

Each state has enacted laws that govern real-estate auctions. Who may bid, how the auctioneer must conduct the auction, and other terms of the auction are clearly established for each state.

Property auctions create urgency and a competition to bid. By their very nature, auctions become exciting events, forcing qualified buyers to a particular moment of decision. Buyers must seize the opportunity on the auction day. Competitive bidding increases interest in the property, and often increases the price. Most important, real-estate sales are confirmed within minutes, sales that could have otherwise taken months or even years to generate and finalize.

Understanding the Terms of the Sale

You must fully realize the terms and conditions of the sale at a real-estate auction. For example, you must usually provide a minimum of 10 percent of your bid in certified funds or cash to the auctioneer at the time your bid is accepted. You must pay the other 90 percent of your bid within a specified time. In some jurisdictions this is seven days, while in other areas it is as long as thirty days. In Florida it is the next day; you only have until 12 P.M. the following day to pay the balance of your bid along with the closing fees.

QUESTION?

How long do real-estate auctions last?
Real-estate auctions often last just a few minutes. The entire procedure might wrap up in just a few moments. You will often be amazed at how quickly the procedure can be completed. Most foreclosure real-estate auctions start and finish in a matter of minutes.

Keep in mind that you must close on the property as required by local laws. There are no extensions, and no excuses are accepted.

As you can see, this is not a beginner's game. If you do not wrap up the purchase of the property, you lose and you forfeit your 10 percent down payment.

Cancellations

Foreclosure auctions are notorious for being canceled or postponed. You could spend a lot of time searching and planning to buy a property at a public auction, and then the auction does not occur. When you arrive at the place of the auction at the scheduled time, you may only learn then that the auction will not occur. This happens quite often in foreclosure auctions.

Sometimes as a desperation move the defaulting property owner files a bankruptcy action. This will stop the foreclosure property auction, at least temporarily.

The property owner might also have located a buyer for the property, and the lender realizes the purchase will close. Often this is another reason property auctions are postponed or canceled.

Just because a property is scheduled for auction doesn't mean that you can't still present an offer to purchase it. However, you would need to close before the auction date.

First Bids

At the property auction the first bid offered is often what is owed on the property to the lender. This bid is usually placed by an attorney representing the lender. To buy the property at the auction, you must offer a bid for more than the amount owed on the loan.

Properties with low amounts owed, and a high fair market value, are the ones that will get plenty of bids. In other words, the more equity that is on the table, the more people (investors) will bid. Expect serious competition and bidding when there is a lot of equity available for someone to grab. As the bids run up, the amount of profit for you diminishes.

Don't expect to buy a $200,000 property for just pennies on the dollar. That's the kind of thing late-night TV infomericals offer as reasons to buy their expensive real-estate investing courses. In reality, this does not happen at foreclosure auctions.

All Sales Are Final

One of the problems with a real-estate auction is that the sale is final. Find a problem in the property and it's your problem, not the seller's. You must still purchase the property. It doesn't matter if the problem is with the title, undisclosed liens, or the property itself: You bought it, and now you own it. It's that simple. Your newly acquired property might have polluted drinking water or be coated with lead-based paint. Whatever it has, there is no recourse or right of recession on your part.

None of the sales terms are negotiable on your part. If you don't agree with the terms, don't bid. You cannot later try to negotiate with the county sheriff or the clerk of courts over how, when, or how much you will pay for the property. If you bid, you have agreed with the terms and conditions of the sale.

Shills and Collusion

It is possible for you to be victimized at a public auction. Shills are people who deliberately drive up the price of the property without the intention of buying it. The purpose is to get a higher price out of you. Shills have been used by unscrupulous auctioneers or a defaulting property owner. By driving up the price, they make more money.

Experienced real-estate investors sometimes deliberately drive up the price of a property to deliberately hurt or damage a new investor. Hoping to stick the new investor with an overpriced property, the idea is to keep the new investor from showing up at future auctions.

You should always keep in mind that bid rigging or collusion could be going on and that you may not even know it. Experienced bidders are known to sometimes meet before a scheduled sale and decide the maximum they will pay for the property. They play a game of driving a price up and let you overpay for the property.

Before the Auction

Prior to a foreclosure property auction, you need to evaluate the property. The purpose, of course, is to determine if you want to buy it. Most, if not all, real-estate auctions include the term "as is." This means what you see, and don't see, is what you are buying when you bid on the property.

The best advice to anyone thinking about buying a property at a public auction is to be well prepared. You must do your own due diligence prior to the date of the auction.

Remember that you will not have time to ask questions about the property at the sale. Always expect and anticipate that the property is to be sold "as is and where is." There will be no concessions or negotiation at the auction. What you bid is what you must pay (if you are the high bidder) for the property. If you later discover the roof leaks, you get to fix it at your expense. The seller of the property is not responsible for any structural problems of the property.

ALERT!

Try to inspect the property thoroughly before the auction. But beware! The property could still be occupied by the defaulting owner. And most likely the property owner is not going to be too happy about a prospective buyer looking around the property.

Your inspection could be curtailed if the property is still occupied by a hostile owner. This also could mean, if you are the successful bidder, that you will have to go through the eviction process to get the property owner out of the house.

Foreclosure properties may not be insurable. Their condition might be such that no casualty insurer will issue a property damage coverage policy. Trashed properties, for example, are often uninsurable. If you are relying on financing to finalize the purchase of the property, without casualty insurance you will not be able to borrow the money.

Some foreclosure properties might be offered for sale at an auction without the opportunity to inspect it. You are truly buying the property sight unseen. Your purchase is on the blind trust of what the property might be.

Failing to get inside to see the property before bidding on it makes little sense. Without a preliminary inspection you could be buying a nightmare. The property could be in pristine condition, or the owner might have stripped it and damaged it beyond repair.

Title Issues of Auctioned Properties

Always check the title before the auction. Check on liens and other possible title clouds. If you have questions or believe the title cannot be easily cleared, you should probably pass on making a bid at the auction.

Many times title insurance is not easily obtained on properties sold at public auctions. The title insurers, especially the underwriters, consider it risky to issue title insurance on properties that are sold at auction. They are concerned that if the auction was not properly conducted there could be an underlying claim to the property. This presents a real possibility for you that you might not be able to purchase insurance that the property title is free and clear of any claims.

Title insurers might declare the property to have an extraordinary and unusual risk. If they detect any errors in the auction sale process, you can be sure they will decline to issue title insurance.

Knowing When Auctions Are Held

You learn about the time, date, and location of foreclosure auctions the same way you do about foreclosures: from the public notices posted in the courthouse and legal notices advertised in the local newspapers. By watching and reading these notices, you will know when and where the foreclosure auctions will be held.

They are routinely held during business hours at the courthouse. However, local tradition and law will determine the time and place.

Cash for Purchase

If you have the cash to purchase the property outright at the auction, you are in a powerful position to bid and close on the property. Depending on the jurisdiction, you may need to show that you have the cash before you can place a bid.

Bidding on a property without the cash to pay for it is difficult and sometimes impossible. When you don't have the cash and are relying on financing, you could quickly find yourself in a precarious situation. Any deposit you placed on the property could be forfeited if you can't close on the property within the time frame allowed.

Remember that the lender will require not only that you are approved as a borrower, but also that the property be suitable as collateral. Should you not be able to get title insurance or casualty insurance, or the property needs extensive repairs, your lender may decline your loan. Your bid is usually accepted without the condition of your being able to obtain suitable financing. Before you realize it, your deposit is forfeited.

Purchasing property at public auctions without the cash and relying on financing is often perilous and too risky for most real-estate investors.

To exclude people without the money necessary to purchase the property, some jurisdictions require that you provide proof of funds before they will accept your bid. The purpose is to prevent unqualified buyers from jamming up the real-estate auction process.

Right of Redemption

Earlier you learned about how some states offer the right of redemption. If the state where the property is located does have this provision in its law, you could lose the property to the defaulted property owner if she can come up with all the money necessary to pay the costs and amount you paid for the property. It's not likely this will happen, but it could.

In Alabama the redemption period is a year. You could lose your investment property at anytime during this period if the defaulted borrower can come up with the money to get the property back. Quite a few states currently have redemption periods for defaulted property owners. For a state-by-state summary, see Appendix A.

Cashier's Check

To purchase a property at an auction you most likely will need a cashier's check (or cash) in a specific amount. This is standard procedure in real-estate auctions.

FACT

Never use a certified check from your account. Once the check has been certified, the bank will always keep those funds from your account available to pay for that check. If the check is lost, you cannot get your money back. Choose a cashier's check rather than a certified check.

In some jurisdictions a flat fee might be required. In lieu of a 10 percent check, you might be required to present a flat fee of $10,000 (or some other amount) before you are allowed to bid. After depositing that amount, you are then considered a qualified bidder.

Your Competition

Despite the problems with real-estate auctions, you can be certain that your competition—other real-estate investors—will be there to bid on properties.

Remember that your competition could have a lot more cash readily available than you do. The person with the most cash always has the best chance to win at real-estate auctions. You can't easily leverage your 10 percent down money with a 90 percent loan to secure a property at the auction. There are too many uncertainties about getting a loan, and the short time to get the loan, to make leveraging work for you. Properties with thin profit margins do not generate the interest that a property with a larger profit margin does.

> If there is no competition from other investors or the lender, you have to ask yourself why aren't others interested in the property. Most likely something is truly wrong with the property. Sometimes lenders won't purchase the property, a sure indication that they believe the property has serious, expensive flaws.

Those real-estate investing gurus that are featured on television infomercials like to boast about the huge profits available from public foreclosure real-estate auctions. In reality, it is not as easy to make money as you might first think. If you don't have the cash to make the purchase outright, it is a risky undertaking. This doesn't mean that you can't make money with foreclosure auctions. It is just not as easy and far more risky than those gurus like to say it is.

Tax Sales

A special kind of foreclosure sale is the tax sale. This occurs when a governmental unit is not paid money it is owed and seizes the property, selling it to collect what is owed.

Many municipalities or counties conduct tax sales once or twice a year. They are generally advertised in the legal sections of the newspaper.

Properties scheduled for tax sales are often removed from the list at the last possible moment. If there is a mortgage, the lender will usually pay the overdue tax and then collect it from the borrower. The lender is not going to lose its collateral because of an unpaid tax bill.

When there is no lien holder, the property owner can lose the property at the tax sale. Realizing this, property owners often pay the overdue amount at the last possible minute to avoid the sale of their property.

Fast Payment Required

It is not unusual for the tax sale to require prompt payment of your bid if you are the winning bidder. For example, the IRS requires payment in full within one hour after the winning bid has been accepted. Some tax sales require payment in full at the time the property is sold. Be prepared to pay the amount of your purchase promptly.

Redemption Periods on Tax Sales

Some municipalities allow property owners to redeem their property. This is to prevent widows or others from losing their properties for the nonpayment of a tax bill. Just as in a foreclosure sale, you could lose the investment property if a property owner uses her redemption right. You do get your money back, as well as interest, but you lose your right to the property. Ask your attorney to explain the redemption law used at tax sales in your jurisdiction.

When There Is No Mortgage

When the property is owned free and clear and the tax sale is held, you can purchase the property free and clear for the unpaid taxes. The bidding usually starts at the amount of the tax bill. If there are others interested in the property, the bidding continues between those interested in the property. Any amount paid by the successful bidder in excess of the tax bill goes to the former property owner.

Tax sales are flaunted on TV as a way to buy a property for pennies on the dollar. The reality is that it occurs rarely and not routinely.

Many government agencies stopped mailing lists or sending notifications of tax sales. The tax sale auctions are now listed only on the agency's offical Web sites.

FACT

A lien holder's interest on the property is often protected by law. In some jurisdictions the tax sale could remove the lien holder's right or interest to the property.

Fair Market Value

The bidding process does not determine the fair market value of the foreclosure property. There are many reasons for this, but if only investors are bidding on the property, the final bid amount is usually less that the market value. The reason is simple: The investor is buying the property at a wholesale price in the hope of selling it for a retail price.

You must also consider that the property is most likely not as pristine as most properties offered for sale. The property probably has issues that affect its marketability and ease of selling. For example, it could still be occupied by a hostile defaulted borrower. The property could have major issues, such as being damaged.

Don't base the value of a property on what it sold for at a public foreclosure auction. The actual sale price at the auction has little to do with a property's fair market value.

When You Are the Successful Bidder

Congratulations! You are the winning bidder at the foreclosure auction. Now what do you do? Your first steps are:

- Receive a copy of the deed after paying for the property.
- Record the deed, placing the property in your name.

- Purchase casualty insurance for the property immediately.
- Obtain title insurance.
- Remove the tenants if any still reside on the property.
- Remove trash, furniture, and other items from the property.
- Inspect the property thoroughly and commence any necessary repairs.

Now you can move forward with your plans for the property. You can either sell it or rent it to earn your profit on the property.

Chapter 16

Purchasing REO Properties

REO properties, those properties now owned by the lender, are always for sale. There are bargains to be made with REO properties. Lenders are not in the business of owning properties. Once they take ownership of them, they want to get rid of them, and usually as quickly as they possibly can. And they will often sell them at a discount. Savvy real-estate investors know that REO properties can yield good profits.

Contacting Mortgage Companies and Banks

As you learned earlier, it pays to contact local lenders, mortgage companies, and banks. As an active real-estate investor, you need to alert the REO departments of these companies that you're interested in their properties.

Most will automatically alert you of any new properties they have available. Personnel in the REO departments move on or change, so it is a good idea for you to make periodic contact. This is especially true if you stop receiving alerts or information from any particular REO office.

Lenders sometimes make sudden and dramatic changes in selling REO properties that appear inexplicable to the outsider. It is important to keep in close touch with your local lenders. This is particularly true if you have identified an REO property that you would like to buy.

Changing Inventories

Within the REO office of any lender, the inventory of REO properties can change dramatically from one day to the next. As an outsider, you never know what opportunities might be available.

An REO department might have only a few properties one day, but then suddenly double or triple the properties they have to sell within a day. This can happen easily when an investor can't close on properties already purchased or an investor (someone with multiple properties) suddenly turns properties over to the lender.

Inventory of foreclosed properties can suddenly increase at specific times of the year. This is usually because of when foreclosure auctions are conducted. Because of the auctions, the REO department takes control of additional properties.

Changing Positions

One of the most vexing issues of working with REO departments is their sudden change in attitude. As an active real-estate investor, you could be working with an REO department trying to purchase a property. Every concession or point is a major struggle. Then suddenly, without any notice or explanation, the REO department seems to change. They can't do enough for you, and they seem to be bending over backward to help you purchase the property for the terms and conditions you want.

QUESTION?

Why do REO departments suddenly change their policy?
You don't know what happens behind the scenes. Management at the lender keeps an eye on the REO properties. For whatever reason, the lender's management team has ordered the REO properties to be liquidated as quickly as possible. The REO properties are now available at better terms, with bigger discounts.

It is just as likely that the lender's management declares it is losing too much on properties it owns and is selling. Therefore, the REO management orders a tightening of the sales of the properties. They demand harder negotiations so as to reduce their losses.

It's a dynamic of REO departments. A change in management can bring about a flurry of REO sales as a new manager tries a different approach to managing various aspects of the lending institution. Deals today disappear tomorrow only to reappear soon. It's nothing you, the real-estate investor, are doing to make the REO department treat you this way; it's just the way they do business.

Other business considerations can impact a lender's decision to sell a property quickly. Lenders are subject to periodic audits by federal regulators. Lenders are required to maintain reserves based partially on nonperforming assets, such as their REO properties. A lender may elect to eliminate some REO properties before an upcoming audit.

Ownership Creates a New Ball Game

Until the property actually becomes an REO, the lender cannot make money on the property. Because the foreclosure process is so closely controlled by state laws and court rules, the lender can only try to recover the money it loaned, as well as its collection fees and costs associated with collecting the loan. The lender will tack on every expense, fee, and any associated cost it spent during the collection process. But the lender is not allowed to profit during the foreclosure. All it can do is collect what it is owed.

Keep in mind that during foreclosure the lender cannot profit or take advantage of the defaulting property owner. After the lender becomes the property owner, it can sell the property for whatever it wants and earn as much of a profit as possible.

But that all changes once the lender actually owns the property outright. Now it can do whatever it wants as the rightful and legal owner of the property. If the lender has $100,000 in the property and can sell it for $250,000, why shouldn't it? As the property's new owner, it can hold on to it, rent it, or sell it.

Real-Estate Agencies

Some real-estate agents and their agencies specialize in listing and selling REO properties. Almost every real-estate agency has one or two agents that closely follow and work foreclosure properties. Working with one or two of these agents can help you maintain a steady flow of investment properties.

Agents are in the business to make money. They will feed you leads and property information as long as they believe there is a legitimate chance of selling you a property. If you start to show signs of not being sincere or professional, they will move on to other investors that are willing and able to purchase investment properties. A local real-estate agent can help you locate the REO properties in your investment farm area.

Many Web sites list REO real estate. It is becoming more common for lenders to list their REO properties on their Web sites. Some of the Web sites of REOs will connect you directly to their local real-estate agent.

FACT

Be prepared to move quickly with any foreclosure property offered for sale, but especially those represented by a real-estate agent. Keep in mind that the agent only makes money when the agent sells the property. Most likely the agent has a list of local real-estate investors, and the properties being shown to you are being marketed to other potential investors.

U.S. Government REOs

The federal government also lists their REOs—properties that the Federal Housing Administration (FHA) or the Department of Veterans Affairs (VA) received because of loan guarantees. These and other homes offered for sale by the federal government are available online at *www.hud.gov/homes/homesforsale.cfm.*

The United States Department of Agriculture (USDA) often has properties available. Foreclosures from their Rural Housing program are available. The USDA offers financing to potential buyers that want to purchase their REOs to live in the property and to investors. Here are the available financing options directly from the USDA:

Eligible Applicants (Program)

Credit is available for program-eligible applicants on program properties. Loans are made for thirty-three years at the present interest rate of 6.0 percent (effective June 1, 2006). Payments are based on the total family income. Eligibility is also based on credit history, repayment ability, and the availability of other credit.

Nonprogram Applicants

Properties that will be occupied by the purchaser can be financed for a term up to thirty years at the present interest rate of 6.5 percent. Purchasers must pay a 2 percent down payment. Investors can obtain a loan for ten years at the present interest rate of 6.5 percent. If more favorable terms are necessary to facilitate the sale, the loan may be amortized over a period of up to twenty years with payment in full due not later than ten years from the date of closing.

Purchasers must pay a 5 percent down payment. The USDA REO properties are available online at *www.resales.usda.gov/sfhdirect/SFHPropMain.cfm*.

State and Local Government REOs

Your state and county may also list properties for sale on their Web sites. Spend some time with your favorite search engine to look for these properties. Check out your local county government sites. It may take some work on your part, but you can find REOs.

Borrower out of Home

By now you realize the importance of getting the defaulted borrower out of the foreclosed home. While many will have left before the property is controlled by the REO department, some will remain.

Not until a sheriff or constable knocks on the door and serves legal papers will some defaulted borrowers even think about moving. Some will continue to stall the process. Depending on the jurisdiction and the local laws, the eviction process can take months.

Don't be afraid to talk directly with the defaulted owners. Often no one has offered them any money to move out. Find out what it would take to get them to move.

Some REO departments won't list properties when the defaulted property owner is still in the property. Real-estate agents often will not list the property until it has been vacated because it is next to impossible to show the property while the defaulted borrower is still living there. This can present an opportunity for the savvy real-estate investor.

Buying the property with the foreclosed owner still occupying the property could mean a substantial discount on the price. The trick is to get the occupants to move quickly and without causing additional damage.

Buying them out of their home might seem distasteful to the REO department (the defaulting borrowers already cost the lender too much money), but for the active real-estate investor it could make a lot of sense. A few hundred dollars could buy control of the property, without damage, and the ability to begin making money with the property sooner rather than later. For more on evictions, see Chapter 14.

Buying Below Market

The main reason why you want to consider purchasing REO properties is the ability to buy them for less than the current fair market value. It goes back to that basic principle of buying low and selling high. REOs can often be purchased for less than fair market value.

Don't fear an REO with a high listing or asking price. Many REOs start with a higher price only to be sold later to an investor with a price much less than the original asking price.

FACT

Your first offer to buy below market value may be rejected. That does not prevent you from submitting second and subsequent offers. You can submit as many offers as you want.

When local real-estate markets are slow, REO properties are likely to be sold more quickly at favorable terms. The last thing REO departments want is for their inventory of houses to grow. Their primary goal is to sell their properties.

Don't expect super deals on properties that are likely to sell quickly. Properties located in hot markets, such as resorts or fast-growing urban areas, are not going to be highly discounted. Properties located in deteriorating areas or unstable neighborhoods will likely be offered at fire-sale prices.

If your local area is experiencing a general real-estate market slowdown, the REO department is likely to offer better terms and accept a lower price for its property.

Negotiating for the REO Property

Don't hesitate to negotiate for the REO property. It is almost expected by the REO department.

One of the differences of negotiating with an REO department versus other real-estate sellers is the lack of counteroffers. Property owners will often submit a counteroffer when they reject a purchase offer. Many REO departments simply reject the purchase offer. Others will routinely submit a counteroffer.

Always offer less than the asking price for an REO property. Offer what the property is worth to you, not what it is worth to the rest of the world. Don't be surprised if your initial offer is rejected and if no counteroffer is presented.

Negotiate as an Investor

When submitting your offer to the REO department, point out the repairs and the costs associated with bringing the property back to life. Make sure they know you are a real-estate investor. This alerts them that they are not going to get a retail price but rather a wholesale price of the property.

Active real-estate investors often report that they spend a good deal of their time making purchase offers on prospective properties. They use computer software to submit their offers, which makes it easier to resubmit a follow-up offer to the REO department.

As part of your negotiation technique, always ask for concessions from the REO department. For example, ask the REO department to pay part (or all) of the closing costs. They may say no, or to your benefit they may say yes. You don't know until you ask. Sometimes they won't pay all the closing costs but will reduce the price of the property in their counteroffer.

Presenting Multiple Offers

Don't hesitate to present multiple purchase offers at the same time. For example:

- **Offer #1:** $185,000 with a closing in forty-five days
- **Offer #2:** $187,700, with a closing in ninety days

By presenting the offers at the same time, the REO officer will generally focus on which is the better offer rather than rejecting both. When an offer is presented to the REO department, it can either accept it, reject it, or present a counteroffer.

Lender Financing

Unless you have an unlimited availability of cash, one of the biggest considerations of purchasing the REO property is financing. Real-estate investors always attempt to purchase properties with the least amount of cash out of pocket. The REO departments recognize this and expect offers from investors to have little out-of-pocket money required.

Not only are you looking for the best possible price for the property, but you are also looking for the best possible financing terms. Of course, it depends on what you intend to do with the property as to what kind of financing terms you want to seek. If you are planning to hold the property and rent it, then you want financial terms that will allow you to enjoy a positive cash flow each month. If you plan to flip the property, then a balloon payment in a year or two will not concern you since you will no longer own the property.

You don't need to ask the lender that owns the REO property for the money. Sometimes it works better if you have other financing arranged. Other times the REO property is sold to an investor faster if the property is going to be financed by the lender that owns the property.

It is often possible to acquire attractive financing, especially if the lender is anxious to sell the property. Turning a defaulted loan into a performing loan is often the most attractive offer you can make to a lender.

Making the Purchase Offer

Depending on whether you are dealing directly with the REO department or a local real-estate agent, your purchase offer will be submitted directly by you or the agent. Your negotiations will either be with someone in the REO department or the real-estate agent.

Don't be foolish and offer such a ridiculous price that all it does is insult the agent or the personnel at the REO department. A perfectly decent property that everyone agrees is worth $200,000 is not going to be sold to you for $20,000. It just doesn't work that way. You are not going to be able to "steal" a property from an REO department of any lender.

ALERT!

Don't make a big deal out of minor damages or problems with the property. A loose cabinet door or a scuff on the wall is not going to reduce the value of the property. Making a great deal out of minor issues quickly brands you as an unprofessional investor. You will not be taken seriously.

REO personnel dislike dealing with arrogant or rude real-estate investors that proclaim they just want to help by taking the property off their hands. They are not going to want you to rub in that they made a mistake making the loan to the defaulted borrower. Be businesslike, professional, and ready to purchase the property if it makes sense to you to do so.

Real problems or issues with the property should be addressed. For example, damaged windows or severe maintenance issues need to be brought to the REO department's attention.

Always start with an offer that is below current market value. A general rule of thumb is to offer about 25 percent below the average market value for comparable properties. Expect the lender to consider your offer over several days. Don't expect an immediate response to your initial offer. Most likely your first purchase offer will be less than the lender wants to accept. It is likely to be passed around within the lender's REO department until someone with the authority to accept or reject the offer has the time to mull over your offer.

The lender already knows the property because it had been appraised before the lender loaned money to the defaulted borrower. They also had the property inspected recently, and had a local real estate broker provide an opinion of the value of the property as is and with repairs.

Some REO departments will return a counteroffer, perhaps proposing a higher dollar amount and attractive financing. It is now up to you to accept or reject their offer. You might want to consider accepting the financing offer but rejecting the purchase price. This give and take, all part of the negotiation, can move quickly or slowly. It all depends on the REO department's method of operation and how fast you respond to the counteroffers.

Your goal is to get:

- Lowest possible selling price
- Lowest possible closing costs
- Best possible financing terms

Your offer and counteroffers are always submitted in writing. If you are negotiating though a real-estate agent, you will likely use the agent's forms to submit offers. When you are dealing directly with the REO department, you can use whatever form or format you want insofar as submitting offers. Appendix D includes a sample purchase offer letter used for submitting an offer to an REO department.

Closing on the REO Property

Be prepared to close quickly on an REO property. Always try to close on an REO property within two to four weeks. This is often one of the most appealing parts of your offer, especially if you agree to close as early as possible. To the lender, this moves the property from a nonperforming asset to a profitable asset.

Be prepared to take over control of the property quickly, including starting the process of eviction if the property is still occupied by the defaulting borrower. Have all the necessary funds and documents ready to conclude the transaction in the least amount of time.

Chapter 17

Financing Your Foreclosure

Unless you have a boatload of cash, you're going to need to finance your investment properties. Your strategies of how you finance your acquisitions will often determine your profit or loss on each property you acquire.

17

The No-Money-Down Myth

It is impossible to buy real estate with no money. It is not impossible to purchase real estate using someone else's money.

Even if someone were willing to lend you 100 percent of the purchase price of the property, there are still costs associated with acquiring the property. There are transfer taxes and recording fees that need to be paid. Maybe you won't be paying these costs, but someone will. Don't overlook things like casualty insurance. A policy needs to be purchased, and someone has to pay for that insurance. The point is that it does take *some* money to buy and sell real estate.

FACT

As a real-estate investor, you always want to use as little of your own money as possible to buy and sell properties. Holding on to your cash is always desirable.

Often you will make decisions about acquiring new properties based on how much cash it will take to purchase it. You are likely to pass on properties that will take too much of your cash to complete the acquisition. This holds true of properties in pre-foreclosure status and those that have been foreclosed.

You will need to use either your own money or someone else's to make your real-estate transactions work. Whether you can convince others to pay the required fees and arrange financing without any down payments will determine how little cash from your own funds you will need.

Savings

The first place to look for money is in your own accounts. What you have available in savings and other accounts is always your first source of funds.

Whether you have a little or a lot of money available, you always want to structure your purchases so that you need to use as little of your cash as possible. You want the property to pay for itself. By reserving your cash, you have it available to acquire additional investment properties.

For example, suppose you purchased one property for $100,000 and put $20,000 (or 20 percent) into it as a down payment. You have a traditional $80,000 mortgage. There is nothing wrong with that, but suppose you could buy three more identical houses. Do you have $60,000 available for the three additional down payments? In this scenario it was better for you to have only used $5,000 as a down payment and financed 95 percent of the purchase price. With the same $20,000 used to purchase the first property you could have purchased four properties. Assuming you could achieve the same profit from each property, your final profit would be four times as large by using the same $20,000.

Having money readily available in your bank accounts is always good for a real-estate investor. It certainly allows you to move forward on more deals quickly.

Family Partnerships

Another important and often viable source of funds is your family. Because you know each other, it is generally easier to form a partnership to acquire and invest in real estate. Before you move forward with any family partnership, all members of the newly formed partnership should enter into a formal partnership agreement. The only way to do this properly is with an attorney. See Chapter 9 for more information on working with family as investors.

There is a temptation not to formalize a partnership agreement with family members. This is a serious mistake. You should never enter into any partnership without a formal written agreement. This is perhaps even more valid with family members.

Partnerships can be formed with any distribution of profits. It does not need to be a 50-50 split or an even split among all partners. If there are an even number of partners, decide who will make the final decision when an issue becomes one of both sides being evenly divided. Also determine how the partnership will be dissolved. All of these issues need to be decided before a partnership is formed.

Have your attorney explain the partnership law in your state. Consult with your tax advisor about the implications of being a partner. Fully understand your duties and obligations of the partnership. Your attorney or your tax advisor might suggest forming a limited liability partnership (an L.L.P.) rather than just a partnership.

Determine profit splits before the partnership is formed, not afterward. And always put the agreement in writing.

Other Partnerships

You are not limited to family members to form a partnership. Following the same suggestions and procedures as a family partnership, you can form a partnership with total strangers. The goal is always the same: to make a profit from acquiring foreclosure properties. Partnerships can be formed to acquire one property, multiple properties, or for specific goals, such as acquire and rent properties or acquire and sell properties.

QUESTION?

How many partnerships can I form?
Legally speaking, you can form and be a partner in more than one partnership. Of course, the more partnerships you have, the more paperwork, tax implications, as well as legal obligations you'll have.

The number one rule with any partnership is to work out problems before they arise. And this always means that you need to have your partnership agreement in writing. Always have an attorney prepare the partnership agreement for you.

Once you have proven yourself as a successful real-estate investor, others will quickly want to become your partner in deals. Everyone likes to make money. If you are consistently making a profit by acquiring foreclosure properties, expect to receive partnership offers. Whether you should enter into a partnership is up to you of course.

Some real-estate investors only use partnerships until they have enough cash resources not to need them any more. Others continually use partnerships as a way to invest in foreclosures. Some real-estate investors never enter into partnerships.

Borrowing the Money

If you do not have the cash from either your own funds or the collective funds of a partnership, it's time to find the money by borrowing it. You might be surprised how easily you can borrow hundreds of thousands of dollars to purchase real estate.

The reason it is so easy to borrow the money is simple: The loan is secured by the real estate. The real estate has value. If you don't pay the loan, the lender will foreclose on you!

Your Personal Credit Rating

The better your personal credit rating, the easier it will be for you to borrow money. If you have lousy credit, don't expect it to be easy to borrow. It's that simple.

Three major credit bureaus report what is in their files about your past credit history. The three major credit bureaus are:

- Equifax   1-888-766-0008   *www.equifax.com*
- Experian (formerly TRW)   1-888-397-3742   *www.experian.com*
- TransUnion LLC   1-800-888-4213   *www.tuc.com*

Past performance of your credit allows an underwriter to evaluate and determine how you will likely perform in the future. The credit bureaus provide a score based on the information in their files. These credit scores are commonly called *FICO scores* because the credit bureau scores are produced from software developed by the Fair Isaac Company.

FICO scores have other names. The three major credit bureaus providing the scores use different names for their numerical score:

These scores are used by most real-estate lenders to determine your overall credit worthiness. Each credit score is based on the information the credit bureau receives from lenders and maintains in their computerized files about you. As this credit information changes, your credit FICO scores change as well.

FACT

Most lenders use a combination of the three scores (one from each credit bureau) to determine your credit rating (some lenders use the middle score, others use the top two).

Obviously it is to your advantage as a real-estate investor to maintain as high of a credit score as possible. The better your credit score is, the better interest rates and loan programs you will be offered by real-estate lenders.

Credit scores range between 300 and 850. The actual ratings and what they mean are:

- **Excellent:** over 750
- **Very Good:** 720 or more
- **Acceptable:** 660 to 720
- **Uncertain:** 620 to 660
- **Risky:** less than 620

As an active real-estate investor, your goal is to achieve and maintain a credit score of 720 or better.

Free Credit Reports

Each person is now entitled to receive one free credit report each year from each of the three major credit bureaus. Each of the three credit bureaus has policies of how to request copies of your credit report. You must request your credit report in one of these three ways:

- Call 877-322-8228.
- Visit *www.annualcreditreport.com*, which is the only authorized source for consumers to access their annual credit report on the Internet for free.
- Complete the form on the back of the Annual Credit Report Request brochure, available from the Federal Trade Commission (online or by writing), and mail it to:

Annual Credit Report Request Service
P.O. Box 105281
Atlanta, GA, 30348-5281

Keep in mind that you have the right to contest any faulty information contained on your credit report. According to federal law, each of the bureaus must investigate and verify the information or remove it. If you find an error on your credit report, contact each credit bureau. Even the smallest error could seriously hurt your credit score and would likely cost you more money for a loan. Do not be denied the purchase of your real-estate investment property because of inaccurate information on your credit report. Take the time necessary to maintain a close watch over what is included in your credit report.

Repairing Problem Credit

Even if you have questionable or difficult credit, it does not mean that you can't improve it. It does take time, but it is quite possible to change your credit from negative to positive. According to the Fair Isaac Company, there are many things you can do to improve your FICO score. They suggest:

- Always pay your bills on time and as you have agreed to do.
- Stay current with your accounts. If you have missed any payments, get current.
- Maintain low or no balances on your credit cards and other revolving credit. High outstanding debt will lower your credit score.
- Don't open unnecessary credit cards or accounts.

Always attempt to manage your credit accounts responsibly. Protecting your credit score will always help you as a real-estate investor.

You should also begin work on your credit report immediately. It does not matter if you plan to acquire your first investment property in the next week or six months from now. It is never too early for you to begin monitoring and improving your credit scores.

Lines of Credit

One good source of funds for the working real-estate investor is an open line of credit. This is a preapproved loan, one that you can use for any purpose you choose.

When you use your equity in your primary residence, the loan is often called a HELOC (home equity line of credit). You might also consider refinancing your residence and taking the cash out to use for your investment property acquisitions.

Some savvy foreclosure investors use their credit cards as a readily available source of funds. Using credit cards that include a cash advance, these investors always have the money they need to make purchase offers or for down payments.

Borrowing from the REO Lender

As you learned in Chapter 16, the REO lender is often a source of financing when buying the foreclosure property. This is particularly true if the REO department outright owns the property.

When the REO department owns the property, that lender is usually the best place to look for financing. Through negotiation it might be possible to get more favorable terms than what is normally offered through regular loan programs.

The REO department may be able to arrange a quick loan for you. It is often possible to close on an REO property within days rather than the normal time of weeks or months.

Investment Loans

Real-estate investment loans are sought by lenders, but they are not as safe as a primary residence loan. Lenders believe that most borrowers will do everything they can to save their primary residence. When the property is an investment, it is much easier for a borrower to walk away from the property.

That doesn't mean that a lender won't make a loan to a real-estate investor. It just means the lender will look closer at the loan and mull over its merit before approving.

Nonowner Occupied

Investor loans are often called NOO, which stands for nonowner occupied. The proposed loan will not fund the primary residence of the borrower. In other words, it is a loan for a real-estate investor.

One of the advantages of the NOO loan is that often the loan to value (LTV) is favorable. The LTV is determined by dividing the loan amount by the property's appraised value. For example, a $100,000 loan versus a $150,000 appraised value computes to a LTV of 66.7 percent. Because investors usually purchase below fair market value, the LTV is usually in line. Investors want as high an LTV as they can get—100 percent is best—because they need no money down to buy the property.

Because there is a higher risk of default for the NOO loan, lenders usually charge a higher interest rate on the borrowed money.

Loan Fraud

To qualify for a loan, unscrupulous borrowers lie on their loan application and provide false information to the lender. The purpose is simple: By providing false information, the borrower is trying to induce the lender to make a loan it would not normally make. When applying for a loan by providing false information, the lying borrower is committing loan fraud.

As the U.S. Department of Housing and Urban Development (HUD) says, "When you apply for a mortgage loan, every piece of information that you submit must be accurate and complete. Lying on a mortgage application is fraud and may result in criminal penalties."

As an active real-estate investor acquiring foreclosure properties, don't even think about providing a lender with false information. It doesn't make sense to build a business on a criminal footing. Eventually you will suffer the consequences.

It's far better to be straightforward and work through the system. Having honor and integrity in all your business transactions only makes sense. Some real-estate gurus recommend to their students to lie about the use of the property. Of course, they don't use the word "lie," but they suggest you do not need to tell the lender that the property will be an NOO unit. Never commit loan fraud. It's just not worth it.

Mortgage Banks and Mortgage Brokers

There are regular banks—those that have the branch offices, drive-up teller windows, and ATMs—and there are mortgage banks. Mortgage banks only deal in real-estate loans. Mortgage brokers specialize in arranging loans for their clients.

You will often find totally different treatment from mortgage banks and mortgage brokers compared to the treatment you get from a regular bank. The loan officer at a traditional bank will smile and offer sympathy but will not grant your NOO loan unless you have a substantial down payment and pristine credit. Give a reason not to make the loan, such as one or two dings on your credit report, and expect a fast but polite rejection of your loan application.

On the other hand, mortgage banks and mortgage brokers will gladly seek your business. Although you might not get as good a deal as someone with perfect credit, most likely you will get the financing you need. Some mortgage banks deal directly with the public, while others originate loans only through mortgage brokers.

A good mortgage broker can help you advance your real-estate investing quickly and easily. A mortgage broker is a person or company that specializes in originating mortgage loans.

Most mortgage brokers have special programs for the real-estate investor needing an NOO loan. The mortgage broker is compensated by receiving a commission for matching the borrower with a lender. The mortgage broker usually performs some or most of the loan processing functions such as taking the loan application and ordering a credit report, appraisal, and title report. The mortgage broker does not underwrite the loan but rather presents it to a lender for approval.

Loans for Every Type of Borrower

Borrowers with damaged or imperfect credit, or with an unusual loan need, turn to a mortgage broker to help them find a loan. Because a broker has multiple contacts with different lenders, the broker can usually locate a loan program that works for the borrower.

Mortgage brokers have expanded their business over the past decades, and now they compete with your local bank for business. Mortgage brokers offer A loans (perfect credit), Alt-A (loans to those with almost perfect credit but perhaps with a few small blemishes), B, and C loans. Most local regular banks will only lend on A or Alt-A loans.

Loans for Real-Estate Investors

Mortgage brokers match loans for real-estate investors. For example, fewer banks are willing to make a loan for the acquisition of a mixed-use property, such as a building with retail space on the first floor and residential units on the second floor. Mortgage brokers can secure the financing for these types of investment properties.

A mortgage broker receives compensation when the loan closes. The broker receives origination fees (points) from you or a yield spread premium (YSP). This is a fee paid by the lender for originating the loan based on the interest rate of the loan. For example, a loan with a 9 percent rate might pay the broker two points of the loan amount in a yield spread premium. The same loan with an 8 percent rate might pay just one point, while a 7 percent rate may pay the broker nothing. You should never pay a retainer or any other fee up front to a mortgage broker. The only money a loan applicant should give to a broker on making application for financing is an amount sufficient to pay for the formal credit report and an appraisal. As an active real-estate investor, most mortgage brokers should be interested in your business because you offer the opportunity for repeat loans.

The states license mortgage brokers where they operate. They must comply with their state as well as federal regulations. A benefit to using mortgage brokers is that they are more likely used to dealing with problem applications. They have the experience to assist a borrower with credit problems or other issues. Do not overlook the value a mortgage broker can offer to you in finding suitable financing.

Most mortgage brokers offer special programs designed specifically for real-estate investors.

Prime and Subprime Loans

A subprime loan is a real-estate loan made to someone with less than perfect credit, or someone who cannot easily verify income. Subprime loans also are those that are not prime in some way. For example, there may not be mortgage insurance on loans that are more than 80 percent LTV.

Subprime loans are often available to real-estate investors. Although the interest rate may be higher, the mere fact these loans are available opens up the possibility of many more investment deals. Don't scoff at the notion of getting a subprime loan. It often has nothing to do with the borrower. You could qualify for a subprime loan because of the property or the terms you seek.

Most subprime loans are originated by mortgage brokers. However, some subprime lenders have their own loan officers originating loans, and you can apply directly to the lender.

Many subprime lenders have special programs for investors. Some allow 100 percent financing or liberal first and second mortgages, which become the equivalent of 100 percent financing. Programs for investors are constantly changing, and new ones become available from subprime lenders.

Private Funds

Another source of financing for real-estate investors acquiring foreclosure properties is private funds. Rather than borrowing money from traditional sources (such as banks, credit unions, or mortgage companies), you borrow money from private individuals.

There are people with significant cash reserves that are willing to lend money, particularly on the short term, at rates higher than they get by keeping their money on deposit at the local banks. The best way to find these loan sources is to ask for referrals from your real-estate attorney, title company, insurance agent, tax advisor, and others in the real-estate business in your community.

Private investors can also be located by advertising for them in the local newspaper. Loans secured by real estate always pique the interest of those willing to lend money for interest income.

Hard Money Lenders

There is a special type of lender that makes special loans to real-estate investors. They are called *hard* moneylenders. These lenders make loans to real-estate investors that need a large amount of money quickly.

They are often used when the property is not likely to be acceptable to a traditional lender because of its condition. For example, the property needs a new roof and without it no lender would accept it as collateral.

When a hard moneylender makes a loan, it is not inexpensive. Often hard moneylenders ask for (and get) four points plus a high interest rate. In addition, there is usually a balloon payment required within a year. But these types of loans can sometimes be used effectively by the real-estate investor.

Consider this situation: You acquire a property for $65,000 that should be worth $100,000 when repaired. You use a hard moneylender because the property needs major repairs that cost $10,000. You borrow $65,000 at four points (4 percent), which costs $2,600. You use your money to complete the repairs and flip the property in two months. The final profit to you looks like this:

$65,000	price of property
$10,000	repairs
$2,600	points for loan
$1,082	interest on loan
$78,682	total expenses
$100,000	received from selling property
$21,318	gross profit

You can readily see how expensive a hard money loan is. By the same token, without it you cannot earn the final profit on the deal.

Other Investors

You should maintain a list of other real-estate investors that are working in your area. Sometimes they have cash available, or know of cash resources, and will work with you. It might be possible to commence a partnership for the pending deal.

Another option is for you to sell your deal to the investor. By using an *assignment* in your sales contract, you can transfer your deal to the investor. You take part of the profit by assigning the contract, and the other investor closes the deal. You might make the assignment for a fixed amount, such as $5,000, or as a percentage of the final profit, such as 25 percent. The idea is to get the deal into the hands of another investor who has the financial resources to close it when you don't have the cash available to make a deal work.

Always make sure that whomever you assign your contract to has the capacity to make the deal work and can close on the property. Without the closing, you may not see any profit for your work.

Chapter 18

What to Do with Your Buy

Now that you acquired a foreclosure property, what are you going to do with it? You have several different options: You can keep the property and live in it, flip it for a profit, rent the property out and become a landlord, or even sell your purchase contract to another investor.

Own It and Keep It

Sometimes you might acquire a foreclosure property that you like so much that you keep it rather than use it as an investment property. While all real estate you purchase is an investment, it's not uncommon for the real-estate investor to decide to move into a foreclosure property.

You need a place to live, so why not enjoy one of the gems you found while working in your real-estate investing business? It only makes sense, especially if it is a place where you want to live and it is affordable.

For tax purposes, it is always easier to change a property from a private residence to an investment property as opposed to changing an investment property to a noninvestment property. Should you ever change an investment property to your primary residence, be sure to consult with your tax advisor.

Flip the Property

Many foreclosure properties are flipped by real-estate investors. After acquiring the property, the investor sells it immediately as is or repairs it and then offers it for sale.

Flipping properties is now the subject of several reality television shows. The concept is simple: Buy at a lower price and then sell it for a higher price. On television, the shows emphasize the fix-it-up part of the process. As a real-estate investor, you have two choices when flipping a property: selling as is or selling after the renovation.

Renovating, remodeling, or fixing up a foreclosed property often becomes a passion for the real-estate investors that work at flipping properties. It can make the overall transaction more complicated. It requires additional credit or cash to pay for the repairs and renovations. It takes longer to have your payday, but it can result in a bigger return on your investment.

Some units will require work before the property can sell. For example, if you acquired a foreclosure property without a working furnace, you are likely going to need to repair or replace the current furnace. Unless you are selling to another investor who does not need financing, this type of basic fix-up is required. To sell the property to a noninvestor, it will need a working heating unit. No lender will approve a loan with the property as collateral unless that property has a working furnace.

Flipping Starter Home Properties

It takes some experience to recognize the full potential of a profitable flip deal. Of course, there is only one way to get this valuable experience: by doing it.

Flipping works in all real-estate markets, in bad or good neighborhoods, and on all types of properties. However, if you are just getting started and learning the process, you should concentrate on flipping starter homes. Starter homes always remain in demand. First-time homebuyers and other investors are particularly interested in decent and affordable houses.

ALERT!

Don't allow yourself to get bogged down to the point of inaction. Many beginning real-estate investors are afraid of making mistakes and over-analyze a property. By doing so, they never make an offer to purchase the property. They develop analysis paralysis and do nothing.

There are several reasons why starter homes make sense for the beginning real-estate investor:

- Starter homes just cost less.
- The demand for starter homes may slow down, but it never really stops. New families always need (and accordingly search for) a place to live.
- Most people understand the real-estate dynamics of a starter home because they have lived in one at some point in their life.
- There are simply more starter homes than expensive homes available.
- Starter homes make better rentals. While there is a market for someone to pay $4,000 a month for a high-end, pricey mansion, there are far more people that are willing and able to pay $800 a month for more modest housing.

It is important to know what a starter home is and what it sells for in your chosen investment farm area. In one real-estate market a starter home might be $85,000. In other markets a starter home might be $250,000.

FACT

There are no set standards as to what determines the price range of a starter home in any given market. It varies from locale to locale.

Starter homes include the basics of decent housing: two or three bedrooms, a bathroom, a kitchen, and a living room. Other items taken for granted include the mechanical systems (heating, plumbing, electrical), roof, working windows and doors, and the other standards of a decent house, such as a usable kitchen. Many starters could have other features and amenities, such as a fireplace, air conditioning, garage, or an extra bath (or a half bath).

Properties to Avoid as Flips

There are certain properties that you should avoid. They just don't make good properties to flip. Consider these suggestions:

- Don't submit purchase offers on unconventional properties.
- Avoid buying commercial property or other special-use properties that require a specific user, such as a restaurant.
- Don't buy the oddball property in the neighborhood. If all the houses on the block are three-bedroom, two-bath, split-level homes with garages, don't buy a one-bedroom, one-bath cottage with no garage.
- Don't purchase properties that are missing essential components. For example, don't buy a property without a working sewerage system.
- Avoid purchasing properties that do not have the basics. As an example, there has to be a safe water source. Air conditioning is not

important for properties in Maine, but in Arizona and Florida it's a necessity.

- Pass on the properties that don't fit well in the neighborhood. If all the properties in a subdivision are colonial two-and-a-half-story homes, don't buy the sprawling contemporary style home that looks out of place.

Quality Versus Shoddy Repairs

If you are going to fix, remodel, and repair properties before you resell them, consider the importance of making quality improvements. Creating problems for future homeowners might mean a bigger profit for you, but is that ethical or fair?

It is easy to make economic decisions without thinking about how they might hurt a future property owner. By all means make a fair profit, but you should consider your ethics in your real-estate transactions. Treat others as you want to be treated.

Consider the need to replace a stove in your property you are going to flip. You could purchase a very basic model for $350 or a more expensive one at $600. Most likely you would opt for the lesser-priced model, even though it has less features. Now consider a leaky roof. Rather than fix it you cover up the leak evidence with some paint. Avoiding the more expensive repair might make economic sense, but the hapless new homeowner probably can't afford to replace a roof. And while they can see the stove they are buying, they can't see the leaks that were intentionally covered up.

Hold and Rent

Another money-making strategy for real-estate investors buying foreclosure properties is to hold on to and rent them. Each month the renter sends you a rent check. A part of that monthly payment is profit for you.

As a working real-estate investor and landlord, you can quickly acquire multiple rental units. One Midwest investor used this strategy and grew his investing business to a total of 1,400 rental units on hundreds of properties. He started with a two-unit property that was foreclosed.

FACT

Being a landlord has its own unique problems that you must manage. From keeping the property maintained to managing tenants, the work never ends. Yet many people have become self-made millionaires by acquiring property and renting it to others.

As a property owner, you must comply with federal, state, and local laws. You must maintain files, be well organized, and pay attention to details. You must have a current and legally binding lease with your tenants. You must also be ruthless in your collection of the rent.

Depending on your jurisdiction, you might not be able to commence eviction proceedings until the tenth day after the rent is due. On the eleventh day you must start evicting your nonpaying tenant. While you will hear all kinds of excuses as to why your tenant cannot pay, you must collect. If you allow a tenant to be late, he will of course be late.

Some people are not cut out to handle this rigid policy of collecting rent. If you are one of these types, you can always employ the services of a property management company to do this work for you. For a monthly percentage of the rent, your rent will be collected, your tenants selected and managed, and the property maintained. All you need to do is cash the checks you receive. Of course, paying for this service cuts directly into your profit. However, some real-estate investors find it a worthwhile expense. It allows the investor more time to search for and acquire additional foreclosure properties.

While you can rent any property you own, some are more conducive as rental units than others. Some properties offer many expensive amenities. Rental units usually are less plush. Accordingly, some properties might be more appropriate as rental units than others.

Multifamily properties are always intended to be rental properties. With separate living units on the property, multiple tenants can live on the property. For the real-estate investor seeking to build long-term growth and a steady monthly income, multifamily units are smart investment properties.

Collecting the rent on time is paramount to your success as a landlord. Give no margin and permit no excuses.

One advantage of holding and renting properties is that you can get to a point where you can stop acquiring new properties if you want and continue receiving income. As a real-estate investor that flips properties, you must always continue to flip if you want to maintain your income.

Sell Your Purchase Contract

Imagine working as a real-estate investor without needing any credit or ability to close a loan, yet you are able to make thousands of dollars on each transaction. This can be done by simply selling your purchase contract to another real-estate investor.

There are some advantages to selling your purchase contract:

- You do not need much money to get started as a real-estate investor.
- You do not need the credit or funds to close on the property.
- You receive your money at the settlement.
- You can do as many as these deals as you can find and assemble; you are not limited by your available cash or credit situation.
- You do not pay any closing costs.

The procedure is simple: You offer to purchase a property, and then after your purchase offer is accepted you sell your purchase contract, assuring your profit on the transaction.

Understanding Assignment

To be able to sell your purchase contract to another investor you must have the legal authority to do so. In most states, if a purchase agreement does not have specific language in it that says it is not assignable, then the purchase agreement is assignable without the consent of the other party.

Some purchase agreements have assignments built in to the contract. Some purchase agreements prohibit assignments.

Often the assignment can be made simply by including it as part of the purchase. For example, if Susan Johnson is the purchaser, she is identified in the purchase offer agreement as "Susan Johnson and/or her assigns." To be sure you can assign the contract, always include a clause in your agreement giving you permission to make the assignment.

Make sure you know what the law is in your state by discussing real-estate purchase agreement assignments with your lawyer. Follow your attorney's advice to make sure you can legally transfer the assignment.

You should always structure your foreclosure deals so you can assign the purchase offer agreement to another person or entity. Even if you don't intend to sell the purchase agreement to anyone else, it is always best to have the ability to do so.

Earnest Money Amount

When you are presenting a purchase offer agreement that you plan to assign to another investor, you want to include as little as possible of your earnest money. You must make an earnest money deposit in order to make the contract binding. Some investors follow these guidelines:

- Never offer more than $100 as earnest money.
- Use a $50 bill, stapled onto the purchase offer, as earnest money.
- Use a $100 promissory note.

Whether you are dealing with a real-estate agent, the defaulting borrower, or the REO department, keep your earnest money low. When someone asks for a larger earnest deposit, quickly respond with the question, "Why do you need more earnest money?"

Using Your Assignment

Once you have your purchase offer with an assignment accepted by the current owner of the property you can begin the process of selling it. Assigning the purchase agreement is accomplished quickly by signing an agreement with your purchaser.

Experienced real-estate investors that use assignments for flipping properties know to whom they are going to sell the property when they make their purchase offer to the property owner. This is because they maintain an active list of real-estate investors that will purchase properties regularly.

QUESTION?

Will an investor accepting the assignment balk at paying a profit to me?
The answer is no, as long as there is room in the deal to make a reasonable profit.

Consider this scenario: You find a property worth $160,000. You make a purchase offer of $117,500, which is accepted. The property needs $11,000 of renovations and repairs, which means the property costs $128,500. You add on your profit and fee of $6,500, which still leaves potential profit of $25,000. There is $25,000 of profit on the table. If you were in a position to make the purchase, wouldn't you take the deal? If deals make sense, real-estate investors will take them. They don't mind paying for them via an assignment.

Conditions of the Assignment

Before you make an assignment of one of your purchase agreements, there are several things to consider:

- Don't make the assignment to an investor that can't close on the property. This does no one any good—not the property owner, the investor that you assigned the purchase agreement to, or yourself.
- Don't be greedy in what you want for your fee when the loan closes.
- Don't become complacent with your deals. If you cannot close on the purchase agreement, you are only out your earnest deposit (although some attorneys might be able to pursue a breach of agreement suit against you). Nothing will ruin your reputation faster than not closing your transactions.

As your business grows and you become more familiar with investing in foreclosures that have been assigned to you, expect to accept these types of deals from others. As long as a purchase makes sense and is profitable, most real-estate investors will make the deal.

A typical assignment letter is included in Appendix C. This is only for illustration purposes. Consult with your attorney as to what your assignment letter should contain for your area.

Professional Bird-Dogging

Another way to make money as a real-estate investor is to do nothing more than find deals for other investors. This is called *bird-dogging*. All you need to do is to turn information over to investors and collect a fee for any deal they close. The standard finder's fee as a bird dog is $500.

Many new real-estate investors start this way. They have no risk; they are not signing purchase contracts or doing anything other than providing information and building a network of investors. Along the way they are earning cash for their efforts. Once they have enough funds on deposit they can start taking on their own deals.

Chapter 19

Determining Your Actual Costs and Profits

With some work, perseverance, and a little luck you will start to see profits from investing in both pre-foreclosure and foreclosure properties. Congratulations! It's always nice to have positive cash flow and paydays. Of course, as an active real-estate investor you are going to have both fixed and adjustable costs associated with your business. The fixed costs are things like your home office expense, telephone service, and daily newspaper subscriptions. Other costs will fluctuate depending on your business activity.

Time

One of the things you want to consider is how much time it is taking you to put together your transactions. In the beginning, while you are still learning and developing your contacts, it will take longer. As you become more experienced and established as a foreclosure investor, you should be able to structure deals faster.

Some deals will fall in place quickly, while others will take much more of your time. It's just the nature of the foreclosure investing business.

Many times you cannot control the time problems you will experience. You have to wait for people to get back in touch with you. You leave messages, they leave messages, and the cycle continues. Every bit of information you need never comes easy. You wait for faxes, phone calls, and letters. Other times you can put together a deal in a few hours.

Rather than look at what you are earning per hour, it might be better to look at what you are making per week or per month.

If your goal is to make $60,000 per year, then you need to bring in $5,000 per month. (Actually, you will need to receive more than this amount to cover your expenses.) If you are making $25,000 per foreclosure deal, you only need to do three a year. Of course, you make adjustments based on your income goals, your expenses, and the amount you make per deal.

Keep track of your time in two ways. Record how much total time you spend on your real-estate investing activities. The best way might be to use an appointment book. As a deal develops and you start a file folder, create a simple time sheet so you can determine later how much total time you spent on the actual transaction.

Any time-keeping system that works for you to maintain a record is suitable. You can use either a paper or computerized system.

After a while you will find valuable information in your time-keeping records. You will know what is working and what is not. You can identify time wasters and redirect your time to more profitable endeavors. For example, you might discover you are spending ten hours a week to do paperwork. By hiring an assistant and paying $125 per week, you have an extra forty hours a month to make two more deals because you are taking about twenty hours to put together a transaction. As you can see, this type of careful watch over your time can produce more income for you.

Tax Information

One part of your foreclosure investment business that you must always keep in mind is your tax liability. Making money is the goal, but when you do, the tax collector wants a cut of your profit. Your goal is to pay 100 percent of what you owe on your taxes, not a penny more or a penny less.

Recordkeeping Is Important

It is easy to put off maintaining your business records: a parking receipt here and a document copying fee there. Before long, receipts are misplaced, unrecorded, or lost forever. The result is you have to pay more than you need to for your taxes.

FACT

Meticulous recordkeeping is your best tactic to pay less in taxes. This requires discipline on your part.

With the use of bookkeeping software and your personal computer, the task of maintaining your expenditures is much easier. It is usually best to set up a separate checking account to track your business expenses for your foreclosure investments. It is easier to watch what you have spent as necessary business expenses with a separate account.

THE EVERYTHING GUIDE TO BUYING FORECLOSURES

Deduct every legitimate business expense available to you. Don't overlook the obvious, such as what you pay to your attorney as legal fees. Other expenses might not be as clear.

Home Office Deduction

Some of the expenses you are entitled to take include a home office expense. Although the Internal Revenue Service has tightened the rules for deducting this expense, it is still a legitimate deduction. Follow the IRS rules to make sure you qualify. No one would question that a real-estate investor would need a home office. Make sure you have clearly set up an area in your residence that qualifies. Take photos to prove your claim that it is your office.

Some expenses you have now are likely to be deductible as legitimate business expenses. Your cell phone, newspaper subscriptions, and Internet connectivity fees are likely to be deductible. Discuss these expenses with your tax advisor.

Be sure to keep track of your utility bills too. A portion of these are likely deductible as part of your home office deduction.

Automobile Expenses

Another major expense that is deductible is the business use of your automobile. You are entitled to deduct the actual expense or a flat rate for each mile you drive. To claim the deduction you must maintain a log of your mileage and your expenses.

It's probably best to keep this log in your automobile. Keep a simple record of the date, time, where you drove and why, and the total miles. Also keep a separate record of your expenses, such as oil changes, fuel, repairs, and tires. Retain the receipts. At tax preparation time you can then determine what the best way to claim your deduction is. The only way you can do so is to maintain accurate records of the use and expense of your car.

Incorporate Your Investing Business

Most real-estate investors start out not as a business but as a mere attempt to profit from buying a property. Foreclosure investors are more likely to turn their real-estate investing into a business enterprise.

Perhaps it's because foreclosures are bought to flip or to turn into rental-income-producing properties that foreclosure investors often seem to grow their business. Starting off as a sole proprietor is fast and easy. As time progresses, it may make sense to incorporate your business.

After consulting with both your attorney and your tax advisor, you might decide that it makes sense to form a corporation. Your corporation could be a limited liability corporation (LLC) or a full corporation.

FACT

The corporation becomes a distinct legal entity, separate and without ties to the individuals that own it. As a legal structure, corporations are attractive to small business owners.

There could be advantages or disadvantages to forming a corporation in a state other than where you are located. Popular states to incorporate are Delaware and Nevada. Both have laws and tax structures favorable to corporations. Whether it would benefit you to incorporate within your state or not is determined by discussing your situation with your trusted advisors.

Before deciding on your final form of legal organization, you should certainly discuss your ability as a corporation to form partnerships with others to acquire and sell properties. Make sure you understand your duties, obligations, and restrictions.

Some advantages of forming a corporation are:

- **Limited liability:** The corporation stands on its own legally.
- **Ongoing concern:** Should the founder or principal of the company die, the business continues to exist as a separate legal entity.
- **Selling stock to raise capital:** It is relatively easy to sell shares of stock to raise capital and split ownership of the company.

- **Tax advantages:** Sometimes the tax rate is less for corporations.
- **Professional appearance:** Operating as a legal corporation may enhance your appearance and stature in the community.

Some of the disadvantages of forming and operating as a corporation are:

- **Extensive government regulations:** There are many reports required by all levels of government.
- **Tax disadvantages:** Sometimes the tax rate is actually higher for corporations.
- **Limited activities:** Your corporation may be limited as to what it can do based on its charter or various laws.

Always seek competent counsel before starting a corporation for your real-estate investing business. It is easy to start as a real-estate investor operating as a sole proprietor. After several profitable transactions, you can then explore the possibility of becoming a corporation.

Pricing the Repairs

What does it cost to repair a foreclosed property? The answer is usually found by deciding on who does the work.

Some of the work you will likely do yourself, especially in the beginning. Whether it be a room that needs painting, replacing a leaky faucet, or fixing a faulty doorbell, small projects are often a Saturday afternoon project. Wearing your paint-spattered jeans, the work is done step-by-step as you wade through the minor fixes. You will also find yourself throwing away unbelievable mounds of trash.

As you progress in your foreclosure investment career, you will soon identify which projects you will do yourself and which are better handled by a professional. While you might be trying to save money to increase your profit, when you are in over your head, call a professional. For example, if you know nothing about oil burners, don't try to fix one yourself. Call a pro!

Landscaping is one area that you might try to tackle yourself. With some teenagers, a plan, and plants, you can quickly improve the appearance of your property. Painting is another area that can quickly improve a property without huge expense or tremendous difficulty. Keep in mind that the size of the project could mandate the hiring of a professional. It is one thing to paint a porch and another to paint an entire house. Fixing the landscaping in a small yard is a different project from replanting and reseeding a two-acre lawn.

Roofs can be problematic. When there are signs of problems, get a professional to repair it. Mold, mildew, wet basements, and soggy crawlspaces also signal problems. Plumbing, electrical, cooling, and heating systems can also be expensive.

As you work to develop your contacts, you also want to be on the lookout for reliable and reputable tradespeople. From the handyman to the electrician, having reliable service people that will get the work done, on time and on budget, are important assets. If you can test your new contacts with a smaller job, do so.

Obviously it makes sense to get the best job done for the least amount of money. However, shoddy workmanship is never worth buying. Keep in mind that your reputation is on the line with each real-estate transaction. Don't purchase substandard repairs or renovation.

Placing Your Properties on the Market

Investment properties are bought to be sold. Sooner or later the properties you acquire as foreclosures will be sold. This is true even for those you bought and held for rental income.

There could be any number of reasons why you want to dispose of the properties you bought as foreclosure bargains. Some real-estate investors sell their properties right away, taking the profit by flipping the property. Others hold and sell later.

When you decide to sell, you have two options: sell it yourself, or sell it by using a real-estate agent.

Many people try to sell a property first without engaging the services of a real-estate agent. They soon learn that agents earn their commissions. It takes a lot of work to sell a property. Advertising and marketing it, handling the inquiries and showings, and working with potential buyers to make an offer takes time and work. Most people give up, realizing it is easier to allow an agent to handle the property.

As an active real-estate investor you may find it easier to sell your own properties than noninvestors do. You are working a business and are accepting calls all the time. You may already know people that are likely to purchase the property. You are regularly looking for properties, and showing one to prospective buyers is not an issue. Plus you may want the leads of potential buyers.

QUESTION?

Should I sell my properties myself?
If you have the time to do so, it might be beneficial. This is particularly true if you are looking for clients either for your rental units or to purchase other properties. If you find good contacts and you cannot meet their needs, offer to turn them over to your favorite real-estate agents. Providing leads to agents only helps your status with them.

Of course, just like noninvestors you can always engage the services of a real-estate agent. You might decide to employ the agent immediately so you can remain focused on acquiring additional foreclosure properties.

Finance Costs

Buying a property without using your own money requires financing. Those with the money to lend will charge you fees to borrow from them. It is not inexpensive to finance a foreclosure property. Some of the fees and costs regularly charged include:

- Credit report
- Property appraisal
- Underwriting fee
- Document preparation fee
- Interest points
- Origination fee

Other fees include title insurance, casualty insurance, and certifications. The lender may also require escrow accounts for the payment of taxes, homeowner association fees, and insurance premiums. All of these fees add up quickly and require additional out-of-pocket expenses.

Look for ways to minimize or eliminate costs. Some tips for reducing finance costs include:

- Don't agree to loans with origination fees. Usually one point (1 percent of the loan amount) is charged by lenders to compensate their loan officer.
- Ask for a reissue rate from the title company. Often available if the title insurance was issued within the past year, this can reduce your title insurance cost by 50 percent or more.
- Seek discounts from your casualty insurer by purchasing a multiple-property policy. One policy will give you blanket coverage on all your properties.
- Don't pay points to lower your interest rate. Pay a higher interest rate on the loan, especially if you are not planning to keep the property for a long period.
- Take advantage of special financing deals. Lenders often offer no-fee loans. Consider these over their loans that have a fee.
- Negotiate lower fees from the lender. Document preparation fees and underwriting fees are often negotiable and can be eliminated if there is a likelihood of repeat business.

Chapter 20

Making Money with Short Sales

As an active real-estate investor you will come across properties with little or no equity. The amount owed by the property owner exceeds the market value of the real estate. Most real-estate investors walk away from these properties. However, it is possible to make a profit from properties with little or no equity. As an investor you can proceed with what is known as a short-sale investment. The short-sale investment occurs when the outstanding obligations—all the loans against a property—exceed what the property can be sold for. In these situations lenders are sometimes willing to accept less than the full amount due.

Understanding a Short Sale

It is not difficult to understand how a short sale works. Simply stated, the lender agrees to accept less than the amount owed on the property. For example, if the borrower owes $150,000, the lender agrees to accept $120,000. You can then resell it or keep it as an income-producing property by collecting rent.

ESSENTIAL

The late-night-television investment gurus hawk cash back at settlement as one of the reasons why you should purchase their expensive CDs or real-estate courses. Short sales are one of the techniques they are using, but they don't say it in their infomercial. You get cash back by immediately flipping the property (or assigning the purchase agreement).

On the surface, a short-sale transaction is not hard to understand. In reality, they take a lot of work to put together. Your work can pay off by providing you with substantial profit on your investment. Too many investors think they can buy the property from the lender after the foreclosure is over. That attitude is flawed because:

- There will be increased competition from other real-estate investors.
- There is a possibility to make a larger profit before the pending foreclosure than afterward.
- Lenders will agree to a short sale when it makes sense to do so.

In a short sale you will actually be acting as mediator between the borrower and the lender. Your job will be to negotiate a settlement of the loan made by the lender to the borrower. You will be trying to get the two sides to agree to take less money than what is actually owed.

QUESTION?

Why would a lender accept far less than what is owed on the property?

It's a simple strategy for the lender and is based on that old saying that "a bird in the hand is worth two in a bush." It is better to get the money now and get rid of the property than to wait with the expectation of making more money later.

From the lender's viewpoint, a short sale saves the ongoing costs associated with the foreclosure process. Eliminating the growing attorney fees, the eviction process, the inevitable delays from the borrower filing bankruptcy, having to repair extensive damage to the property, and the costs associated with resale is a lofty goal.

In a short-sale opportunity, the lender gets the property back much faster from the borrower. By doing so, it is able to cut its losses on the loan that has gone bad. Your job as an active real-estate investor is to convince the lender that it will likely do better by accepting less money now than waiting for the property and sale many months later.

Borrower Issues

From the borrower's position, the need to do something about his pending foreclosure is pressing. A short sale is a quick answer for the defaulting borrower. It allows the borrower to put the foreclosure behind him. The borrower has to agree first to the short sale. You'd think he would readily agree, but he probably won't. There are some problems from the borrower's point of view:

- He must move immediately (or very soon).
- He receives no money from the sale of the property.
- He's probably in dire financial straits, and must admit it.

Most borrowers do not want to recognize their current financial situation. Their denial of the circumstances only makes it more difficult to resolve the crisis. Some defaulting borrowers will readily agree to discuss their pending foreclosure and will do whatever is necessary to get over their current loan default. They eagerly concur that their best strategy is to get the pending foreclosure over and start over. Other defaulting borrowers will refuse to do anything, allowing the foreclosure process to move forward. As an active real-estate investor, sometimes the toughest part of the short sale will be to convince the defaulting property owner to agree to leave the property with nothing.

Lender Issues

From the lender's position, the acceptance of the short-sale offer means the loss of money that it is owed, and lenders do not like losing money. To walk away from the property in early foreclosure is courageous. Lenders are not known to show a lot of daring when it comes to losing money, especially their own money.

Lenders usually have a strict policy when it comes to accepting a short sale. They often will publicly state that they seldom, if ever, accept any short-sale offers. In reality they will entertain any offer on a property in foreclosure and seldom accept the first short-sale offer they receive.

Don't confuse short sales in real estate with shorting in finance. Shorting is a method to profit from the decline in the price of a security. Most investors "go long" (as opposed to go short) on an investment by hoping the price of a stock or bond will rise.

Before a lender will consider a short-sale offer, a BPO (broker's price opinion) is usually ordered. The BPO is less expensive than a full appraisal. The lender is likely to rely heavily on the BPO as to what the probable market value of the property is.

From the point of view of the loss mitigation department of the lender, it is safer to accept an offer close to the BPO than it is to accept an offer thousands of dollars less.

Some of the reasons why a lender is more likely to accept a short sale include:

- The property is in poor condition.
- The neighborhood has generally depreciated.
- Newer homes in the market area are being chosen over existing homes.
- The defaulted borrower has serious hardships and cannot afford the home payments.

In addition, there must not be a reasonable expectation that the defaulted borrower's financial situation is likely to change in the immediate future.

Working with the Borrower

The first step in a short sale is to get the defaulting borrower to agree to the transaction. Most times the borrower has called you because of your marketing efforts. She has seen your bandit sign or small classified advertisement. She is hoping that you will buy her property for more than she owes on it.

Most likely you are not the first real-estate investor she has talked to about her current financial situation. The reason the defaulting property owner has called you might be that another real-estate investor has declined to purchase the property.

ALERT!

The property owner with little or no equity usually cannot afford to list the property with a real-estate agent because of the agent's commission. The defaulting owner has probably thought about selling her home, but the market value and listing price determined by the agent is less than what she owes.

Adding on the real-estate agent's commission for selling the property places the defaulting borrower further into debt. The property owner is looking for some other way to get rid of the property. Keeping all of this in mind, remember too that most real-estate investors will simply walk away from a potential short sale. You could also, but there could be a chance to earn a profit from the transaction.

At first it may not be apparent that a short sale is a possibility. The conversation is likely to start by the property owner pitching his property to you, hoping to sell it. One of your questions will be, "What is your asking price?"

After receiving the price of the property, you should ask if there is any mortgage on the property and if the payments are current. When the property owner indicates there is no (or very little) equity and the payments are in default, start thinking short sale.

Ask the defaulting property owner if he would consider a short sale. Most owners will have no idea what you are suggesting. They will be clueless and ask for more information. "I might be able to help you out with a short-sale transaction," are your next words. "A short sale is when the lender is willing to accept less than what is owed on your loan."

Too many defaulting borrowers think that when a lender is willing to accept less than what is owed (a short sale), it means the possibility of receiving money.

Your next step is to visit and inspect the property and meet with the borrower. Give yourself some extra time at the property as you need to gather as much information as possible during your inspection.

Visiting and Inspecting the Property

A property that you will attempt to acquire needs a careful and thorough inspection. You need to identify every potential problem. Take careful notes and, with the property owner's permission, photograph everything that needs to be fixed, repaired, or updated.

Don't perform a cursory walk-through. You need to check everything. It is highly likely you will need this information later as you intensify your negotiations with the lender.

Permission from the Borrower

During your initial meeting with the defaulting borrower, you need to review several important issues. A frank discussion with the homeowner is the best approach. During the discussion you should cover the following topics:

- Your position as an investor
- Your offers/negotiations with the lender
- What you need from the property owner
- Issues for the property owner to consider

A frank and open discussion works best. The defaulted borrower needs to understand what you can and cannot do and what will happen if his lender accepts your offer.

Tell the Borrower What You Do

One of the first points you must make clear with the homeowner is that you are a real-estate investor, and the only reason you would attempt to purchase the property is to earn a profit. If you cannot make a reasonable return, you will certainly move on to another property and another opportunity.

Explaining a short sale to the defaulted homebuyer is not difficult. Your discussion should include the information that she will receive no money from the transaction, and she will have to move from the property quickly if the lender accepts your purchase offer.

The deal with the homeowner is simple. Whatever you decide to offer for the purchase of the property will go to her lender. She will receive nothing. You need to get the homeowner to sign an authorization to release form. This will be used to discuss her loan with her lender.

Without a signed authorization to release form, the defaulting borrower's lender will not discuss any part of the loan with you. It is critical that the homeowner sign the release form for you.

A generic authorization form looks like this:

AUTHORIZATION TO RELEASE CREDIT INFORMATION
Date: _____
To: _____
Account #: _____

As a holder of the above referenced loan with you, I (we) hereby authorize and request that you release my (our) credit history with your firm and forward it to Mary J. Johnson. You are also authorized to discuss the sale of my property secured by your loan with Mary J. Johnson. Please be advised, this letter serves as my (our) authorization for the release of my (our) loan information with your firm. Thank you for your assistance and cooperation in this matter.

_____   _____
Signature   Signature of Joint Applicant (if any)

_____   _____
Social Security Number   Social Security Number

_____
Address, Line 1 Address, Line 1

_____
Address, Line 2 Address, Line 2

Homeowner Ramifications

There are two major concerns for the homeowner when his lender accepts a short sale:

- IRS tax considerations
- Default judgment sought by the lender

As part of your discussions with the homeowner you should explain that the discounted amount (the difference between the mortgage balance and the short sale) might have to be declared as income on his income tax return if the lender issues a 1099 form (miscellaneous income) to the borrower. The IRS often becomes involved with short sales because they are seen as a relief of debt and may be treated as income.

FACT

You should not offer tax advice, but rather refer the homeowner to his accountant or tax advisor for advice. Since he is having severe financial problems, the income reported on a 1099 may have little consequence to him. Always refer homeowners to a tax advisor.

Remember that the agreed upon price for the property is payment in full. You will receive title and possession of the property. However, the defaulted borrower may still owe the difference between the mortgage balance and the discounted amount you paid for the property. This is a deficiency judgment. Unless specifically prohibited in the state where the property is located, you should inform the property owner of this probability.

Should the lender pursue a deficiency judgment, it will affect the homeowners and their credit report just as any other judgment. Inform the defaulting borrower that your purchase offer will include a condition that the lender accepts payment in full without pursuit of any deficiency judgment.

Avoid any future legal complications from the defaulting property owners by sending a follow-up letter reiterating that they check with their tax advisor about the potential of the tax owed on a 1099 and that a deficiency judgment might be possible. A letter provides proof you told them about these consequences during your meeting.

Hardship Letter from the Borrower

Another document you will need from the borrower is a hardship letter. It is best if it is handwritten. In this letter the borrower must tell her story why she is so desperate for the short sale, how she has no financial resources to bring the loan current, and that there is little if any likelihood that the loan could be brought current in the future.

Structuring Your Offer

As you continue with your effort to purchase the property, you need to calculate your potential profit with the transaction. Consider the costs associated with the acquisition of the property and what you intend to do with the property. Whether you plan to buy and hold the property or flip it should determine how you want to structure your purchase offer.

Although your purchase offer is with the owner of the property, the amount you pay is what the lender is being asked to accept as the payoff of the loan.

Your next step is to verify the value of the property. Do your own market analysis of the area and the property. Use recent comps to determine the realistic value of the property.

As part of your calculations, add up all the costs of selling the property. Use this number as part of your negotiations with the lender.

Work the calculations. Subtract the total amount owed against the property from the estimated proceeds of the sale. On a short sale, this will (or should) be a negative number. Look for other loans and liens against the property.

Don't accept the total amount owed from the defaulting borrower. Only use verified numbers, which are provided directly by the lender. Borrowers are often confused and disengaged by the time their property has reached foreclosure status.

Working with the Lender

During the process you must keep the defaulted borrower under control. You should be in regular contact and keep the borrower informed. By doing so you are more likely to achieve success with your offer. Part of your effort to acquire the property will include two time-consuming sections:

- Determining who at the lender has the authority to negotiate
- Assembling a short-sale package for submission to the lender

In today's world of voice mail, do not be surprised how long it may take you to determine who has the authority to negotiate on behalf of the lender with you. Although you should not have too much trouble contacting the loss mitigation department of the lender, locating the person that has the authority to accept a short sale offer may prove to be frustrating.

ALERT!

Don't be surprised if some customer service representatives say that they do not accept any short-sale agreements. They might have been trained to say that, or they may not even know what a short sale is. Keep trying.

You may want to try some different terms to find the right person at the lender. Ask if the lender has a workout, foreclosures, short-sale, loan modification, or reinstatement department. The reason to ask for different departments is that often a new employee is working the customer service telephone. Hopefully one of the terms will click and you will ultimately get to the right person.

Be prepared for a frustrating experience. Even though you may think you have the right person, don't be surprised that the contact you reached does not have the authority to negotiate a short sale. Negotiating any short sale with a lender is often thorny only because it is a daunting task finding the correct person with the authority to accept a discount on a loan payoff. It could take days to figure out who this person is. Often the person you need to speak with is a vice president or similar executive who hides behind voice mail.

Refer to the defaulting borrowers by their first names. This makes them more than just another defaulted loan to the lender's representative. By using the first names you are more likely to get an emotional decision.

Avoid wasting your time by talking to anyone other than the person that can authorize the short sale. Sending your short-sale packet to anyone else at the lender's office is generally a waste of time. Once you are finally in touch with the right person at the lender's office, only then can the negotiating begin.

The person at the lender's office will make or break your short-sale deal. It's time for you to be cordial and professional. Your initial telephone conversation should go something like this:

"Hello, my name is Mary J. Johnson and I am calling on behalf of Tom and Sue Jones. I have an authorization-to-release-information form I'd like to fax to you right now so we can discuss their loan deficiency. What is your fax number?"

Try to keep the lender's representative on the phone while the authorization is retrieved from the lender's fax machine. When you are back on the phone, continue the conversation.

"As you know, Tom and Sue are in foreclosure. I recently met them, and they seem like good folks with a serious financial problem. When I learned about their current dilemma, I said I would try to assist them. They want to sell their property immediately and move on with their lives and someday rebuild their credit. I have a rental unit in the area and I am willing to purchase Tom and Sue's property, but there is a big problem. They owe much more than what their property is worth."

Be prepared to back up the value issue with current comps. Offer to provide the proof you have assembled to the lender's representative. Continue the discussion by saying something like, "I am willing to help Tom and Sue out of their foreclosure as well as help you get a defaulted loan off your books. But there is no way I could possibly pay the mortgage balance. Will you consider a short payoff?"

Keep quiet as the lender's representative mulls over your proposal. If you get a positive response, ask what you need to submit. If the lender's representative turns your short-sale proposal down, suggest that your name and contact information be maintained in the file.

Submitting Your Short-Sale Package

Following your initial contact with the lender's representative, it is time to submit your short-sale purchase offer. Your package should include:

- Authorization to release form, signed by the homeowner
- Cover letter that summarizes the proposed short-sale transaction
- Defaulting borrowers hardship letter
- List of comps (comparables)
- List of repairs/problems with the property
- Photos of needed repairs and property deficiencies (photos show as-is condition)
- Borrower's current financial statement
- Supporting documents to support the financial statement (bank accounts, pay stubs, tax returns, unemployment insurance payments, workers comp payments, medical bills, divorce decree)
- Purchase agreement between you and property owner
- Completed proposed HUD-1 Settlement Statement

The most recent version of the HUD-1 Settlement Statement is available free at *www.hud.gov/offices/adm/hudclips/forms/hud1.cfm*. (A fill-in version is also available on HUD's Web site.)

Your cover letter should resemble something like this:

Dear Mr. Martin:

It was a pleasure speaking to you earlier today about Tom and Sue's unfortunate financial situation.

I have enclosed the short-payoff package for your review. This is for the payoff of your loan number 111112 for the property located at 191919 Sandy Drive, Philadelphia, PA.

My proposed purchase price of $102,550 is based on the following:

1. Your borrower is insolvent.
2. The recent comparables set the value of this property at $118,000.
   (See attached list.)
3. Two contractors have estimated needed repairs at $15,000.
4. Property values in the area are falling. See the enclosed newspaper article that was recently published about the real-estate prices in the area declining since the loss of three local employers.

I am ready to close on this property within five days of your acceptance of my offer. I have the funds available to make full cash payment. My purchase offer remains in effect for the next three days. Please call me with any questions. I look forward to hearing from you.

Sincerely,
Mary J. Johnson

Negotiating Your Deal

After submitting your short-sale proposal, call the next day to make sure it was received. Offer to answer any questions. Expect your first offer to purchase the property to be rejected. Most likely the lender's representative will counteroffer or tell you to come back with a higher offer.

At that point you can offer more or walk away. Persistence will pay off. The lender's representative needs to show that a higher offer was attempted. Negotiate over the price, emphasizing your position as to the value of the property in its current as-is condition. The negotiation for the property can go fast or be excruciatingly slow.

FACT

If you are able to make a deal, reduce it to writing right away. Ask the lender to issue a letter of acceptance of your offer.

Other Considerations about the Short Sale

There are many so-called short-sale experts on television and on the Internet championing the profits available for investors closing short-sale transactions. In reality short-sales are a lot of work, often fall through, and are not nearly as prevalent as the gurus would want you to believe. Lenders are not likely to give you the $30,000 to $40,000 just because you asked for it. While you can make a profit with a short-sale transaction, it will not be as large as gurus profess it can be.

Additionally, almost all short-sales transactions are cash sales. Seldom will the lender approve any purchase agreement with an assignment clause. Most lenders, before accepting a short sale, are likely to ask for proof of funds from you. They want to see that you have enough money on hand to close the transaction.

The Property's As-Is Condition

The current condition of the property is a primary concern for the lender. The BPO will guide the decision to accept a short sale. The more problems with the property, especially if it is in a deteriorating neighborhood, the more likely the lender will consider a short sale. Owning properties that are going to be tough to sell and need significant repairs is not what the lender wants.

The Hardship Factor

Most lenders have a rigorous hardship test that borrowers must pass before they will consider a short sale. In most cases the defaulting borrower must be experiencing one or more of these financial hardships:

- Death of a spouse, and without the spouse's income the borrower is unable to make the monthly loan payments.
- Divorce and the borrower has been abandoned by the spouse. Without the other spouse's income, the borrower could not make the monthly loan payment.
- Serious catastrophic illness has wrecked the borrower's personal finances.
- One of the borrowers has been called away for active military service.
- The borrower's employer has gone out of business, and high unemployment in the area prevents the borrower from finding similar employment.
- The borrower has been incarcerated and can no longer work.
- The borrower has become insolvent and has no realistic way to make payments now or in the future.
- The borrower has been injured, or is so seriously ill that working again seems unlikely.

Providing photographs of the as-is condition can help speed along the negotiation process. The pictures can support your value of the property. The more deficiencies the lender's representative can see with the property, the more likely your offer will be accepted.

Private Mortgage Insurance Factors

Lenders require borrowers to pay for private mortgage insurance. It insures against the lender's loss in the event that a loan is foreclosed.

The insurer may be the one that decides to accept or reject a short sale. The lender may make a claim against the mortgage insurance. At that point the insurer might advance funds to bring the loan current or purchase the loan from the lender. Another option for the mortgage insurer is to approve the short sale and reimburse the lender for any loss up to the amount of the coverage.

FACT

The lender will require that any short sale be an *arm's length transaction*. That means the buyer cannot be a family member, relative, or friend of the defaulting borrower. The lender does not want someone close profiting from the loss. If a lender finds out later that it was not an arm's length transaction, it will likely file a lawsuit to rescind the sale.

FHA and DVA Short Sales

Federal Housing Administration (FHA) short sales are called pre-foreclosure sales. The FHA has established substantial guidelines and regulations about short sales that are available at *www.hudclips .org/sub_nonhud/html/pdfforms/00-05.doc.*

Investors are not permitted to bid on HUD properties during the first offer period. HUD, as part of its mission, prefers to offer and sell its foreclosure properties to owner-occupants. If an owner-occupant buyer is not found during the first round of bidding, HUD then offers their properties to both owner-occupants and investors.

Properties acquired directly from HUD are a different kind of short sale. With these properties you will not be dealing with the former property owner. Rather you are simply offering to purchase the property for whatever you offer.

The Department of Veterans Affairs (VA) short sales are called compromised sales. According to the VA, when the borrower is unable to sell his or her property for an amount greater than or equal to the current outstanding loan balance plus closing costs, the VA may pay the difference to allow the sale to take place. Compromise sales are approved if the sales contract meets several criteria and results in a cost savings compared to a foreclosure. These factors must be considered:

- The property must be sold for fair market value.
- The closing costs must be reasonable and customary.
- The compromise sale must be less costly for the government than foreclosure.
- There must be financial hardship on the part of the seller.
- There must be no other liens, second mortgages, or judgments unless the amount is insignificant. In situations with other liens, the seller can request that the lien holder consider releasing the lien and converting the loan to a personal loan.
- The seller must obtain a sales contract in order to be considered for the program.
- To protect the seller's interest, the seller should make the sales contract contingent on the approval of the VA.

When awarding bids, HUD considers the bottom line: what its net proceeds will be on the sale of the property. Bidders seeking fewer concessions have the advantage.

See Appendix D for a listing of the Department of Veterans Affairs regional loan centers.

Chapter 21

Your First and Next Steps

Now that you have learned about foreclosures what you do next will determine your ability to make money as a real-estate investor investing in foreclosure properties. You can play it safe and do nothing or jump in and test the waters. Doing nothing will cost you nothing. Or you might make some offers on properties, spend some money, and earn significant profits as an active real-estate investor. It's time to dig in and get started investing in foreclosures. Here are your next steps in the process of becoming an active investor.

Get Your Team in Place

No matter which direction you want to go with investing in foreclosures, the next step is to get your team in place. It doesn't matter whether you want to flip properties for profit; invest in apartment buildings; or buy, fix-up, and sell—you must get your team formed and ready.

Hiring a Competent Real-Estate Attorney

The first part of the team is your attorney. You should locate and employ the services of a competent real-estate attorney. Remember that it always costs less to stay out of legal trouble than it does to get out of trouble later.

You should give top priority to securing the services of a competent and experienced real-estate attorney. You want a specialist, not a lawyer that does some real-estate transactions as part of many other aspects of practicing law. Just as you would not want a podiatrist performing an operation on your heart, you do not want a personal injury lawyer working on your real-estate transactions.

Many states offer special certifications for lawyers. If your state does, consider hiring an attorney that has been certified in real-estate law. Often it takes five years of practice, with over 50 percent of the time in real-estate law, for an attorney to gain this certification. When considering the hiring of a lawyer, you should always independently investigate the lawyer's credentials and ability. You should not rely on the advertisements or any self-proclaimed expertise.

QUESTION?

What if I cannot afford to hire a lawyer?
The answer is simple: You can't afford not to hire a lawyer! Don't even think about trying to be an active real-estate investor without having a competent attorney representing you.

Schedule a meeting with the attorney. Be willing to purchase an hour of the lawyer's time if necessary. Tell the attorney what you want to do, and ask how the attorney can be part of your team. Determine during your initial meeting how frequently the attorney will be available to you. Make it clear that you are not looking for a once-and-done transaction but intend to invest in as many foreclosure properties as possible. Ask the attorney to describe her experience in handling foreclosure settlements.

Make sure the attorney's personality matches yours. Remember that the attorney is in business to provide legal service. The lawyer should be willing to help you grow your investing business and should look at you as a long-term client.

Other Team Members

Your other team members include a title company, insurance agent, lender or mortgage broker, real-estate agent, and accountant. Don't be surprised if it takes longer than you might first realize to put your team together. It is not uncommon to take a little bit of time to assemble your resources.

Locating other real-estate investors is also part of the start-up period. It should be your goal to locate as many investors as possible. Maintain a good working list of these investors. Using your computer will make it easier to develop and keep your investor list in proper order.

Get involved in your local real-estate investor club or organization. Getting out there and making contacts makes sense. You may have to travel to attend a club. It's worth the effort to find and attend club meetings.

Depending on your credit worthiness and cash availability, you might need to locate potential partners who can bring the cash or money to the deal. Many investors need the help of a partner or mentor to conclude their first real-estate investment transaction.

Remember to treat this as a business. Real-estate investing is a business just like any other. It takes time to develop resources, clients, associates, partners, and so on. You need to be disciplined and professional. Work hard and with serious effort and your real-estate investing business will prosper.

Build Your Credibility

One of the intangibles you need to establish is your credibility. You have to decide how you are going to present yourself to your local real-estate market. Your success will likely depend on how others perceive you within your market area. Having a used-car salesperson mentality will gain you little. You want to present an image of a professional investor.

Never closing deals presented to you by a local real-estate agent will result in the agent moving on to others. Real-estate agents are in the business of selling property. You can't expect an agent to keep feeding you deals if you cannot or will not close any of them.

You will soon be considered an oddball if you try to buy property with no money, lousy credit, and insignificant income. Running around and spinning your wheels is not getting deals done.

Be Smart

Working as a real-estate investor requires patience, entrepreneurial skills, and vision. It is easy to make expensive mistakes as a real-estate investor. Just like any other business, you can fail by investing in the wrong property or not having the skills to sell your investment property at a profit.

ESSENTIAL

Operating your real-estate business requires you to be smart. Just as in running any other business, you should focus on your goals and long-term growth.

There any many stupid things you can do in the operation of your business. For example, one real-estate investor decided to go cheap and download forms on the Internet. In his exuberance to make a deal work, he opted to use a generic, free purchase-offer form he had located online. The defaulting property owner signed the forms provided by the investor-to-be. But it was not long until things turned sour. The property owner's attorney soon contacted the hapless investor. The attorney realized immediately that a requirement of state law required certain disclosures in the agreement, which were not included in the investor's purchase agreement. The investor made a settlement, or in other words paid damages, to prevent a lawsuit. In this case the investor was not smart enough to have his attorney provide the proper purchase-agreement forms. The thousands of dollars he paid in damages could have been better spent to acquire properties.

Too many real-estate investors simply want to get rich quick. They imagine quitting their day jobs, working a few hours a month, and spending the rest of their time on yachts and beaches. If only operating a business were so easy.

It Takes Time

Anyone intending to become a real-estate investor should realize it takes time and persistence to achieve success. It would be wonderful if you could purchase one property and make hundreds of thousands of dollars on the transaction. In reality your profit is going to be significantly less.

You should develop a business plan. The big decision is whether you operate your real-estate investing business as a hobby or a full-time endeavor. Some investors only have one or two investment properties in addition to their own home. Others develop significantly larger portfolios.

So many new real-estate investors want instant success and desire to make thousands of dollars weekly. They intend to make that big splash as investors. Some succeed, but many fail. The main reason for their failure is their inability to plan for success.

Many people will tell you it is impossible to make money as a real-estate investor. These naysayers are certain that you cannot achieve financial freedom.

One of the most important aspects of real-estate investment is time. If you are buying and holding foreclosure properties, your investment will enjoy appreciation due to the fact that most real estate appreciates. If you buy, fix, and sell a foreclosure property, you have improved the value of the property. It takes time to find the properties, acquire them, and then turn them into profitable transactions. Seasoned real-estate investors know that in the real-estate game there are no instant dollars. While everyone wants to make a quick buck, every transaction takes time.

Real estate is a great form of investing, but it takes a lot of work and time on your part. This is often true if your resources are limited, and they usually are when you are getting started.

FACT

Working full-time usually means working forty hours each week. However, full-time investors live off the income they develop from investing in real estate and often have no other source of income or are not employed by anyone else.

Persistence is one of the most important skills you can develop. Few real-estate deals are consummated on the first attempt. Relentless real-estate investors that are not hesitant to follow up with multiple attempts to put the most foreclosure deals together. A follow-up system that includes a running history of conversations can help you put together an acceptable purchase agreement and close the foreclosure deal. Too many new investors want to make one phone call and fall into a $25,000 profitable deal. They do not have the willingness to persevere and work hard to put deals together. It takes time to be successful as a real-estate investor.

Get Started Now

If you want to be a successful real-estate investor that specializes in acquiring foreclosure properties, get started now. The worst thing you can do is sit on the sidelines while others play the game. By doing so all you are really doing is allowing other real-estate investors to make money.

You can sit on the sidelines for months, or years, and never invest in foreclosure properties. During that time someone else in your marketing area will have been acquiring foreclosure properties. They will have bought them, sold them, fixed them up, rented them, or lived in them. You have two choices: either get into the game or not.

ALERT!

The risk is less than you think. Of course, you can make serious and expensive mistakes. To avoid them, hire and rely on competent professionals to help you through the process.

Assume for a moment that you had $100,000 to invest in the stock market. Where would you invest it? How much could you make on this investment? And perhaps most importantly, have you ever heard of someone losing her stock investments?

Now invest that $100,000 in real estate. If you acquired ten properties with that $100,000 and rented the properties, allowing the renters to pay the mortgage, in ten to fifteen years what would the properties be worth? Which gave you the best result, investing in the stock market or foreclosure properties that you bought and held?

The one thing you cannot do if you want to make money by investing in foreclosure properties is to do nothing. You have to get into the game. Within these pages you have learned many ways to profit from investing in foreclosure properties. It's time to make those investments. Don't sit on the sidelines. Get into the game. Remember that you will not make any money as a real-estate investor unless you commence investing.

Start today. Good luck!

Appendix A

State Foreclosure Summary

Alabama

Type of Foreclosures Permitted
Both judicial and nonjudicial foreclosures are permitted.

Average Foreclosure Time
Approximately three to four months to complete the foreclosure.

Common Practice
Nonjudicial foreclosures are the most common.

Special Notes
The borrower has the right to pay off the debt at any time and stop the foreclosure until the day of the sale.

Judicial Foreclosures
There are few judicial foreclosures in Alabama. They usually only occur when there is a title problem that needs to be corrected or if a mortgage does not permit nonjudicial foreclosure.

Nonjudicial Foreclosures
Non-judicial foreclosures are the most common type of foreclosure in Alabama.

Sale Information
The lender must strictly follow any notice of sale requirements that are specified in the mortgage. The notice of the public sale is published for three weeks in a newspaper or posted at the courthouse door and three other public places. The sale is conducted at the courthouse. Following the foreclosure sale, and upon payment of the bid and costs, a deed is granted to the winning bidder.

Redemption
The defaulted borrower has the right to redeem the property after the foreclosure

sale for up to one year after the foreclosure sale date.

Alaska

Type of Foreclosures Permitted
Both judicial and nonjudicial foreclosures are permitted in Alaska.

Average Foreclosure Time
Approximately four months to complete the foreclosure.

Common Practice
Nonjudicial foreclosures are the most common.

Special Notes
Before an out-of-court foreclosure can commence, the borrower must be in default for thirty or more days. The default notice is recorded and sent to all parties. It must contain the deed of trust information, a description of the property, the debt owed, and the date, time, and location of the public sale. This default notice is also posted on the encumbered property. The borrower has the right and may resolve the default before the sale by paying the amount in default plus all applicable expenses.

Judicial Foreclosures
When the judicial foreclosure is used in Alaska, the borrower does not need to be thirty days in default. A foreclosure complaint and lis pendens are filed in the court and delivered to the borrower. If the borrower does not respond within twenty days, the court can rule the borrower is in default and direct the property to be sold.

Nonjudicial Foreclosures
The lender's attorney usually conducts the foreclosure sale.

Sale Information
In Alaska, for both types of foreclosures the public notice of sale must be posted in three public places at least thirty days before the actual sale. One of the locations must be the nearest U.S. post office. The public sale notice is also required to be published in a local newspaper once a week for four consecutive weeks.

When the nonjudicial foreclosure is used, the location of the public sale varies. After the sale, the trustee provides the winning bidder with the deed, which transfers ownership from the borrower to the purchaser. Any other liens against the property are usually cleared from the title for the purchaser at an out-of-court auction.

When judicial foreclosures are used, the winning bidder receives a certificate of sale and the sale must be confirmed.

Redemption
For judicial foreclosure sales, (and not nonjudicial sales), borrowers have the right of redemption for twelve months after the sale confirmation. The borrower is required to pay the amount of the sale price plus 8 percent interest and all other applicable costs. If the property is not redeemed by the borrower, the winning bidder obtains full ownership of the property.

Arizona

Type of Foreclosures Permitted
Both judicial and nonjudicial foreclosures are permitted.

Average Foreclosure Time
Approximately three to four months to complete the foreclosure.

Common Practice
Nonjudicial foreclosures are the most common.

Special Notes
Court foreclosures commence when the lender files for foreclosure and records a notice of the pending lawsuit (lis pendens). If the borrower does not respond to the court action, the court rules against the borrower and sets the amount owed to the lender. The county clerk then directs the county sheriff to conduct a sale of the property to recover the amount the court determined is owed to the lender.

Judicial Foreclosures
Judicial foreclosures are permitted.

Nonjudicial Foreclosures
Nonjudicial foreclosures occur if the trust deed permits the lender to sell the property if the borrower defaults. The sale is not permitted until ninety days after the notice of sale is recorded.

Sale Information
Until 5:00 P.M. the day prior to the scheduled sale, the borrower may stop the foreclosure by paying the default amount, fees, and costs.

For court-directed foreclosures, the sheriff conducts the sale approximately forty-five days after the county clerk directs the public auction. The final bid price must be paid to the sheriff by 5:00 p.m. the day after the sale. A certificate of sale is issued to the winning bidder.

Redemption
The redemption period is six months from the sale date. To redeem the property, the total amount owed plus fees and costs must be paid. If there is no redemption, the sheriff transfers ownership to the winning bidder. There is no right of redemption for the borrower after a nonjudicial foreclosure auction.

Arkansas

Type of Foreclosures Permitted
Both judicial and nonjudicial foreclosures are permitted.

Average Foreclosure Time
Approximately two to four months to complete the foreclosure.

Common Practice
Nonjudicial foreclosures are the most common

Special Notes
The lender must have an appraisal of the property taken prior to the scheduled foreclosure date.

Judicial Foreclosures
The court determines the amount in default and grants the borrower a short time to pay the determined debt to the lender.

Nonjudicial Foreclosures
Power-of-sale clauses in mortgages allow lenders to foreclose on properties in default without going through the court system.

Sale Information
An auctioneer conducts the public sale. The highest bidder must pay the bid price within ten days of the sale. The mortgaged property must sell for

no less than two-thirds of the appraised value. If this value is not met at the public sale, the property must be offered again within twelve months of the original sale date. When this occurs, the second sale awards the property to the highest bidder regardless of the appraisal value.

Redemption
For nonjudicial foreclosures, the borrower has no right to redeem the property after the sale. If the property is sold by a judicial foreclosure, the borrower has one year from the date of the sale to redeem the property.

California

Type of Foreclosures Permitted
Both judicial and nonjudicial foreclosures are permitted.

Average Foreclosure Time
Approximately four to five months to complete the foreclosure.

Common Practice
Nonjudicial foreclosures are the most common.

Special Notes
At least twenty days before the public sale, the notice of sale must be posted both on the property and in one local public location. The notice of the sale is also published once a week for three weeks in the local newspaper, starting at least twenty days before the sale date. The sale notice is also mailed to the borrower at least twenty days prior to the sale and to anyone who requests the notice. The notice of sale is also recorded with the county recorder at least fourteen days before the sale.

Judicial Foreclosures
Sale occurs as directed by the court.

Nonjudicial Foreclosures
Three months after the notice of default is filed the lender can schedule a trustee's sale of the property.

Sale Information
The defaulted borrower may pay off the default plus any applicable costs of foreclosure five days prior to the sale and stop the foreclosure process. The sale is a public auction and the property is sold to the winning bidder. The trustee may require bidders to pay the full bid amount in cash or cashier's check.

Redemption
None. After the sale is complete, the trustee transfers ownership to the winning bidder.

Colorado

Type of Foreclosures Permitted
Both judicial and nonjudicial foreclosures are permitted.

Average Foreclosure Time
Approximately six to seven months to complete the foreclosure.

Common Practice
Nonjudicial foreclosures are the most common

Special Notes
Colorado uses a public trustee. The trustee for each county is either appointed by the governor or elected by the public.

If the borrower intends to pay off the default and stop the foreclosure, he must notify the public trustee at least fifteen days prior to the sale.

Judicial Foreclosures
As directed by the court.

Nonjudicial Foreclosures
The nonjudicial foreclosure process commences when the lender files with the public trustee to request a sale of the property. Following the public trustee recording the foreclosure action, the public sale is scheduled.

When the public auction is scheduled, the lender must still obtain a court order allowing the sale. The court schedules a hearing. If the court finds the borrower is in default, the court allows the sale.

Sale Information
The notice of the public sale is published in a local newspaper for five weeks prior to the sale. The public trustee usually conducts the sale at the courthouse. At the public sale the public trustee reads the written bid submitted by the lender. Anyone may offer a higher bid.

Redemption
Following the public sale, the defaulted borrower has seventy-five days to redeem the property. If there is no redemption, the public trustee transfers ownership of the property to the winning bidder.

Connecticut
Type of Foreclosures Permitted
Only judicial foreclosures are permitted.

Average Foreclosure Time
Approximately two to six months to complete the foreclosure.

Common Practice
Connecticut has two types of court-directed foreclosure procedures: strict foreclosure and foreclosure by sale. A judge decides which procedure will be used.

Special Notes
The court assigns an attorney to oversee the sale, and the attorney publishes the public sale notice and conducts the sale.

Judicial Foreclosures
A court action is commenced by the lender against the borrower. The court decides the debt, market value of the property, costs, and whether a strict foreclosure or a foreclosure by sale will be used.

A strict foreclosure is ordered if there is no borrower equity in the property. The borrower is given a specified date when the debt must be paid. If the borrower does not pay the debt in full, the ownership automatically goes to the lender.
A judgment of foreclosure by sale occurs when there is equity in excess of the amount the borrower owes and a public auction is needed to recover the debt.

Nonjudicial Foreclosures
Not used in Connecticut.

Sale Information
At any time prior to the sale the borrower may stop the foreclosure by paying the amount owed on the mortgage. The court sets the sale date about sixty days from the date it makes its initial ruling. In Connecticut the sale typically occurs on

the property on a Saturday. A 10 percent deposit of the successful bid is required from the winning bidder. After the court approves the sale, the winning bidder is granted thirty days to pay the balance of the winning bid.

Redemption
Normally within two weeks following the sale the court decides whether to approve the sale. Until the sale is approved by the court, the borrower can redeem the property by paying the amount owed plus costs.

Delaware

Type of Foreclosures Permitted
Only judicial foreclosures are permitted.

Average Foreclosure Time
Approximately seven months to complete the foreclosure.

Common Practice
A complaint is filed in court to commence the foreclosure procedure.

Special Notes
After the complaint has been filed, the borrower is given instructions to appear in court within twenty days and provide evidence as to why the foreclosure should not occur. The court determines if the borrower is in default.

Judicial Foreclosures
The lender can submit a request to the county sheriff to conduct a sale eleven days after the court determines the borrower is in default.

Nonjudicial Foreclosures
Not permitted in Delaware.

Sale Information
Public sales are held either at the property or the courthouse by the sheriff. Typically the sale occurs two to three months after the court determines the borrower is in default. The notice of sale is published in two local newspapers. The notice of the sale is also delivered to the borrower at least ten days before the sale date. After the auction, confirmation of the sale occurs within one to three months. The sheriff then transfers ownership to the winning bidder.

Redemption
The borrower has no right of redemption.

District of Columbia

Type of Foreclosures Permitted
Both judicial and nonjudicial foreclosures are permitted.

Average Foreclosure Time
Approximately four months to complete the foreclosure.

Common Practice
Nonjudicial foreclosures are the most common.

Special Notes
The defaulting borrower may reinstate his loan up to five days before to the foreclosure sale by paying the default amount, including late charges and costs. This can occur no more than once in any two years.

A licensed auctioneer conducts the public sale. The foreclosure sale occurs at the auctioneer's office. After the sale is completed, the deed is recorded.

Judicial Foreclosures
Judicial foreclosures are seldom used.

Nonjudicial Foreclosures
The lender starts the nonjudicial foreclosure proceeding by sending a notice to the borrower that the terms of the mortgage or deed of trust have been violated.

Sale Information
The lender is required to send a notice of foreclosure sale by certified mail to the owner of the property at least thirty days prior to the public sale. The lender must also record the notice of sale with the recorder of deeds and must also mail a copy to the mayor's office.

The mortgage or deed of trust may specify a particular time and place of the sale. If so, the procedure must be followed. If the mortgage or deed of trust does not specify the time and place of the public sale, the lender or trustee acquires a court order specifying the sale terms.

The lender follows any advertising requirements stipulated in the mortgage or deed of trust. If there are no requirements included in the documents, the lender traditionally advertises the foreclosure sale in the *Washington Post* or the *Washington Times* five times prior to the actual sale date.

Redemption
There is no right of redemption.

Florida

Type of Foreclosures Permitted
Only judicial foreclosures are permitted.

Average Foreclosure Time
Approximately five months to complete the foreclosure.

Special Notes
The borrower can stop the foreclosure action until the date of the sale by paying the total amount owed to the lender.

Judicial Foreclosures
A lender commences a foreclosure by filing a court action and recording a notice of a pending lawsuit (lis pendens) against the borrower. The lender notifies the borrower by mail. The court sets the foreclosure sale date if it determines the borrower is in default.

Nonjudicial Foreclosures
Not used in Florida.

Sale Information
The clerk of the court typically conducts the sale, which ordinarily occurs at the county courthouse at 11:00 A.M. The successful bidder must immediately pay a 5 percent deposit. The balance must be paid by the end of the day.

Redemption
The borrower has no right of redemption.

Georgia

Type of Foreclosures Permitted
Both judicial and nonjudicial foreclosures are permitted.

Average Foreclosure Time
Approximately two months to complete the foreclosure.

Common Practice

Nonjudicial foreclosures are the most common.

Special Notes

Lenders are not required to notify the borrower before starting the foreclosure process unless the mortgage or deed of trust requires notification. The borrower may stop the foreclosure by paying the total loan balance prior to the public sale.

Judicial Foreclosures

Judicial foreclosures are rare in Georgia, but they are used to correct title problems. After a court filing, the borrower is required to pay the defaulted amount to the court within thirty days. If the money is not received, a foreclosure sale is set by the court.

Nonjudicial Foreclosures

Nonjudicial foreclosures are common. The lender starts the foreclosure by scheduling the public sale.

Sale Information

Georgia schedules foreclosure sales at the county courthouse on the first Tuesday of the month between 10:00 a.m. and 4:00 p.m. The notice of sale is published each week for four weeks before the sale. The notice of sale is also sent to the borrower a minimum of fifteen days prior to the sale date. The winning bidder must pay the full bid amount to the person conducting the sale immediately following the sale.

Redemption

The borrower has no right of redemption.

Hawaii

Type of Foreclosures Permitted

Both judicial and nonjudicial foreclosures are permitted.

Average Foreclosure Time

Approximately six months to complete the foreclosure.

Common Practice

Nonjudicial foreclosures are the most common.

Special Notes

The timeline for a judicial foreclosure is typically eleven months. Within three days prior to the public sale the borrower may pay any default and stop the public sale.

Judicial Foreclosures

A judicial foreclosure begins when the lender files documents with the court and asks the court to rule the borrower in default. The borrower may appeal a default finding within thirty days.

Nonjudicial Foreclosures

Nonjudicial foreclosures must be in accordance with all the sale clauses contained within the mortgage. These terms may require the lender to notify the borrower of any default on the loan before starting the foreclosure process.

Sale Information

With nonjudicial foreclosures, the notice of foreclosure sale is posted on the property twenty-one days prior to the sale. The sale is a public auction where the highest bidder buys the property.

For judicial foreclosures, the court appoints a commissioner to sell the property at public auction. Any party may bid at the public auction. The winning bidder is required to pay 10 percent of the bid in cash or a cashier's check. In Hawaii the highest bidder does not automatically get the property. Additional bidding may occur at a confirmation hearing. If the court determines the sale price as fair, the sale is confirmed.

Redemption

There are no redemption rights for the borrower.

Idaho

Type of Foreclosures Permitted

Both judicial and nonjudicial foreclosures are permitted.

Average Foreclosure Time

Approximately five to nine months to complete the foreclosure.

Common Practice

Nonjudicial foreclosures are the most common.

Special Notes

The borrower has a minimum of 115 days to resolve the default and stop the foreclosure process by paying the lender the full amount due, including costs.

Judicial Foreclosures

Judicial foreclosures are seldom used except to clear the property title.

Nonjudicial Foreclosures

The lender commences the nonjudicial foreclosure by mailing a notice of default to the borrower. The lender also files the notice of default with the county recorder. After the notice of default is recorded, the foreclosure sale is scheduled and advertised.

Sale Information

At least 120 days before the public sale date, a notice of sale is mailed to the borrower. The lender also publishes the notice of sale in the local newspaper once a week for four weeks. The final publication has to be at least thirty days prior to the sale date.

The trustee's attorney conducts the sale. Anyone may bid, and the trustee transfers ownership of the property to the winning bidder after receiving payment. Idaho law establishes the winning bidder is entitled to possession of the property within ten days after the sale.

Redemption

There are no redemption rights for the borrower.

Illinois

Type of Foreclosures Permitted

Only judicial foreclosures are permitted.

Average Foreclosure Time

Approximately twelve months to complete the foreclosure.

Special Notes

A borrower can stop the foreclosure within three months of being notified of the court action by paying the default amount plus all the fees and costs.

Judicial Foreclosures

A lender commences a foreclosure by filing a court action. The borrower has thirty days to respond to the court action or the lender will continue to pursue the foreclosure by requesting the court make a ruling on the matter. When the court rules against the borrower, the lender is then able to schedule a public sale to recover the amount owed on the loan plus applicable costs.

Nonjudicial Foreclosures
Not permitted in Illinois.

Sale Information
The sheriff typically conducts the public auction. The property is sold to the highest bidder. The person conducting the sale issues a certificate of sale to the winning bidder, subject to confirmation by the court. If the property is still occupied by the property owner, eviction is commenced. The winning bidder is entitled to possession of the property within thirty days of the sale.

Redemption
The borrower can redeem the property for at least seven months after the auction.

Indiana

Type of Foreclosures Permitted
Only judicial foreclosures are permitted.

Average Foreclosure Time
Approximately nine months to complete the foreclosure.

Common Practice
Foreclosure periods vary based on the age of the mortgage. After the pre-foreclosure period expires, a copy of the order of public sale and judgment are issued and certified by the clerk to the sheriff. After receiving the court order, the sheriff proceeds with the foreclosure sale.

The defaulting borrower may satisfy the foreclosure judgment at any time before the foreclosure sale by paying the amount owed, interest, and fees.

Special Notes
In Indiana there is no waiting period for properties abandoned by their owners. Immediately after the public sale, the sheriff transfers the property ownership to the winning bidder.

Judicial Foreclosures
A lender commences a foreclosure by filing a court action.

Nonjudicial Foreclosures
Nonjudicial foreclosures are not available.

Sale Information
The sheriff appoints an auctioneer to conduct the public foreclosure sale. The notice of sale is published three times in a local newspaper. The sheriff must post the notice in at least three public places and in the county courthouse.

Redemption
There are no redemption rights.

Iowa

Type of Foreclosures Permitted
Both judicial and nonjudicial foreclosures are permitted.

Average Foreclosure Time
Approximately four months to complete the foreclosure.

Common Practice
Nonjudicial foreclosures are the most common.

Special Notes
The lender typically delivers a written notice of default to the borrower thirty days before starting the foreclosure process. Foreclosure sales often

occur within two months; however, the borrower can demand a delay for six to twelve months.

Judicial Foreclosures

The court issues a judgment for the entire amount due and directs the property to be sold to satisfy the judgment.

Nonjudicial Foreclosures

Uncomplicated out-of-court foreclosures are permitted if the lender does not pursue a deficiency judgment against the borrower.

Sale Information

The sheriff organizes and conducts the public sale, which occurs between 9:00 A.M. and 4:00 P.M. The sheriff receives sealed written bids, along with a refundable payment. At the public sale the sheriff opens and reads the written bids.

If the lender chooses foreclosure without any redemption, the winning bidder receives a deed without redemption after the foreclosure sale.

Redemption

In Iowa foreclosures may occur with or without redemption rights depending on how the lender pursues the foreclosure. Defaulted property owners enjoy a one-year redemption period if the lender pursues a deficiency judgment.

Kansas

Type of Foreclosures Permitted

Only judicial foreclosures are permitted.

Average Foreclosure Time

Approximately seven months to complete the foreclosure.

Common Practice

A lender commences a foreclosure by filing a court action. After the borrower's right of redemption has expired, the winning bidder exchanges the certificate of purchase for a recorded deed that transfers the property ownership.

Special Notes

The lender dictates the bid price at the public sale.

Judicial Foreclosures

The borrower has at least twenty days to respond to the lender's court action. The borrower then has ten days to pay the amount due before a foreclosure sale is scheduled.

Nonjudicial Foreclosures

Not permitted in Kansas.

Sale Information

The winning bidder receives a certificate of purchase.

Redemption

The redemption period for the borrower begins on the sale date, but the length of time varies from three to twelve months.

Kentucky

Type of Foreclosures Permitted

Only judicial foreclosures are permitted.

Average Foreclosure Time

Approximately six months to complete the foreclosure.

Common Practice
A lender commences a foreclosure by filing a court action.

Special Notes
The notice of pending action (lis pendens) is delivered by the sheriff to the borrower, who has twenty days to respond. If the borrower does not respond, the lender asks the court to rule against the borrower. When this occurs, the court sets a foreclosure sale date. In Kentucky the property must be appraised prior to the foreclosure sale.

Judicial Foreclosures
Kentucky foreclosures only proceed under court order.

Nonjudicial Foreclosures
Nonjudicial foreclosures are not permitted.

Sale Information
The sale usually is held one month after the court issues its ruling against the defaulted borrower. The sale, conducted by a court official called a master commissioner, usually occurs at the county courthouse. The highest bidder purchases the property and may pay in cash or post bond to pay in installments.

Redemption
If the public sale price is less than two-thirds of the appraised value, the property owner has the right to redeem the property from the buyer by paying the sale price plus interest for up to one year from the foreclosure sale date.

Louisiana

Type of Foreclosures Permitted
Only judicial foreclosures are permitted.

Average Foreclosure Time
Approximately six months to complete the foreclosure.

Common Practice
There are two kinds of judicial foreclosure proceedings in Louisiana: executory process and ordinary process. Executory process is commonly used.

Special Notes
The executory process is an accelerated procedure by which the lender uses a mortgage that includes an "authentic act that imparts a confession of judgment." Ordinary process is when the lender files a lawsuit to foreclose on the mortgage.

Judicial Foreclosures
A lender commences a foreclosure by filing a court action.

Nonjudicial Foreclosures
Nonjudicial foreclosures are not permitted in Louisiana.

Sale Information
After the executory process is issued, the borrower is served with a demand for the delinquent payments. The borrower has three days to provide the delinquent payments or the court orders a writ of seizure and sale. The writ is executed by the county sheriff, who will seize the property. Following the property seizure, it is advertised for thirty days. The sheriff then sells the property.

Redemption
There is no right of redemption.

Maine

Type of Foreclosures Permitted
Only judicial foreclosures are permitted.

Average Foreclosure Time
Approximately nine months to complete the foreclosure.

Common Practice
Before the lender can start a foreclosure, the lender must deliver a default notice to the borrower. If the borrower does not pay the default amount within thirty days, the lender may commence a foreclosure action.

Special Notes
If the borrower does not oppose the lender in a court action, there is no hearing. If the borrower opposes the lender, a hearing is scheduled by the court. After a ruling in favor of the lender, the borrower has ninety days to stop the foreclosure by paying all amounts due.

Judicial Foreclosures
A lender commences a foreclosure by filing a court action.

Nonjudicial Foreclosures
Nonjudicial foreclosures are not permitted.

Sale Information
The sale is often held at the office of the foreclosure attorney. The property is advertised thirty to forty-five days prior to the sale. Bidders are required to bring a certain deposit amount (stipulated in the notice of sale) and must pay off the balance within thirty days. After receiving payment, the property ownership is transferred to the successful bidder.

Redemption
There is no redemption period.

Maryland

Type of Foreclosures Permitted
Only judicial foreclosures are permitted.

Average Foreclosure Time
Approximately two months to complete the foreclosure.

Common Practice
A lender commences a foreclosure by filing a court action. The lender must also obtain a decree of sale.

Special Notes
After the winning bid has been established at the public auction, a notice that the sale has occurred is published in a local newspaper to advise interested parties that any objections must be made within thirty days. If no objections are filed, the sale is confirmed by the court and the property ownership is transferred to the successful bidder.

Judicial Foreclosures
The court supervises the foreclosure and sale.

Nonjudicial Foreclosures
Not permitted in Maryland.

Sale Information
The sale must be published in the local newspaper for three weeks prior to the actual sale date. A licensed auctioneer conducts the public sale, which typically takes place outside the courthouse.

Redemption
There is no redemption period.

Massachusetts

Type of Foreclosures Permitted
Both judicial and nonjudicial foreclosures are permitted.

Average Foreclosure Time
Approximately three months to complete the foreclosure.

Common Practice
Nonjudicial foreclosures are the most common. The foreclosure can take less than ninety days after the lender schedules a foreclosure sale. Before the lender may commence the foreclosure, a ruling from the land court must be obtained to ensure the borrower is not subject to protection under the Soldiers' and Sailors' Civil Relief Act of 1940. This law allows a postponement of a foreclosure action for active members of the U.S. military.

Special Notes
The mortgage may require the lender to notify the borrower of any default before scheduling a public foreclosure sale. Massachusetts law does not require any notification.

Judicial Foreclosures
Not used in Massachusetts.

Nonjudicial Foreclosures
The notice of a sale appears for three weeks in the local newspaper, and the first notice occurs no less than twenty-one days prior to the sale date.

Sale Information
A licensed auctioneer conducts the sale at the property. The winning bidder must pay a deposit at the time of the sale and deliver the remaining funds within thirty days. Within thirty days after the public auction, the sale is recorded at the courthouse and the ownership is transferred to the winning bidder.

Redemption
There is no right of redemption.

Michigan

Type of Foreclosures Permitted
Both judicial and nonjudicial foreclosures are permitted.

Average Foreclosure Time
Approximately eight months to complete the foreclosure.

Common Practice
Nonjudicial foreclosures are the most common.

Special Notes
A trustee or the county sheriff conducts the public auction between 9:00 A.M. and 4:00 P.M. at the county courthouse.

Judicial Foreclosures
Permitted in Michigan but are seldom used.

Nonjudicial Foreclosures
The person conducting the sale completes the necessary documents to transfer ownership to the winning bidder at the sale. Those documents must state the property owner's redemption expiration.

Sale Information
The public sale usually occurs about two months after the lender commences the foreclosure process. A notice of sale is published for four weeks in a local newspaper, and the sale may not be less than twenty-eight days from the first publication date. A notice is also posted on the property.

Redemption
The redemption period varies in Michigan, but typically it is about six months from the foreclosure sale date.

Minnesota

Type of Foreclosures Permitted
Both judicial and nonjudicial foreclosures are permitted.

Average Foreclosure Time
Approximately four months to complete the foreclosure.

Common Practice
Nonjudicial foreclosures are the most common.

Special Notes
A court foreclosure commences when a lender notifies the borrower of the default. The lender must next file a court action against the borrower. If the court rules against the borrower, a sale is scheduled.

Judicial Foreclosures
The court may supervise the foreclosure process.

Nonjudicial Foreclosures
The majority of foreclosures are handled through a power-of-sale clause contained in the mortgage. This does not require court supervision of the public sale.

Sale Information
The county sheriff or sheriff's deputy conducts the foreclosure sale between 9:00 A.M. and sundown at a public place, usually the sheriff's office. After the sale has been conducted, the sheriff issues a certificate of sale to the winning bidder. This certificate of sale effectively transfers ownership and possession rights to the successful bidder after the redemption period.

Redemption
In Minnesota a borrower usually has a six-month redemption period.

Mississippi

Type of Foreclosures Permitted
Both judicial and nonjudicial foreclosures are permitted.

Average Foreclosure Time
Approximately three months to complete the foreclosure.

Common Practice
Nonjudicial foreclosures are the most common.

Special Notes
A deed of trust usually includes the specific provision enabling the lender to sell a property if the borrower defaults.

Judicial Foreclosures
Seldom used in Mississippi.

Nonjudicial Foreclosures

The borrower receives a default notice at least thirty days prior to the foreclosure sale. If the default is not paid, the trustee starts the foreclosure sale process.

Sale Information

The trustee conducts the sale, usually between 11:00 A.M. and 4:00 P.M. at the county courthouse. The winning bidder must pay in the form of cash or certified funds at the sale.

Redemption

There is no redemption period.

Missouri

Type of Foreclosures Permitted

Both judicial and nonjudicial foreclosures are permitted.

Average Foreclosure Time

Approximately two months to complete the foreclosure.

Common Practice

Nonjudicial foreclosures are the most common.

Special Notes

After a borrower's default, the lender must follow the notice of default procedure in the mortgage or deed of trust.

Judicial Foreclosures

Court foreclosures are not common in Missouri.

Nonjudicial Foreclosures

Missouri requires that a notice of sale be published in local newspapers.

Sale Information

The deed of trust dictates who conducts the foreclosure sale and when the sale occurs. The sale is usually held at the county courthouse

Redemption

Borrowers have redemption rights only if the buyer at the sale was the lender.

Montana

Type of Foreclosures Permitted

Both judicial and nonjudicial foreclosures are permitted.

Average Foreclosure Time

Approximately five months to complete the foreclosure.

Common Practice

Montana foreclosures are conducted either with a judicial or nonjudicial action depending on the existence of a power-of-sale clause in the mortgage or deed of trust.

Special Notes

The sale must be at least 120 days after the notice of default is filed.

Judicial Foreclosures

The court determines the appropriate amount due to the lender and gives the borrower a certain amount of time to pay the debt. If the borrower does not pay, the lender issues a notice of foreclosure sale.

Nonjudicial Foreclosures

The lender starts the nonjudicial foreclosure process by filing a notice of sale with the county recorder.

Sale Information

For nonjudicial foreclosures, a copy of the notice of sale is posted at the property in an obvious spot at least twenty days before the sale. Foreclosure auctions are held between 9 A.M. and 4 P.M. on the sale date at the county courthouse. The winning bidder receives a deed transferring ownership and takes possession after ten days.

Redemption

There is no right of redemption.

Nebraska

Type of Foreclosures Permitted

Both judicial and nonjudicial foreclosures are permitted.

Average Foreclosure Time

Approximately four months to complete the foreclosure.

Common Practice

Nonjudicial foreclosures are the most common. After the lender files a notice of default and delivers it to the borrower, a thirty-day reinstatement period is created.

Special Notes

Judicial foreclosures are for mortgages, and nonjudicial foreclosures are for deeds of trust.

Judicial Foreclosures

Court-supervised foreclosures can take six months. Mortgages must be foreclosed with a judicial foreclosure.

Nonjudicial Foreclosures

After the thirty-day reinstatement period, a trustee sale is scheduled.

Sale Information

Either a court official, called the master commissioner, or the county sheriff conducts the sale. The sale must be advertised for four weeks. After the sale has been confirmed, a deed is issued that transfers ownership to the winning bidder.

Redemption

Redemption is available for a two- to three-week period following the sale but before a hearing to confirm the sale. After the hearing there is no further redemption available.

Nevada

Type of Foreclosures Permitted

Both judicial and nonjudicial foreclosures are permitted.

Average Foreclosure Time

Approximately four months to complete the foreclosure.

Common Practice

Nonjudicial foreclosures are the most common. Nevada has statutorily required language that must be included in all deeds of trust.

Special Notes

Most mortgages permit lenders to sell a property when the owner defaults without having to file a lawsuit.

Judicial Foreclosures

Judicial foreclosures are rare. In Nevada there is a one-year redemption period when the judicial foreclosure is used.

APPENDIX A: STATE FORECLOSURE SUMMARY

Nonjudicial Foreclosures

A lender commences the foreclosure process by recording a notice of default with the county recorder and mailing the notice to the borrower.

Sale Information

Three months after recording the notice of default, the lender may schedule a public foreclosure sale if the borrower has not paid off the default amount.

A trustee (a third party named in the deed of trust) conducts the public sale. Following the sale, the trustee transfers ownership to the winning bidder.

Redemption

There is no redemption period for the borrower after a nonjudicial foreclosure sale.

New Hampshire

Type of Foreclosures Permitted

Both judicial and nonjudicial foreclosures are permitted.

Average Foreclosure Time

Approximately three months to complete the foreclosure.

Common Practice

Nonjudicial foreclosures are the most common. A mortgage provision gives the lender the right to sell a property once a borrower defaults. New Hampshire mortgages provide a thirty-day grace period for the borrower to cure any default.

Special Notes

If a borrower does not pay off the default during the pre-foreclosure period, the lender may commence the foreclosure process and schedule a foreclosure sale.

Judicial Foreclosures

Judicial foreclosures are seldom used.

Nonjudicial Foreclosures

The sale usually occurs at the property and is conducted by the lender's attorney or an auctioneer.

Sale Information

The notice of sale is published for three weeks in a local newspaper, with the first publication appearing at least twenty-one days prior to the sale date. Within sixty days of the public foreclosure sale the winning bidder must pay the balance of the full bid amount. The lender files the necessary recorded documents to transfer ownership to the winning bidder.

Redemption

There is no redemption period.

New Jersey

Type of Foreclosures Permitted

Only judicial foreclosures are permitted.

Average Foreclosure Time

Approximately nine months to complete the foreclosure.

Common Practice

At least thirty days prior to starting the foreclosure process, the lender notifies the borrower and issues a warning of the impending foreclosure.

Special Notes

The notice of sale must be posted on the property as well as in the county office where the property is located.

Judicial Foreclosures

A foreclosure complaint and lis pendens are filed in the court and delivered to the borrower. If the borrower does not respond within thirty-five days, the court can rule the borrower is in default and direct the property to be sold.

Nonjudicial Foreclosures

Nonjudicial foreclosures are not permitted.

Sale Information

Notice must be delivered to the property owner at least ten days prior to the scheduled public sale. Foreclosure sales are conducted as public auctions by the sheriff. The sheriff transfers ownership to the purchaser within ten days following the sale. The court also reviews and confirms the sale.

Redemption

The borrower retains redemption rights for ten days following the public sale, when objections to the sale are considered by the court.

New Mexico

Type of Foreclosures Permitted

Only judicial foreclosures are permitted.

Average Foreclosure Time

Approximately six months to complete the foreclosure.

Common Practice

Mortgages and deeds of trust for residential property are foreclosed and sold by the court due to the ban of power-of-sale clauses.

Special Notes

The lender is not required by state law to notify the owner before initiating the pre-foreclosure process. However, some mortgages or deeds of trust may include this requirement.

Judicial Foreclosures

A foreclosure complaint and lis pendens are filed in the court and delivered to the borrower. If the borrower does not respond within thirty days, the court can rule the borrower is in default and direct the property to be sold.

Nonjudicial Foreclosures

Nonjudicial foreclosures are not permitted.

Sale Information

The lender or the lender's trustee publishes a notice of the public sale for four weeks in a local newspaper. The sale is scheduled a minimum of thirty days after the court ruling of default by the borrower. The final publication of the public sale notice must occur at least three days prior to the date of the sale. In New Mexico an acceptable bid must be at least 80 percent of the fair market value of the property at the time of the judicial sale. After the property is sold a deed is recorded granting the ownership of the property to the winning bidder.

Redemption

After the sale is approved by the court the original borrower has one month to redeem. In some instances the redemption period can be as long as nine months. Borrowers may redeem their property by filing a notice to redeem and paying the sale price plus taxes and interest.

New York

Type of Foreclosures Permitted
Both judicial and nonjudicial foreclosures are permitted.

Average Foreclosure Time
Approximately fifteen months to complete the foreclosure. New York has one of the longest foreclosure time periods of all the states.

Common Practice
Nonjudicial foreclosures are uncommon. Although permitted, they are seldom used by lenders.

Special Notes
Notification of a pending foreclosure notice is not required to be sent to the defaulted borrower.

Judicial Foreclosures
A foreclosure complaint and lis pendens are filed in the court and delivered to the borrower. If the borrower does not respond within thirty days, the court can rule the borrower is in default and direct the property to be sold.

If the borrower appears in court, the court considers the case before ruling whether the property can be foreclosed. After the hearing, if the court rules against the borrower a foreclosure sale is scheduled. The foreclosure process leading up to the actual court ruling takes seven to nine months.

Nonjudicial Foreclosures
Nonjudicial foreclosures, though permitted, are seldom used.

Sale Information
Public foreclosure sales are usually scheduled at least four months after the court ruling. The notice of sale must be published in a general circulation newspaper at least four weeks prior to the sale. The winning bidder typically pays 10 percent of the final bid immediately following the sale and the remaining balance within thirty days. When the full amount is paid, the winning bidder assumes ownership of the property.

Redemption
There is no right of redemption in New York.

North Carolina

Type of Foreclosures Permitted
Both judicial and nonjudicial foreclosures are permitted.

Average Foreclosure Time
Approximately three months to complete the foreclosure.

Common Practice
Nonjudicial foreclosures are the most common.

Special Notes
A preliminary hearing is conducted before a power-of-sale foreclosure occurs. The lender must notify the borrower, either by mail or in person, as to how much is owed at least ten days before the notice of hearing. After the notice was issued, the county clerk conducts the hearing to determine whether a foreclosure sale will take place.

Judicial Foreclosures
Judicial foreclosures are used when there are title problems.

Nonjudicial Foreclosures
A preliminary hearing is conducted before a power-of-sale foreclosure can take place.

Sale Information
The lender mails the notice of sale to the borrower twenty days prior to the sale date. The lender also publishes the notice in a local newspaper for two weeks. The sale is held between 10:00 A.M. and 4:00 P.M. at the county courthouse.

Redemption
The borrower has a ten-day right of redemption after the sale.

North Dakota

Type of Foreclosures Permitted
Only judicial foreclosures are permitted.

Average Foreclosure Time
Approximately five months to complete the foreclosure.

Common Practice
North Dakota law requires lenders to give the borrower thirty days notice of their intent to foreclose prior to beginning any foreclosure proceedings.

Special Notes
After the pre-foreclosure notice is delivered to the defaulting borrower, the lender may file an action with the court to begin the foreclosure.

Judicial Foreclosures
The court assesses the lender's claim, the amount of the borrower's debt, and gives the borrower a short time to pay what is owed. If the borrower fails to pay the debt within the court's specified

timeframe, the property is offered for sale as advertised by the court clerk.

Nonjudicial Foreclosures
Nonjudicial foreclosures are not used.

Sale Information
Foreclosure sales are by public auction held by the county sheriff or his deputy. The property is sold to the highest bidder. The winning bidder must pay in cash at the auction. The winning bidder is given a certificate of sale until the borrower's redemption period has ended. Following the redemption period, the sheriff transfers ownership to the winning bidder.

Redemption
There is a six month redemption period.

Ohio

Type of Foreclosures Permitted
Only judicial foreclosures are permitted.

Average Foreclosure Time
Approximately seven months to complete the foreclosure.

Common Practice
A foreclosure complaint is filed in the court and delivered to the borrower. If the borrower does not respond within twenty-eight days, the court can rule the borrower is in default and direct the property to be sold.

Special Notes
After the court makes its decision about the foreclosure action, the county clerk issues an order of sale to the sheriff. The sale price of the prop-

erty must be at least two-thirds of the appraised value.

Judicial Foreclosures
The court allows borrowers to pay their debt within a certain time. If the borrower fails to pay the amount owed, the foreclosure process continues.

Nonjudicial Foreclosures
Nonjudicial foreclosures are not used.

Sale Information
Prior to the foreclosure sale, the sheriff must obtain three appraisals and publish an ad in a local newspaper for three weeks. The sheriff conducts a public auction at the courthouse. The court reviews the sale and files an order confirming the sheriff's sale. The sheriff issues a deed transferring ownership to the winning bidder.

Redemption
There is no redemption after the public sale of the property.

Oklahoma

Type of Foreclosures Permitted
Both judicial and nonjudicial foreclosures are permitted.

Average Foreclosure Time
Approximately six months to complete the foreclosure.

Common Practice
Nonjudicial foreclosures are rare in Oklahoma. Judicial foreclosures are the most common.

Special Notes
The notice of sale is recorded in the county where the property is located. Notice is also published in a local newspaper for four consecutive weeks. The first publishing date must be at least thirty days prior to the date of the public sale.

Judicial Foreclosures
A foreclosure complaint is filed in the court and delivered to the borrower. If the borrower does not respond within twenty days, the court can rule the borrower is in default and direct the property to be sold. After the public sale, the court approves the sale in fifteen days.

Nonjudicial Foreclosures
The lender may proceed with a nonjudicial foreclosure as long as the mortgage or deed of trust grants it the authority to do so. There are many restrictions, so judicial foreclosures are typically used.

Sale Information
The property is sold at a public auction overseen by the county sheriff with an opening bid no less than two-thirds of the property's appraised value. The highest bidder must provide cash or certified funds equal to 10 percent of the bid amount.

Redemption
There are no redemption rights.

Oregon

Type of Foreclosures Permitted
Both judicial and nonjudicial foreclosures are permitted.

Average Foreclosure Time
Approximately five months to complete the foreclosure.

Common Practice
Nonjudicial foreclosures are the most common. The usual practice is for the lender to include a power-of-sale clause in the mortgage. This provision allows the lender to sell the property without court approval.

The lender records a notice of default with the county recorder at least four months before the property is scheduled for sale. The property owner is provided with a copy of the notice of default.

Special Notes
The borrower may stop the foreclosure up to five days before the sale by paying all past due amounts owed plus costs.

Judicial Foreclosures
When the lender records a notice of default, if no power-of-sale is included in the mortgage, the court directs the foreclosure proceedings.

Nonjudicial Foreclosures
For out-of-court foreclosures, the notice of sale is published four weeks before the sale in a local newspaper. The last notice is published at least twenty days before the sale date.

Sale Information
The public auction is between the hours of 9 A.M. and 4 P.M. at the location stated on the notice. The property is sold to the highest bidder, who must pay in full in cash at the time of the auction. The trustee transfers ownership of the property to the winning bidder within ten days of the sale. The purchaser is then entitled to possession of the property.

Redemption
There are no redemption rights.

Pennsylvania

Type of Foreclosures Permitted
Only judicial foreclosures are permitted.

Average Foreclosure Time
Approximately ten months to complete the foreclosure.

Common Practice
Before the foreclosure process can begin within Pennsylvania, the borrower must be at least sixty days late on payments.

The lender usually sends the borrower two letters before commencing a foreclosure action. These letters notify the borrower of the impending foreclosure and give the borrower options to prevent the foreclosure. The property owner has a period of sixty days to prevent the foreclosure before the lender takes further action on the foreclosure.

Special Notes
The borrower may prevent the public sale at any time up to one hour before the sale by paying the full amount owed.

Judicial Foreclosures
A foreclosure complaint is filed in the court and delivered to the borrower. If the borrower does not respond within twenty days, the court can rule the borrower is in default and direct the property to be sold.

Nonjudicial Foreclosures
Nonjudicial foreclosures are not allowed.

Sale Information
The sale is a public auction conducted by the county sheriff and takes place one to two months following the court's order. At least thirty days prior to the scheduled sale, the county sheriff serves a notice of the sale by putting a handbill on the property as well as delivering a copy of the notice to the borrower. The sale is advertised for three consecutive weeks in both a local general-interest newspaper and a local legal newspaper.

Redemption
There are no redemption rights.

Rhode Island

Type of Foreclosures Permitted
Both judicial and nonjudicial foreclosures are permitted.

Average Foreclosure Time
Approximately two months to complete the foreclosure.

Common Practice
Nonjudicial foreclosures are the most common. In Rhode Island nonjudicial foreclosures occur easily and efficiently.

Special Notes
Before scheduling the public foreclosure sale, the lender's attorney must give the borrower a notice at least twenty days before starting to advertise for the sale.

Judicial Foreclosures
Judicial foreclosures are used only if there are title problems or some other significant issue.

Nonjudicial Foreclosures
For nonjudicial foreclosures, the process commences when the lender forwards all pertinent documentation to the attorney and a title search of the property is performed.

Sale Information
The notice of the foreclosure sale must be published for three weeks in a local newspaper, and the first notice must appear at least twenty-one days prior to the sale date. An auctioneer conducts the sale. The successful bidder receives a certificate of sale and a deed is recorded transferring ownership.

Redemption
There is no redemption available in Rhode Island.

South Carolina

Type of Foreclosures Permitted
Only judicial foreclosures are permitted.

Average Foreclosure Time
Approximately six months to complete the foreclosure.

Special Notes
The foreclosing lender files a lis pendens, or pending lawsuit, to announce the intent to foreclose.

Judicial Foreclosures
A foreclosure complaint is filed in the court and delivered to the borrower. If the borrower does not respond within thirty days or does not resolve

the default, the case is referred to a hearing officer. The officer orders the property to be sold if the borrower is found in default.

Nonjudicial Foreclosures
Nonjudicial foreclosures are not available.

Sale Information
The public sale is advertised in the local newspaper for three weeks. A court officer or special referee holds the sale, which typically takes place at 11:00 A.M. on a Monday. The winning bidder must provide 5 percent of the winning bid at the sale and usually has thirty days to pay the remaining bid balance.

Redemption
In South Carolina, if the lender waives the right to file a deficiency judgment, the borrower has no right of redemption. If the lender reserves the right to a deficiency judgment, the sale continues for thirty days after the bidding ends. During this period anyone may place an upset bid. After any post-sale bidding period is over and the winning bidder pays the remaining bid balance, the sale official transfers ownership. The court confirms the sale.

South Dakota

Type of Foreclosures Permitted
Judicial foreclosures are permitted.

Average Foreclosure Time
Approximately four months to complete the foreclosure.

Common Practice
Judicial foreclosures are the most common. Certain mortgages may be foreclosed via advertisement, but that is uncommon.

Special Notes
South Dakota has no requirement that lenders must mail a default notice to the borrower before initiating a foreclosure.

Judicial Foreclosures
A foreclosure complaint is filed in the court and delivered to the borrower. If the borrower does not respond within thirty days, the court can rule the borrower is in default and direct the property to be sold.

Nonjudicial Foreclosures
Nonjudicial foreclosures, except foreclosures by advertisement, are not used in South Dakota.

Sale Information
Following the court ruling that the foreclosure may continue, the lender publishes a notice of foreclosure sale in a local newspaper. At least twenty-one days before the sale, the lender must deliver a written copy of sale notice to the borrower.
The county sheriff conducts the public sale. The winning bidder is provided with a sale certificate and receives a deed transferring ownership after the redemption period expires.

Redemption
The redemption period is six months. However, if the property is vacant the redemption period is two months.

Tennessee

Type of Foreclosures Permitted
Both judicial and nonjudicial foreclosures are permitted.

Average Foreclosure Time
Approximately two months to complete the foreclosure.

Common Practice
Nonjudicial foreclosures are the most common.

Special Notes
When the borrower defaults on the required monthly payment, the trustee assigned in the deed of trust has the full authority to begin the foreclosure process and advertise the property for sale.

Judicial Foreclosures
Judicial foreclosures are very rare.

Nonjudicial Foreclosures
Nonjudicial foreclosures are customary. A clause is included in a mortgage or deed of trust that authorizes the lender to sell the property if the borrower defaults.

Sale Information
The public sale notice is published three times in a newspaper, with the first publication appearing twenty days prior to the foreclosure sale. After the sale the trustee transfers the ownership to the winning bidder.

Redemption
Deeds of trust in Tennessee do not permit the borrower to redeem the property after the sale. However, if this right is not waived within the deed of trust, the borrower may redeem the property by paying the total debt plus costs within two years of the sale.

Texas

Type of Foreclosures Permitted
Both judicial and nonjudicial foreclosures are permitted.

Average Foreclosure Time
Approximately three months to complete the foreclosure. Texas laws allows for fast, smooth foreclosures.

Common Practice
Nonjudicial foreclosures are the most common.

Special Notes
The lender files a lawsuit against the borrower to obtain a court order authorizing the lender to foreclose on the property. Once the court approves the foreclosure, the property is scheduled for public sale.

Judicial Foreclosures
If there is no power-of-sale clause included in the mortgage or deed of trust, the foreclosure is handled by the court.

Nonjudicial Foreclosures
Nonjudicial foreclosures are customary. A clause is included in a mortgage or deed of trust that authorizes the lender to sell the property if the borrower defaults. Before commencing the foreclosure process, the lender mails a default notice letter to the borrower. The lender must allow the

borrower at least twenty days to pay the default amount on the loan. If the borrower does not pay, the lender may commence the foreclosure process by mailing a second letter to the borrower, which states that the loan has been accelerated and a sale has been scheduled to recover the full amount due.

Sale Information

The lender must post a notice of sale at the door of the county courthouse and file a foreclosure notice with the country clerk twenty-one days prior to the foreclosure sale. Texas laws do not require the publication of a notice of the sale in local newspapers.

All foreclosure sales are between 10 A.M. and 4 P.M. on the first Tuesday of the month (including holidays) on the county courthouse steps. The public auction is conducted with the property awarded to the highest bidder, who pays in cash. The trustee may allow some time (but only within the same day) for the highest bidder to pay the full amount.

Redemption

There is no right of redemption in Texas.

Utah

Type of Foreclosures Permitted

Both judicial and nonjudicial foreclosures are permitted.

Average Foreclosure Time

Approximately five months to complete the foreclosure.

Common Practice

Nonjudicial foreclosures are the most common.

Special Notes

After the notice of default is recorded in the county courthouse, the borrower has three months before the property is sold at public auction.

Judicial Foreclosures

The lender files a lawsuit against the borrower to obtain a court order authorizing the lender to foreclose on the property. The court determines if the borrower is in default and if so by how much. The court gives the borrower a specific amount of time to pay what is owed. If the borrower fails to pay, the court will approve a foreclosure. Once the court approves the foreclosure, the property is scheduled for public sale.

Nonjudicial Foreclosures

Most foreclosures in Utah are commenced with a nonjudicial foreclosure. The lender commences the nonjudicial foreclosure process by recording a notice of default with the county recorder. A copy of the notice of default is delivered to the borrower.

Sale Information

Three months after the notice of default is recorded and at least twenty days before the sale date, the notice of sale is posted on the property and at the office of the county recorder. In addition, the lender publishes a notice of sale for three consecutive weeks in a local newspaper. The last advertisement must be at least ten days but not more than thirty days before the date of the public auction. The public auction is held at the county courthouse.

Redemption

There is no redemption period.

Vermont

Type of Foreclosures Permitted
Both judicial and nonjudicial foreclosures are permitted.

Average Foreclosure Time
Approximately nine months to complete the foreclosure.

Common Practice
Nonjudicial foreclosures are the most common.

Special Notes
Vermont law authorizes strict foreclosure, which is conducted by the court. After default, a lender files the court documents to start the foreclosure. The borrower receives a summons to appear in court. If the court rules against the borrower, the lender is authorized to take possession of the property or schedule a public sale of the property.

Judicial Foreclosures
Judicial foreclosures are permitted and used. If the lender proceeds through the court, the judge may rule the property in foreclosure and allow for a public sale of the property.

Nonjudicial Foreclosures
The more common type of foreclosure in Vermont is authorized when the mortgage permits the lender to sell the property if the borrower defaults. When the foreclosure is handled with a nonjudicial action, the lender mails a notice of the foreclosure to the borrower. The notice must be sent to the borrower at minimum of thirty days before a notice of sale is published. In a nonjudicial foreclosure, the lender records the notice of sale with town records at least sixty days before the public sale.

Sale Information
The public sale notice is published for three weeks in a local newspaper, with the first notice appearing no less than twenty-one days before the sale date. Within ninety days after a nonjudicial foreclosure sale, the property ownership is transferred free and clear to the winning bidder. Within ten days after a court foreclosure sale, the court reviews the sale and then either confirms the sale or orders a resale. If the court confirms the sale, the property ownership is transferred to the winning bidder by court order.

Redemption
For judicial foreclosures, the borrower has six months from the court ruling to redeem the property.

Virginia

Type of Foreclosures Permitted
Both judicial and nonjudicial foreclosures are permitted.

Average Foreclosure Time
Approximately two months to complete the foreclosure.

Common Practice
Nonjudicial foreclosures are the most common.

Special Notes
The public sale is not permitted to be postponed, but it may be canceled.

Judicial Foreclosures
Rarely used in Virginia, judicial foreclosures can be used to correct title issues. A foreclosure complaint is filed, and a court-ordered foreclosure

and sale is authorized after the court finds the borrower in default.

Nonjudicial Foreclosures

The most common foreclosure process used in Virginia is the nonjudicial foreclosure. The mortgage or deed of trust allows the lender to sell the property without going through the courts. The lender initiates the foreclosure by scheduling a foreclosure sale. The lender first sends a notice of default to the borrower, giving them thirty days to pay off the default to prevent the foreclosure sale.

Sale Information

After scheduling the foreclosure sale, the lender must advertise the sale. In Virginia the notice of sale publication dates vary and are based on the requirements of the deed of trust or state statute. Borrowers must receive notice at least fourteen days before the foreclosure sale.

The trustee typically conducts the public auction at the county courthouse. The trustee announces the opening bid, with the property selling to the highest bidder.

Redemption

There is no redemption period in Virginia.

Washington

Type of Foreclosures Permitted

Both judicial and nonjudicial foreclosures are permitted.

Average Foreclosure Time

Approximately five months to complete the foreclosure.

Common Practice

Nonjudicial foreclosures are the most common.

Special Notes

Until eleven days before the sale, the defaulting borrower can stop the foreclosure by paying the past-due payments plus all expenses.

Judicial Foreclosures

A foreclosure complaint is filed by the lender, and the borrower has thirty days to respond to the complaint. The court ordered foreclosure and sale is authorized after the court finds the borrower in default. The sale is usually scheduled about eight weeks following the court ruling.

Nonjudicial Foreclosures

The lender mails a notice of default to the borrower. The lender must also either post the notice at the property or personally deliver the notice to the borrower. The borrower then has thirty days to respond and correct the default before the property is scheduled for public auction.

Sale Information

If the borrower does not correct the default within thirty days after receiving the notice of default, the lender next records a notice of sale with the county recorder. The notice is recorded at least ninety days before the sale date and is mailed to the borrower. The notice of sale is also required to be published twice in a local newspaper. At the sale, the winning bidder must pay cash for the property.

Redemption

The borrower has no right of redemption following the nonjudicial foreclosure sale. The borrower has redemption rights for one year from the date of a judicial sale. During this redemption period the borrower may remain in the property if it is his primary residence.

West Virginia

Type of Foreclosures Permitted
Both judicial and nonjudicial foreclosures are permitted.

Average Foreclosure Time
Approximately four months to complete the foreclosure.

Common Practice
Nonjudicial foreclosures are the most common. Before initiating the foreclosure process, the lender notifies the borrower via a letter of the impending foreclosure.

Special Notes
Per West Virginia law, the lender may not accelerate the loan or take action to possess the property until ten days following the notification letter to the borrower. However, if a borrower has been notified of the default three or more times he can't stop the foreclosure by paying off the default.

Judicial Foreclosures
A foreclosure complaint is filed by the lender, and the borrower has thirty days to respond to the complaint. The court-ordered foreclosure and sale is authorized after the court finds the borrower in default.

Nonjudicial Foreclosures
The minimum requirement for a nonjudicial foreclosure is that there is a publication of the sale notice for two weeks. If the deed of trust contains different requirements, then those requirements must be followed.

Sale Information
A minimum of twenty days before the scheduled auction, a copy of the notice of sale must be mailed to the borrower. A trustee's deed transferring ownership to the successful bidder is usually recorded within thirty days.

Redemption
There is no redemption period.

Wisconsin

Type of Foreclosures Permitted
Only judicial foreclosures are permitted.

Average Foreclosure Time
Approximately twelve months to complete the foreclosure.

Common Practice
Based on precedent and not law, the lender customarily warns the defaulting borrower that it intends to foreclose before making the filing with the court.

Special Notes
After the court has issued a judgment of foreclosure, the borrower is granted a reinstatement period to stop the pending foreclosure by paying the amount owed. The reinstatement period varies: abandoned properties have a two-month redemption period, while other properties have six to twelve months.

Judicial Foreclosures
A foreclosure complaint is filed in the court and delivered to the borrower. If the borrower does not respond within twenty days, the court can rule the borrower is in default and direct the property to be sold.

Nonjudicial Foreclosures
Nonjudicial foreclosures are not used.

Sale Information
The local sheriff provides notice of the time and place of sale. The notice of sale is published ten months after the court ruling. The foreclosure sale does not occur until after the owner's reinstatement period is completed.

The county sheriff conducts the public auction. Within ten days following the sale, the sheriff files a report and deposits the proceeds with the clerk of the court. The clerk pays the lender and delivers the deed transferring ownership to the winning bidder, who must pay the balance of the sale price. Should the buyer fail to pay the balance of the sale price within ten days after the confirmation of sale, the deposit is forfeited and another sale is conducted. Should the court not confirm the sale, the clerk refunds the buyer's deposit and another sale is ordered.

Redemption
There is no redemption period.

Wyoming

Type of Foreclosures Permitted
Both judicial and nonjudicial foreclosures are permitted.

Average Foreclosure Time
Approximately two months to complete the foreclosure.

Common Practice
Nonjudicial foreclosures are the most common.

Special Notes
The notice of sale must be published in a local newspaper for four consecutive weeks.

Judicial Foreclosures
In Wyoming most mortgages include a power-of-sale clause. If it is not included in the mortgage, foreclosure is conducted through the courts. After the court declares a foreclosure, the property is offered for sale.

Nonjudicial Foreclosures
If a power-of-sale clause is included in the mortgage, the lender has the right to sell the mortgaged property without initiating court action to pay off the balance of the loan in the event of default. All public sales are at the front door of the courthouse in the county where the property is located.

Sale Information
Written notice of the intent to foreclose on a property must be delivered to the borrower at least ten days prior to the first publication of the notice of sale. The sale is conducted by the person appointed by the county sheriff. The winning bidder receives a certificate of purchase.

Redemption
A redemption period of three months after the foreclosure sale is available in Wyoming.

Sample Purchase Offer Letter for an REO Property

December 21, 2009
Susan Myers, Director
Quarryville National Bank
967 Main Street
Quarryville, PA 17566

Dear Ms. Myers:
I am submitting the following purchase offer for your review and acceptance:

Property:	12225 South North Drive Lancaster, PA 17607
Offer:	$123,875
Considerations:	Purchased as is
Subject To:	Financing of 95 percent provided by Quarryville National Bank; rate of interest 7 percent, 360-month term
Closing Date:	December 31, 2009
Other Terms:	Clear title provided by QNB; all closing/transfer costs paid by Quarryville National Bank

I have carefully inspected the property, and I am ready to close on the property before the end of this month. Please respond to this purchase offer within the next 48 hours.

Thank you for your consideration,

Sincerely,

George Sheldon

Sample Assignment Letter for Purchase Agreement

December 21, 2009
Ralph T. Smith
123 Main Street
Quarryville, PA 17566

Dear Mr. Jones:

As we discussed on the telephone today, I am presenting this assignment agreement. After reviewing, please sign and return a copy to me.

This agreement is made this 21st day of December, 2009, between George Sheldon, known hereinafter as the Assignor, and Ralph T. Smith, known hereinafter as the Assignee. Assignor and Assignee hereby agree as follows:

1. In return for the consideration set forth in this agreement, Assignor hereby assigns, sells, and transfers all of Assignor's title and interest in and rights under the attached real estate purchase agreement entitled, "Purchase Agreement" dated December 19, 2009, hereinafter referred to as the "Purchase Agreement," executed by Susan T. Thomas as Seller and by George Sheldon as Buyer, for the purchase of said property known as 987 North South Street, Lancaster, Pennsylvania, and legally described as: Lot 48, Plot 12, in Deed Book 121 in the Lancaster County, PA, Recorder of Deed's Office.

2. A complete and accurate copy of the Purchase Agreement is attached hereto as Exhibit "A" and incorporated as if fully set forth herein. By accepting this assignment, Assignee agrees to perform the obligations imposed on Assignor, as the buyer, under the Purchase Agreement. Assignee accepts this assignment subject to all terms and conditions contained in the Agreement, and/or those imposed by Pennsylvania law.

3. In return for the rights assigned by Assignor to the Assignee, the Assignee agrees to pay the Assignor the sum of $5,000 (five thousand) dollars at closing on or before December 31, 2009.

All of the provisions of this assignment of purchase agreement shall extend to, and bind to the benefit of the heirs, executors, personal representatives, successors, and the assigns of both the Assignor and the Assignee.

IN WITNESS WHEREOF, the Assignor and Assignee have agreed to the terms set forth by signing this Assignment Agreement.

_____

Accepted and Agreed:

_____

Ralph T. Smith

Additional Resources

Management and Marketing Contractors

Arizona and Nevada

Michaelson, Connor, & Boul
6908 East Thomas Road, Suites 200 & 201
Scottsdale, AZ 85251
Phone: (480) 941-8737; toll free: (866) 941-8737
Fax: (480) 941-9855
E-mail: george.howell@mcbreo.com
✐ *www.mcbreo.com*

Arkansas and Louisiana

Cityside Management Corporation
301 Market Street Suite B
Hammond, LA 70401
Phone: (985) 419-0311
Fax: (985) 419-0310
E-mail: lhotard@citysidecorp.com
✐ *www.citysidecorp.com*

California, Hawaii, and Guam

PEMCO, Ltd.
1600 Sacramento Inn Way, Suite 210
Sacramento, CA 95815
Phone: (916) 927-7313
Fax: (916) 927-7454
E-mail: kimi@pemco-norcal.com
✐ *www.hudpemco.com*

Caribbean (Puerto Rico and U.S. Virgin Islands)

Atlantic Alliance of Asset Managers
Iturregui Plaza, Suite 14A
1135 65th Infantry Avenue
Rio Piedras, PR 00924
Phone: (787) 300-2194
Fax: (787) 300-2199
E-mail: idelacruz@atlanticallianceasset
managers.com
✐ *www.atlanticallianceassetmanagers.com*

Colorado, Montana, Utah, and Wyoming
Michaelson, Connor, & Boul
4500 Cherry Creek Drive, South, Suite 1070
Glendale, CO 80246
Phone: (303) 758-6736; Toll Free: (866) 889-6736
Fax: (303) 758-6748
E-mail: david.huckemeyer@mcbreo.com
✑ www.mcbreo.com

Florida
National Home Management Solutions, LLC
2100 Coral Way, Suite 504
Miami, FL 33145
Phone: (305) 854-1711
Fax: (305) 854-1217
✑ www.nhmsi.com

Georgia
PEMCO, LTD (for new acquisitions as of September 30, 2006)
Piedmont Center
3525 Piedmont Road, N.E.
Bldg. 5, Suite 310
Atlanta, Georgia 30305
Phone: (404) 995-7111; toll free: (800) 881-9260
Fax: (404) 995-7110
✑ www.hudpemco.com

Illinois and Indiana
Harrington, Moran, Barksdale, Inc.
8600 W. Bryn Mawr Avenue, Suite 600 South
Chicago, IL 60631
Phone: (773) 714-9200; toll free: (866) 702-6600
Fax: (773) 714-1669
E-mail: chicago@hmbireo.com
✑ www.hmbireo.com

Kansas, Missouri, and Oklahoma
Pyramid Real Estate Services D3, LLC
4500 S. Garnett, Suite 250
Tulsa, OK 74146
Phone: (918) 660-0800
Fax:(918) 359-7601
E-mail: MortgageeDC@pyramidrealestate.com
✑ www.pyramidrealestate.com

Kentucky and Tennessee
Pyramid Real Estate Services
616 Marriott Drive, Suite 300
Nashville, TN 37214
Phone: (615) 885-2002; toll free (877) 451-4680
Fax: (615) 620-3075
E-mail: MortgageeAE@pyramidrealestate.com
✑ www.pyramidrealestate.com

Maryland and the District of Columbia
HomeSource Real Estate Asset Services, Inc.
8403 Colesville Road, Suite 1250
Silver Spring, MD 20910
Phone: (301) 960-2700
Fax: (301) 563-6236
E-mail: info@hudhomesource.com
✑ www.hudhomesource.com

Michigan and Ohio
Michaelson, Connor, & Boul
5312 Bolsa Avenue, Suite 200
Huntington Beach, CA 92649
Phone: (714) 230-3600
Fax: (714) 230-3699
E-mail: Joan@mcbreo.com
✑ www.mcbreo.com

Mississippi and Alabama
Hooks, Van Holm, Inc.
The Noble Building
1021 Noble Street, Suite 212-221
Anniston, AL 36201
Phone: (256) 241-1415; toll free: (866) 851-5476
Fax: (256) 247-1425; toll free: (866) 851-5479
E-mail: PandP@hooksvanholm.com or
extensions@hooksvanholm.com
www.hooksvanholm.com

New Jersey and New York
National Home Management Solutions of New York, LLC.
Three Advantage Court
Bordentown, NJ 08505
Phone: (609) 981-5500; toll free: (800) 211-0621
Fax: (609) 981-5513
www.nhmsi.com

North Carolina and South Carolina
Harrington, Moran, Barksdale, Inc.
5350 77 Center Drive, Suite 200
Charlotte, NC 28217
Phone: (704) 522-3590; toll free: (866) 316-4624
Fax: (704) 565-6852
E-mail: Charlotte@hmbireo.com
www.hmbireo.com

North Dakota, South Dakota, Nebraska, Minnesota, Wisconsin, and Iowa
Best Assets, Inc.
501 Marquette Avenue, Suite 1200
Minneapolis, MN 55402
Phone: (612) 333-7450
Fax: (612) 333-6474

E-mail: bmasters@best-assets.com
www.best-assets.com

Pennsylvania and Delaware
Hooks, Van Holm, Inc.
1005 West 9th Avenue, Suite A
King of Prussia, PA 19406
Phone: (866) 851-5482 or (610) 491-2420
Fax: (610) 491-2479
E-mail: info@hooksvanholm.com
www.HooksVanHolm.com

Texas (north) and New Mexico
Southwest Alliance of Asset Managers
5040 Addison Circle, Suite 300
Addison, TX 75001
Phone: (972) 788-0026 or (800) 394-1103
Fax: (972) 715-1548
E-mail: jmcduffee@southwestalliance.com
www.southwestalliance.com

Texas (south)
Southwest Alliance of Asset Managers
7718 Wood Hollow Drive, Suite 100
Austin, TX 78731
Phone: (512) 231-2600 or (800) 457-4961
Fax: (512) 231-2699
E-mail: rhutchison@southwestalliance.com
www.southwestalliance.com

Vermont, New Hampshire, Maine, Rhode Island, Massachusetts, and Connecticut
Cityside Management Corporation
22 Greeley Street, Suite #5
Merrimack, NH 03054

Phone: (603) 423-0313; toll free: (877) 289-7433
Fax: (603) 429-1427
E-mail: bmarko@citysidecorp.com
    www.citysidecorp.com

Virginia and West Virginia
Harrington, Moran, Barksdale, Inc.
1600 Wilson Boulevard, Suite 600
Arlington, VA 22209
Phone: (703) 465-1704
Fax: (703) 465-1931
E-mail: arlington@hmbireo.com
    www.hmbireo.com

Alaska, Idaho, Oregon, and Washington
Harrington, Moran, Barksdale, Inc.
20829 72nd Ave. South
Suite 115
Kent, WA 98032
Phone: (425) 378-9500; toll free: (866) 317-4624
Fax: (425) 747-7465
E-mail: Bellevue@hmbireo.com
    www.hmbireo.com

Department of Veterans Affairs Regional Loan Centers

Atlanta
Georgia, North Carolina, South Carolina, Tennessee
Department of Veterans Affairs
Regional Loan Center
1700 Clairmont Rd.
PO Box 100023
Decatur, GA 30031-7023
    888-768-2132
    www.vba.va.gov/ro/atlanta/rlc/index.htm

Cleveland
Delaware, Indiana, Michigan, New Jersey, Ohio, Pennsylvania
Department of Veterans Affairs
Cleveland Regional Loan Center
1240 East Ninth Street
Cleveland, OH 44199
    800-729-5772
    www.vba.va.gov/ro/central/cleve/index1.htm

Denver
Alaska, Colorado, Idaho, Montana, New Mexico, Oregon, Utah, Washington, Wyoming
Department of Veterans Affairs
VA Regional Loan Center
Box 25126
Denver, CO 80225
    888-349-7541
    www.vba.va.gov/ro/denver/loan/lgy.htm

Honolulu
Hawaii, the Pacific Islands of American Samoa, Guam, Wake, and Midway, and the Commonwealth of the Northern Mariana Islands
Spark M. Matsunaga Bldg.
VA Medical and Regional Office Center
Loan Guaranty Office
459 Patterson Road
Honolulu, HI 96819-1522
    808-433-0480
E-mail: lgytsero@vba.va.gov

Houston
Arkansas, Louisiana, Oklahoma, Texas
Department of Veterans Affairs
VA Regional Loan Center
6900 Almeda Road
Houston, TX 77030
  888-232-2571
  www.vahouston.com

Manchester
Connecticut, Massachusetts, Maine, New Hampshire, New York, Rhode Island, Vermont
Department of Veterans Affairs
VA Regional Loan Center
275 Chestnut Street
Manchester, NH 03101
  800-827-6311
  www.vba.va.gov/ro/manchester/lgymain/loans.html

Phoenix
Arizona, California, Nevada
Department of Veterans Affairs
Phoenix Regional Loan Center
3333 N. Central Avenue
Phoenix, AZ 85012-2402
  888-869-0194
  www.vba.va.gov/ro/phoenixlgy/index.htm

Roanoke
District of Columbia, Kentucky, Maryland, Virginia, West Virginia
Department of Veterans Affairs
Roanoke Regional Loan Center
210 Franklin Road SW
Roanoke, VA 24011

  800-933-5499
  www.vba-roanoke.com/rlc

St. Paul
Illinois, Iowa, Kansas, Minnesota, Missouri, Nebraska, North Dakota, South Dakota, Wisconsin
Department of Veterans Affairs
VA Regional Loan Center
Fort Snelling
1 Federal Drive
St. Paul, MN 55111-4050
  800-827-0611
  www.vba.va.gov/ro/central/stpau/pages/homeloans.html

St. Petersburg
Alabama, Florida, Mississippi
Department of Veterans Affairs
VA Regional Loan Center
PO Box 1437
St. Petersburg, FL 33731-1437
  888-611-5916 (out of state); 800-827-1000 (in FL)
  www.vba.va.gov/ro/south/spete/rlc/cv.htm

San Juan
Puerto Rico, U.S. Virgin Islands
VA Regional Office
PO Box 364867
San Juan, PR 00936
  787-772-7312, 787-772-7314, or 787-772-7311

Index

The EVERYTHING Series!

BUSINESS & PERSONAL FINANCE

Everything® Accounting Book
Everything® Budgeting Book
Everything® Business Planning Book
Everything® Coaching and Mentoring Book, 2nd Ed.
Everything® Fundraising Book
Everything® Get Out of Debt Book
Everything® Grant Writing Book
Everything® Guide to Foreclosures
Everything® Guide to Personal Finance for Single Mothers
Everything® Home-Based Business Book, 2nd Ed.
Everything® Homebuying Book, 2nd Ed.
Everything® Homeselling Book, 2nd Ed.
Everything® Improve Your Credit Book
Everything® Investing Book, 2nd Ed.
Everything® Landlording Book
Everything® Leadership Book
Everything® Managing People Book, 2nd Ed.
Everything® Negotiating Book
Everything® Online Auctions Book
Everything® Online Business Book
Everything® Personal Finance Book
Everything® Personal Finance in Your 20s and 30s Book
Everything® Project Management Book
Everything® Real Estate Investing Book
Everything® Retirement Planning Book
Everything® Robert's Rules Book, $7.95
Everything® Selling Book
Everything® Start Your Own Business Book, 2nd Ed.
Everything® Wills & Estate Planning Book

COOKING

Everything® Barbecue Cookbook
Everything® Bartender's Book, 2nd Ed., $9.95
Everything® Calorie Counting Cookbook
Everything® Cheese Book
Everything® Chinese Cookbook
Everything® Classic Recipes Book
Everything® Cocktail Parties & Drinks Book
Everything® College Cookbook
Everything® Cooking for Baby and Toddler Book
Everything® Cooking for Two Cookbook
Everything® Diabetes Cookbook
Everything® Easy Gourmet Cookbook
Everything® Fondue Cookbook
Everything® Fondue Party Book
Everything® Gluten-Free Cookbook
Everything® Glycemic Index Cookbook
Everything® Grilling Cookbook
Everything® Healthy Meals in Minutes Cookbook
Everything® Holiday Cookbook

Everything® Indian Cookbook
Everything® Italian Cookbook
Everything® Low-Carb Cookbook
Everything® Low-Cholesterol Cookbook
Everything® Low-Fat High-Flavor Cookbook
Everything® Low-Salt Cookbook
Everything® Meals for a Month Cookbook
Everything® Mediterranean Cookbook
Everything® Mexican Cookbook
Everything® No Trans Fat Cookbook
Everything® One-Pot Cookbook
Everything® Pizza Cookbook
Everything® Quick and Easy 30-Minute,
    5-Ingredient Cookbook
Everything® Quick Meals Cookbook
Everything® Slow Cooker Cookbook
Everything® Slow Cooking for a Crowd Cookbook
Everything® Soup Cookbook
Everything® Stir-Fry Cookbook
Everything® Sugar-Free Cookbook
Everything® Tapas and Small Plates Cookbook
Everything® Tex-Mex Cookbook
Everything® Thai Cookbook
Everything® Vegetarian Cookbook
Everything® Wild Game Cookbook
Everything® Wine Book, 2nd Ed.

GAMES

Everything® 15-Minute Sudoku Book, $9.95
Everything® 30-Minute Sudoku Book, $9.95
Everything® Bible Crosswords Book, $9.95
Everything® Blackjack Strategy Book
Everything® Brain Strain Book, $9.95
Everything® Bridge Book
Everything® Card Games Book
Everything® Card Tricks Book, $9.95
Everything® Casino Gambling Book, 2nd Ed.
Everything® Chess Basics Book
Everything® Craps Strategy Book
Everything® Crossword and Puzzle Book
Everything® Crossword Challenge Book
Everything® Crosswords for the Beach Book, $9.95
Everything® Cryptic Crosswords Book, $9.95
Everything® Cryptograms Book, $9.95
Everything® Easy Crosswords Book
Everything® Easy Kakuro Book, $9.95
Everything® Easy Large-Print Crosswords Book
Everything® Games Book, 2nd Ed.
Everything® Giant Sudoku Book, $9.95
Everything® Kakuro Challenge Book, $9.95
Everything® Large-Print Crossword Challenge Book
Everything® Large-Print Crosswords Book
Everything® Lateral Thinking Puzzles Book, $9.95

Everything® Literary Crosswords Book, $9.95
Everything® Mazes Book
Everything® Memory Booster Puzzles Book, $9.95
Everything® Movie Crosswords Book, $9.95
Everything® Music Crosswords Book, $9.95
Everything® Online Poker Book, $12.95
Everything® Pencil Puzzles Book, $9.95
Everything® Poker Strategy Book
Everything® Pool & Billiards Book
Everything® Puzzles for Commuters Book, $9.95
Everything® Sports Crosswords Book, $9.95
Everything® Test Your IQ Book, $9.95
Everything® Texas Hold 'Em Book, $9.95
Everything® Travel Crosswords Book, $9.95
Everything® TV Crosswords Book, $9.95
Everything® Word Games Challenge Book
Everything® Word Scramble Book
Everything® Word Search Book

HEALTH

Everything® Alzheimer's Book
Everything® Diabetes Book
Everything® Health Guide to Adult Bipolar Disorder
Everything® Health Guide to Arthritis
Everything® Health Guide to Controlling Anxiety
Everything® Health Guide to Fibromyalgia
Everything® Health Guide to Menopause
Everything® Health Guide to OCD
Everything® Health Guide to PMS
Everything® Health Guide to Postpartum Care
Everything® Health Guide to Thyroid Disease
Everything® Hypnosis Book
Everything® Low Cholesterol Book
Everything® Nutrition Book
Everything® Reflexology Book
Everything® Stress Management Book

HISTORY

Everything® American Government Book
Everything® American History Book, 2nd Ed.
Everything® Civil War Book
Everything® Freemasons Book
Everything® Irish History & Heritage Book
Everything® Middle East Book
Everything® World War II Book, 2nd Ed.

HOBBIES

Everything® Candlemaking Book
Everything® Cartooning Book
Everything® Coin Collecting Book
Everything® Drawing Book

Everything® Family Tree Book, 2nd Ed.
Everything® Knitting Book
Everything® Knots Book
Everything® Photography Book
Everything® Quilting Book
Everything® Sewing Book
Everything® Soapmaking Book, 2nd Ed.
Everything® Woodworking Book

HOME IMPROVEMENT

Everything® Feng Shui Book
Everything® Feng Shui Decluttering Book, $9.95
Everything® Fix-It Book
Everything® Green Living Book
Everything® Home Decorating Book
Everything® Home Storage Solutions Book
Everything® Homebuilding Book
Everything® Organize Your Home Book, 2nd Ed.

KIDS' BOOKS

All titles are $7.95
Everything® Kids' Animal Puzzle & Activity Book
Everything® Kids' Baseball Book, 4th Ed.
Everything® Kids' Bible Trivia Book
Everything® Kids' Bugs Book
Everything® Kids' Cars and Trucks Puzzle and Activity Book
Everything® Kids' Christmas Puzzle & Activity Book
Everything® Kids' Cookbook
Everything® Kids' Crazy Puzzles Book
Everything® Kids' Dinosaurs Book
Everything® Kids' Environment Book
Everything® Kids' Fairies Puzzle and Activity Book
Everything® Kids' First Spanish Puzzle and Activity Book
Everything® Kids' Gross Cookbook
Everything® Kids' Gross Hidden Pictures Book
Everything® Kids' Gross Jokes Book
Everything® Kids' Gross Mazes Book
Everything® Kids' Gross Puzzle & Activity Book
Everything® Kids' Halloween Puzzle & Activity Book
Everything® Kids' Hidden Pictures Book
Everything® Kids' Horses Book
Everything® Kids' Joke Book
Everything® Kids' Knock Knock Book
Everything® Kids' Learning Spanish Book
Everything® Kids' Magical Science Experiments Book
Everything® Kids' Math Puzzles Book
Everything® Kids' Mazes Book
Everything® Kids' Money Book
Everything® Kids' Nature Book
Everything® Kids' Pirates Puzzle and Activity Book
Everything® Kids' Presidents Book
Everything® Kids' Princess Puzzle and Activity Book
Everything® Kids' Puzzle Book
Everything® Kids' Racecars Puzzle and Activity Book
Everything® Kids' Riddles & Brain Teasers Book
Everything® Kids' Science Experiments Book
Everything® Kids' Sharks Book

Everything® Kids' Soccer Book
Everything® Kids' Spies Puzzle and Activity Book
Everything® Kids' States Book
Everything® Kids' Travel Activity Book

KIDS' STORY BOOKS

Everything® Fairy Tales Book

LANGUAGE

Everything® Conversational Japanese Book with CD, $19.95
Everything® French Grammar Book
Everything® French Phrase Book, $9.95
Everything® French Verb Book, $9.95
Everything® German Practice Book with CD, $19.95
Everything® Inglés Book
Everything® Intermediate Spanish Book with CD, $19.95
Everything® Italian Practice Book with CD, $19.95
Everything® Learning Brazilian Portuguese Book with CD, $19.95
Everything® Learning French Book with CD, 2nd Ed., $19.95
Everything® Learning German Book
Everything® Learning Italian Book
Everything® Learning Latin Book
Everything® Learning Russian Book with CD, $19.95
Everything® Learning Spanish Book with CD, 2nd Ed., $19.95
Everything® Russian Practice Book with CD, $19.95
Everything® Sign Language Book
Everything® Spanish Grammar Book
Everything® Spanish Phrase Book, $9.95
Everything® Spanish Practice Book with CD, $19.95
Everything® Spanish Verb Book, $9.95
Everything® Speaking Mandarin Chinese Book with CD, $19.95

MUSIC

Everything® Drums Book with CD, $19.95
Everything® Guitar Book with CD, 2nd Ed., $19.95
Everything® Guitar Chords Book with CD, $19.95
Everything® Home Recording Book
Everything® Music Theory Book with CD, $19.95
Everything® Reading Music Book with CD, $19.95
Everything® Rock & Blues Guitar Book with CD, $19.95
Everything® Rock and Blues Piano Book with CD, $19.95
Everything® Songwriting Book

NEW AGE

Everything® Astrology Book, 2nd Ed.
Everything® Birthday Personology Book
Everything® Dreams Book, 2nd Ed.
Everything® Love Signs Book, $9.95
Everything® Love Spells Book, $9.95
Everything® Numerology Book
Everything® Paganism Book
Everything® Palmistry Book
Everything® Psychic Book
Everything® Reiki Book
Everything® Sex Signs Book, $9.95

Everything® Spells & Charms Book, 2nd Ed.
Everything® Tarot Book, 2nd Ed.
Everything® Toltec Wisdom Book
Everything® Wicca and Witchcraft Book

PARENTING

Everything® Baby Names Book, 2nd Ed.
Everything® Baby Shower Book, 2nd Ed.
Everything® Baby's First Year Book
Everything® Birthing Book
Everything® Breastfeeding Book
Everything® Father-to-Be Book
Everything® Father's First Year Book
Everything® Get Ready for Baby Book, 2nd Ed.
Everything® Get Your Baby to Sleep Book, $9.95
Everything® Getting Pregnant Book
Everything® Guide to Pregnancy Over 35
Everything® Guide to Raising a One-Year-Old
Everything® Guide to Raising a Two-Year-Old
Everything® Guide to Raising Adolescent Boys
Everything® Guide to Raising Adolescent Girls
Everything® Homeschooling Book
Everything® Mother's First Year Book
Everything® Parent's Guide to Childhood Illnesses
Everything® Parent's Guide to Children and Divorce
Everything® Parent's Guide to Children with ADD/ADHD
Everything® Parent's Guide to Children with Asperger's Syndrome
Everything® Parent's Guide to Children with Autism
Everything® Parent's Guide to Children with Bipolar Disorder
Everything® Parent's Guide to Children with Depression
Everything® Parent's Guide to Children with Dyslexia
Everything® Parent's Guide to Children with Juvenile Diabetes
Everything® Parent's Guide to Positive Discipline
Everything® Parent's Guide to Raising a Successful Child
Everything® Parent's Guide to Raising Boys
Everything® Parent's Guide to Raising Girls
Everything® Parent's Guide to Raising Siblings
Everything® Parent's Guide to Sensory Integration Disorder
Everything® Parent's Guide to Tantrums
Everything® Parent's Guide to the Strong-Willed Child
Everything® Parenting a Teenager Book
Everything® Potty Training Book, $9.95
Everything® Pregnancy Book, 3rd Ed.
Everything® Pregnancy Fitness Book
Everything® Pregnancy Nutrition Book
Everything® Pregnancy Organizer, 2nd Ed., $16.95
Everything® Toddler Activities Book
Everything® Toddler Book
Everything® Tween Book
Everything® Twins, Triplets, and More Book

PETS

Everything® Aquarium Book
Everything® Boxer Book
Everything® Cat Book, 2nd Ed.
Everything® Chihuahua Book

Everything® **Cooking for Dogs Book**
Everything® Dachshund Book
Everything® Dog Book
Everything® Dog Health Book
Everything® Dog Obedience Book
Everything® Dog Owner's Organizer, $16.95
Everything® Dog Training and Tricks Book
Everything® German Shepherd Book
Everything® Golden Retriever Book
Everything® Horse Book
Everything® Horse Care Book
Everything® Horseback Riding Book
Everything® Labrador Retriever Book
Everything® Poodle Book
Everything® Pug Book
Everything® Puppy Book
Everything® Rottweiler Book
Everything® Small Dogs Book
Everything® Tropical Fish Book
Everything® Yorkshire Terrier Book

REFERENCE

Everything® American Presidents Book
Everything® Blogging Book
Everything® Build Your Vocabulary Book
Everything® Car Care Book
Everything® Classical Mythology Book
Everything® Da Vinci Book
Everything® Divorce Book
Everything® Einstein Book
Everything® Enneagram Book
Everything® Etiquette Book, 2nd Ed.
Everything® **Guide to Edgar Allan Poe**
Everything® Inventions and Patents Book
Everything® Mafia Book
Everything® **Martin Luther King Jr. Book**
Everything® Philosophy Book
Everything® Pirates Book
Everything® Psychology Book

RELIGION

Everything® Angels Book
Everything® Bible Book
Everything® **Bible Study Book with CD, $19.95**
Everything® Buddhism Book
Everything® Catholicism Book
Everything® Christianity Book
Everything® Gnostic Gospels Book
Everything® History of the Bible Book
Everything® Jesus Book
Everything® Jewish History & Heritage Book
Everything® Judaism Book
Everything® Kabbalah Book
Everything® Koran Book

Everything® Mary Book
Everything® Mary Magdalene Book
Everything® Prayer Book
Everything® Saints Book, 2nd Ed.
Everything® Torah Book
Everything® Understanding Islam Book
Everything® **Women of the Bible Book**
Everything® World's Religions Book
Everything® Zen Book

SCHOOL & CAREERS

Everything® Alternative Careers Book
Everything® Career Tests Book
Everything® College Major Test Book
Everything® College Survival Book, 2nd Ed.
Everything® Cover Letter Book, 2nd Ed.
Everything® Filmmaking Book
Everything® Get-a-Job Book, 2nd Ed.
Everything® Guide to Being a Paralegal
Everything® Guide to Being a Personal Trainer
Everything® Guide to Being a Real Estate Agent
Everything® Guide to Being a Sales Rep
Everything® **Guide to Being an Event Planner**
Everything® Guide to Careers in Health Care
Everything® Guide to Careers in Law Enforcement
Everything® Guide to Government Jobs
Everything® **Guide to Starting and Running a Catering Business**
Everything® Guide to Starting and Running a Restaurant
Everything® Job Interview Book
Everything® New Nurse Book
Everything® New Teacher Book
Everything® Paying for College Book
Everything® Practice Interview Book
Everything® Resume Book, 2nd Ed.
Everything® Study Book

SELF-HELP

Everything® **Body Language Book**
Everything® Dating Book, 2nd Ed.
Everything® Great Sex Book
Everything® Self-Esteem Book
Everything® Tantric Sex Book

SPORTS & FITNESS

Everything® Easy Fitness Book
Everything® **Krav Maga for Fitness Book**
Everything® Running Book

TRAVEL

Everything® **Family Guide to Coastal Florida**
Everything® Family Guide to Cruise Vacations
Everything® Family Guide to Hawaii
Everything® Family Guide to Las Vegas, 2nd Ed.
Everything® Family Guide to Mexico
Everything® Family Guide to New York City, 2nd Ed.
Everything® Family Guide to RV Travel & Campgrounds
Everything® Family Guide to the Caribbean
Everything® **Family Guide to the Disneyland® Resort, California Adventure®, Universal Studios®, and the Anaheim Area, 2nd Ed.**
Everything® **Family Guide to the Walt Disney World Resort®, Universal Studios®, and Greater Orlando, 5th Ed.**
Everything® Family Guide to Timeshares
Everything® Family Guide to Washington D.C., 2nd Ed.

WEDDINGS

Everything® Bachelorette Party Book, $9.95
Everything® Bridesmaid Book, $9.95
Everything® Destination Wedding Book
Everything® Elopement Book, $9.95
Everything® Father of the Bride Book, $9.95
Everything® Groom Book, $9.95
Everything® Mother of the Bride Book, $9.95
Everything® Outdoor Wedding Book
Everything® Wedding Book, 3rd Ed.
Everything® Wedding Checklist, $9.95
Everything® Wedding Etiquette Book, $9.95
Everything® Wedding Organizer, 2nd Ed., $16.95
Everything® Wedding Shower Book, $9.95
Everything® Wedding Vows Book, $9.95
Everything® Wedding Workout Book
Everything® **Weddings on a Budget Book, 2nd Ed., $9.95**

WRITING

Everything® Creative Writing Book
Everything® Get Published Book, 2nd Ed.
Everything® Grammar and Style Book
Everything® Guide to Magazine Writing
Everything® Guide to Writing a Book Proposal
Everything® Guide to Writing a Novel
Everything® Guide to Writing Children's Books
Everything® Guide to Writing Copy
Everything® **Guide to Writing Graphic Novels**
Everything® Guide to Writing Research Papers
Everything® Screenwriting Book
Everything® Writing Poetry Book
Everything® Writing Well Book